THE LONG GAME

THE LONG GAME

1996-2003:
THE INSIDE STORY OF HOW THE BBC BROUGHT BACK **DOCTOR WHO**

PAUL HAYES

TEN ACRE FILMS

The Long Game – 1996–2003:
The Inside Story of How the
BBC Brought Back Doctor Who

First published November 2021 by Ten Acre Films Ltd.

ISBN 978-1-908630-80-3

Copyright © 2021 Paul Hayes.

The rights of Paul Hayes to be identified as the author
of this work have been asserted in accordance with
the Copyright, Designs and Patents Act 1988.

All rights reserved. No part of this publication may be reproduced,
stored in or introduced into a retrieval system, or transmitted, in
any form or by any means (electronic, mechanical, photocopying,
recording or otherwise) without the prior written permission of the
publisher. Any person who does any unauthorised act in relation
to this publication may be liable to criminal prosecution and civil
claim for damages.

A CIP catalogue record for this book is available from the
British Library.

Project Editor: Stuart Manning.
Printed in Great Britain by 4Edge Ltd.

This book is sold subject to the condition that it shall be not,
by way of trade or otherwise, be lent, re-sold, hired out, or
otherwise circulated without the publisher's prior consent in any
form of binding or cover other than that in which it is published
and without a similar condition including this condition being
imposed on the subsequent purchaser.

CONTENTS

INTRODUCTION		7
1.	"R.I.P. DOCTOR WHO"	11
2.	THE CLASS OF '97	31
3.	SET THE CONTROLS FOR THE SILVER SCREEN	49
4.	"I THINK THAT'S DEAD"	69
5.	COTTAGE INDUSTRY	87
6.	THE VELVET WEB	107
7.	"A JACUZZI OF SPARE PUBLIC CASH"	129
8.	NOT DOCTOR WHO	155
9.	RUNNING IN WEDGES	177
10.	WHAT DO WE WANT?	189
11.	THE BIDDERS	201
12.	DO I HAVE THE RIGHTS?	229
13.	"RUSSELL. DOCTOR WHO. WE'RE DOING IT"	253
14.	MIDNIGHT	283
BBC POSITIONS		299
TIMELINE		301
SOURCES		315
INDEX		341

INTRODUCTION

MAY 1996 TO SEPTEMBER 2003 does, I fully appreciate, seem like a very odd choice of period in *Doctor Who*'s history about which to want to write a book. From the point at which it went off-air – again, after only having been back for just under an hour-and-a-half in the first place – to the day when its long-awaited return was finally announced by the BBC.

Yes, seven long years in which *Doctor Who* was conspicuously not being made.

I won't be so ludicrous as to claim that this somehow constitutes a favourite era of the show, for me or for anybody else. But looking back from the safe vantage point of *Doctor Who* having once again become a successful and long-running television series, it's fascinating to see how it happened, and how all of the elements finally came together to enable its return to take place.

It's an era through which I lived from a distance; starting as a twelve-year-old boy in my first year at secondary school, to a 19-year-old student just beginning my second year at university – a period which, at that age, feels like a lifetime in and of itself. So many of the stories and events recounted here I first experienced as they were related at the time via the news pages of *Doctor Who Magazine* and later the Outpost Gallifrey website. Little traces and glimmers of optimism or, more usually, dashed hopes. But always wondering what was really happening at the BBC, and if there was any chance that the show I loved so much might ever come back.

This then, is my attempt to relate, as accurately as I can, what was really going on throughout those years.

Like many *Doctor Who* fans, almost ever since I can remember,

THE LONG GAME

I have had an insatiable curiosity about the making of the series; a desire to open the bonnet and explore how it works. The long period of development which led up to the launch of the show in 1963 has fascinated me since I was a child, but it's a journey that has already been very well-chronicled by many other writers and researchers. I don't think, though, that the equivalent period 40 years later necessarily has been – which is why I wanted to write this book.

Similarly, the period up to and including the TV Movie and the actual making of the 21st Century series have both been thoroughly covered, quite excellently, elsewhere. But this part of the show's history – the years in between – has not. At least, not all together in one place.

There have been many interviews, articles and documentaries which have told assorted elements of the story. Over the years I have enjoyed trying to put all of these pieces together, purely for my own interest. Eventually, it occurred to me that nobody else seemed to have done this yet, so why not attempt to get it all down in book form? Why not try my best to pull all of those parts into one narrative? Why not explain how *Doctor Who* went from that one-night stand on BBC One in late May 1996, to that wonderful September morning seven years later when we finally learned that it was really, truly coming back again?

This is the story of the changes in the BBC which allowed that to happen, and how the careers of those who brought it back put them in the right places at the right time to do so. It's also the story of the false hopes and non-starters along the way, against the broader backdrop of the changing face of British television.

Looking back from 2021, it's all history now. It belongs to another era, another world – yet one which suddenly echoes into *Doctor Who*'s future, as once more Russell T Davies is announced as the programme's showrunner on the last Friday in September.

The journey begins again.

1

"R.I.P. DOCTOR WHO"

HOPES OF *DOCTOR WHO* RETURNING as a regular series died both a quick and a slow death over the late spring and summer of 1996.

It was a quick death in the sense that any prospect of the TV Movie leading to further episodes was gone pretty much as soon as the American viewing figures were in, before it had even been shown by the BBC. For its broadcast on the Fox Network on May 14, the movie earned 8.3 million viewers and a nine percent share of the night's audience. This left it in 75th place for the week in the US television charts, with a Nielsen ratings system score of 5.5 - only just over half the figure that Fox's previous 'Movie of the Week' had gained, and much lower than it would have needed for the network to want to consider developing it into a series.

So in a sense, the BBC One broadcast of the film, on the Bank Holiday Monday of May 27, was almost irrelevant. It did good business in the UK, though; earning 9.08 million viewers and gaining a Top Ten place among the programmes broadcast by the BBC that week. Overall it was 15th in the weekly chart of programmes from all channels and won its slot - albeit by a hair's breadth - against ITV's Victorian medical drama *Bramwell*, also denting the rival show's audience by ten percent compared with the previous week's episode.

But the hopes then died a slow death because, at the time, nobody outside of the BBC knew quite what these figures meant for the future of *Doctor Who*, or even found out about them very quickly. The internet certainly existed at this point, but many fans were not yet online. Those who were connected communicated mostly via the rec.arts.drwho newsgroup, but there was no instant picking-apart of overnight figures from the BBC broadcast. Fans had to wait for the final consolidated ratings to be reported in the trade press the following month, and then – in something of an information vacuum – try to work out what it all meant.

Someone with a much better idea of whether or not *Doctor Who* would go any further after the TV Movie was Alan Yentob – the man who was then the Controller of BBC One. Yentob had offered a glimmer of hope for the show's future in his appearance at the end of the anniversary documentary *30 Years in the TARDIS* in 1993, and was seen by some fans as a rare BBC executive who was on the side of the angels as far as *Doctor Who* was concerned. However, Yentob says that when the TV Movie finally happened, his feelings towards the project were at best lukewarm.

"I never had any real conviction about that," he admits. "I had other things to deal with at that time. Clearly, I could have said that we wouldn't do it or that we weren't interested, but it was driven – and paid for, more or less – by BBC Worldwide and their partners Universal and Fox. So really, I think BBC Television just let it happen to some extent."

BBC Worldwide was the Corporation's commercial arm, existing as a wholly-owned subsidiary company. This was the part of the BBC which oversaw tie-in merchandise and home media releases, sold programmes to broadcasters in other countries, and generally made money for the BBC on top of that which came in from the licence fee. Worldwide also invested in co-productions, and had been one of the partners in the TV Movie deal.

Yentob had in fact been involved in discussions with them about another *Doctor Who* project during his time at BBC One. In Worldwide's previous incarnation as BBC Enterprises, the name under which they had operated until 1994, they had seriously attempted to enter into drama production themselves for the first time with a *Doctor Who* thirtieth anniversary special, *Lost in the Dark Dimension*. Yentob had been prepared to invest a quarter of a million pounds of BBC Television money into this, to enable what was originally intended as a straight-to-video drama to be broadcast on BBC One for the anniversary in November 1993. However, as it turned out, this contribution inadvertently ended up bringing about the project's collapse. Enterprises mistakenly included the £250,000 from BBC One in their calculations for both the budget and the projected revenue, resulting in a massive shortfall in the figures – a basic error which can't have reassured anyone on the television side about Enterprises' ability to make the move into actual programme-making.

"So I wasn't really behind this," Yentob continues of the TV Movie. "I was interested in what would happen to *Doctor Who* and where it would go, but it was really very much Worldwide's initiative. I have to admit the movie with Paul McGann wasn't, to me, the most perfect answer to this.

"The film was essentially a way of seeing if *Doctor Who* had a future. Could it be revived as a series? Because that would be the most valuable thing for Worldwide and the BBC, if it actually revived interest in it."

So, what if the film *had* revived interest to the extent that it had been an enormous hit on BBC One? What if it had gained, say, twelve or fifteen million viewers instead of nine? Could there ever have been a possibility of the BBC going it alone with a follow-up series off the back of it?

Jo Wright was the BBC's executive producer on the movie – and within weeks of its transmission became the Corporation's Head of Drama Series, so would almost certainly have had responsibility over any such home-made show. She, however, thinks it would have been highly unlikely, whatever the ratings.

"It didn't hang on anything, really, because nobody really wanted it back. That's the real truth of all of it. Because *Doctor Who* felt like something that'd had its time and it had not been very good towards the end. From my point of view, having done the TV Movie and it being a nightmare from beginning to end, it wasn't something that I was rushing to go back to. There were just so many problems with it."

THE LONG GAME

In Wright's view, Yentob's enthusiasm for *Doctor Who* had waned after Steven Spielberg's Amblin Entertainment had ceased to be involved in the development of what eventually became the TV Movie.

"Alan liked the idea of it, but he liked the idea less when Spielberg disappeared. It was fantastic PR for the BBC. It's not because he personally wanted *Doctor Who* in any way, but he just loved the idea of Spielberg, and getting it to be expensive and American and all those things that Alan thought were a good idea. Whereas the rest of the BBC were just not interested in the slightest."

Wright does concur with Yentob's view that it was the BBC Worldwide camp who were the main impetus behind the film from the Corporation's side of things.

"They made a fortune out of *Doctor Who*," she says. "Suddenly it came crashing down, and they hadn't got anything to sell all the old stuff on. That was the problem for them. They were in a position where they couldn't actually hang their biggest cash cow on anything. So they were absolutely desperate to make it and were incredibly disappointed because they wanted a series. They didn't want a TV movie."

Wright and Yentob are both also in agreement that the only reason the movie happened at all was due to the persistence of its US-based expatriate producer Philip Segal, and his love for the show. "There was Philip Segal who was really pushing it, and was talking to big American distributors," says Yentob.

"Phil was the keeper of the keys and a complete Whovian, and was just obsessed with getting it made," agrees Wright. "But there was nobody else except Phil who was as keen."

Outside of the knowledge of what was going on within the BBC, and as is perhaps typical for *Doctor Who* fans, online speculation and reaction to the performance of the TV Movie posted that summer varied wildly, from "I overheard a rumour that BBC Worldwide picked up the series and is starting pre-production on new episodes" to "R.I.P. *Doctor Who*, 1963–1989. All that's left is for us sad fans to bury it, forget about it and get a life."

"R.I.P. DOCTOR WHO"

One of those engaging in such online discussion at the time was Canadian fan Shannon Patrick Sullivan, who also ran one of the early *Doctor Who* news websites. He sums up what he recalls of the mood in fandom immediately following the movie.

"By the time of the UK broadcast, there was already a sense that the whole project was dead in the water," says Sullivan. "There was a general awareness that the BBC wasn't going to move forward if the Fox Network wasn't interested in more *Doctor Who*, and the American ratings clearly didn't justify that. There was some hope that Fox might opt to use *Doctor Who* as a replacement for *Sliders*, which seemed to be perpetually on the brink of cancellation. But when *Sliders* got renewed a couple of weeks after the broadcast of the TV Movie, even that faint hope evaporated."

Gary Gillatt was the then editor of *Doctor Who Magazine*, and had travelled to Vancouver to write on-set reports during the TV Movie's production. His recollection is that this pessimistic outlook was already present while the movie was still being made, even from the man who had been most responsible for it happening – producer Philip Segal.

"When I left Vancouver at the end of the shoot, it was pretty clear that it wasn't going any further," Gillatt recalls. "Segal had wanted to make *Doctor Who* by hook or by crook, but the deal he ended up with – the only one left after every other door had closed – was a one-shot and, by its nature, a dead end. When speaking to him at the studio, he was pretty muted. True, they were running over schedule and budget and he was surely knackered, but he wasn't giving me the same huckster 'sell' for the future of a series I'd had from him before.

"However, there was no point in being pessimistic, especially in the pages of *Doctor Who Magazine*, and damning the thing before even the studio lights cooled. 'Backdoor pilot' was the term, wasn't it? That was the hope we could cling to – that someone in power somewhere would see the TV Movie, reach for a cigar and say: 'I love this Limey shit! Get me 26 episodes for Fall sweeps!' But it was pure fantasy. The likelihood of that happening was vanishingly small. It was and is incredibly rare. Segal knew it, and was

THE LONG GAME

communicating it in his manner, if not his words.

"So, in *Doctor Who Magazine* we stayed positive for as long as was dignified, then quietly moved on."

Indeed, Issue 241 of the magazine, published in July 1996, did its best to be optimistic when it reported that:

> "A BBC Worldwide spokesperson told us: 'Reports that BBC Worldwide have no intention of producing new *Doctor Who* are untrue. However, we cannot confirm a commitment to making more films until we know for certain how the film has fared in the ratings, and how the video has sold. Everything is still very much up in the air.' A publicist for BBC Drama more bluntly but more encouragingly added: 'We're not going to have poured all this money into it to wash it straight down the drain.'"

Those of a more cynical bent who followed the progress of BBC Drama at the time might, perhaps, have raised an eyebrow at that latter quote. The department was then in something of a state of flux, with nobody to lead it and finding itself at the centre of a divisive and confusing series of behind-the-scenes changes in the structure of the BBC.

It is against this backdrop of change and uncertainty that the first attempt at a television comeback for *Doctor Who* therefore came to a swift halt. But it was also where the long journey began towards the next, more successful revival.

When the return of *Doctor Who* as an ongoing series did eventually come, the BBC television drama landscape into which it was born was very different to that which the series had left in 1989. So it's worth looking at just what had changed, and why things had evolved in the manner that they did – a process which was already well underway by the time of the TV Movie's broadcast in 1996. Although, at that point, the department still carried the legacy of previous changes which had been made at the time of *Doctor Who*'s very beginnings.

"R.I.P. DOCTOR WHO"

Those who have read about the creation of *Doctor Who* are probably familiar with the fact that when Sydney Newman arrived at BBC Television as Head of Drama in January 1963, he decided that the department – or the 'BBC Drama Group', to give it its rather quaint official title – was too large and unwieldy for him to handle all of a piece. He therefore divided it into three separate sections, each with its own head reporting to him – Series, Serials and Plays.

'Series' consisted of those shows in which each episode generally had a self-contained storyline, although of course there would be a regular cast of characters and other ongoing elements which would continue throughout. Successful drama series, often police or medical procedurals or perhaps soap operas, might return year after year for long runs.

'Serials' referred to what might also be called 'miniseries' – a show with a run of a limited number of episodes, where a single main storyline was told across those episodes and concluded in the final one. These might typically be either literary adaptations or contemporary thrillers. *Doctor Who*, being a series of serials, was a production of the Drama Serials department for most of its original run.

In 1979, series and serials were combined into a single joint department within the Drama Group; this merger then lasted for most of the 1980s. In 1989, they were separated again and remained that way throughout most of the 1990s and into the 2000s – with a brief exception in 1993-1994.

And then there were 'Plays'.

In the early days of BBC Television and, still at the time when Newman had arrived in 1963, one-off plays were a staple of BBC Drama. They were its most prestigious, discussed and critiqued output among reviewers, and indeed to begin with had been almost British television's sole dramatic form – with series and serials only gradually becoming more common through the 1950s. Plays remained important on television throughout the 1960s and 1970s, but by the end of the 1980s had almost entirely disappeared. BBC One's *The Play on One*, which lasted into 1991, was the last gasp of the form as a regular event on the Corporation's main channel; although BBC Two's *Screenplay* and *Performance* anthology series still provided very occasional examples for more niche audiences into the 1990s.

The old-style British television play was made in the same way as classic *Doctor Who*, and almost all other BBC television drama of the era. They were rehearsed by the cast in a similar manner to a stage play, then recorded over perhaps at most two or three days using a multi-camera set-up in a television studio; some productions would also have a limited amount of pre-shooting done in advance, usually on location. Up until the early 1960s, aside from any pre-filmed sequences, they would have been broadcast live; even for many years after that, they would usually be recorded pretty much as-live in one go. Even with an increased shift to out-of-sequence recording in the 1970s and 1980s, BBC studio productions still favoured long, rehearsed takes, edited in-camera during the recording via the vision-mixing desk. Videotape editing remained technically challenging and cumbersome compared to the versatility of assembling filmed material shot-by-shot.

This type of studio production did survive into the 1990s, routinely used for sitcoms, but for drama, it was very much a dying art. Occasional multi-camera studio plays were still being made, but they were now rare beasts. The same was true of the way in which series and serials were produced, too. The BBC had made *some* dramas entirely on film for decades, but these productions had always been in the minority. By the 1990s that ratio had flipped in almost all areas of the BBC's drama output. Outside of soaps, the BBC's last major multi-camera studio drama series – or 'series made using classic *Doctor Who*-like methods,' if you prefer – was the costume drama *The House of Eliott*, which came to an end in 1994.

Even *Doctor Who* had been moving away from the studio towards the end of its original run. Over half of its final series in 1989 had been made on location, including two whole stories, *The Curse of Fenric* and *Survival*. Of course, all of this location work was recorded using an Outside Broadcast video unit rather than film. The 1996

"R.I.P. DOCTOR WHO"

TV Movie, unsurprisingly for an American television endeavour, had been shot on expensive 35mm film; although as was often the case with film-shot television productions of this era, its post production was done on videotape, rather than being assembled as a completed physical film copy.

As the techniques which had usually been used for the old television plays fell out of favour across British drama, so the nature of these one-offs also changed. The BBC's main series of plays, *Play for Today*, had been laid to rest in the 1980s, succeeded by the *Screen One* and *Screen Two* strands. The production methods of these more often used single-camera, shot-by-shot techniques; they were also usually made entirely on film, on location or on sound stages, rather than in TV studios.

Probably the best-known *Screen Two* production was Anthony Minghella's *Truly, Madly, Deeply* – made for television in 1990 and premiered at that year's London Film Festival. It then earned great critical acclaim from a limited cinema release, before eventually being broadcast on BBC Two in March 1992. Although it was not a major box office hit, the positive reception the film gained – not to mention the interest from US distributors – helped to cement the BBC's new desire to be involved in feature film production and investment.

The Plays department at the BBC had itself ceased to exist when the final Head of Plays, Peter Goodchild, left the job after internal restructuring at the end of the 1980s. At that point, only Series and Serials remained, with the Head of Drama himself overseeing films for BBC Two and Richard Broke appointed to work as executive producer for films on BBC One. However, by 1993 the idea of having a separate head of department within Drama to take charge of all these one-offs had been resurrected, albeit under a new title. The term 'TV movie' would never have gained much traction within the BBC, as to British ears it suggested something American rather than home-grown. Thus the person in charge of one-offs in the BBC Drama department in the mid-1990s – George Faber – held the title 'Head of Single Drama'.

So, at the time of the *Doctor Who* TV Movie's broadcast in 1996, the main BBC Drama Group in London still, roughly-speaking, had much of the same structure – and even the same name – as when Sydney Newman had arrived over 30 years earlier. In the group were departments for Drama Series, Drama Serials and, if not plays, then Drama 'Singles' in the TV industry terminology of the 1990s.

In addition to these main departments in London, the BBC had also maintained a dedicated drama production unit at its Pebble Mill Studios in Birmingham since the early 1970s, which had been responsible for several popular and acclaimed programmes. There were also the production centres in Scotland, Wales and Northern Ireland, each of them contributing some dramas for UK-wide broadcast. These were important as in April 1994 the BBC had set itself a target that by 1997 a third of all network programme spending should be going on productions made outside of London and the surrounding south-east of England, in order to better represent different areas across the country. Then finally, there was newcomer BBC Films; a unit created with such successes as *Truly, Madly, Deeply* in mind, to run the BBC's investment in productions for the cinema – which placed it in direct competition for scripts with television's Drama Singles department.

The BBC also no longer made all of its own programmes itself. The British government's 1990 Broadcasting Act had obliged the Corporation to, by 1993, source at least 25 percent of its original, UK-made, non-news television output each year from independent production companies. The idea was that this would increase competition within the industry and help to create opportunities for smaller programme-making businesses. This quota was only a minimum, and by 1994 *Broadcast* magazine reported that 45 percent of BBC television drama was now being made by independent companies, although it also stated that the Head of Drama Charles Denton wanted to reduce this to 30 percent.

The minimum quota from independents was measured in hours delivered, and that from outside London was measured in budget. But altogether, it meant that by the mid-1990s the central in-house BBC Drama Group – which, just a few years beforehand, had

"R.I.P. DOCTOR WHO"

been responsible for the vast majority of all BBC drama production – was now making less than half of the BBC's output in the genre.

To facilitate the new requirement to buy programmes from independent companies, the BBC appointed separate commissioners in the various genres to work with these outside suppliers; in Drama, this role was held by Tessa Ross from 1993 until 2000. From 1997, Ross did the job as a member of the 'Independent Commissioning Group', gaining drama commissions for outside companies without the involvement of the in-house drama department. This meant that the BBC's in-house staff would be competing with the ICG for commissions from channel controllers. Reportedly, on one occasion, this rivalry reached the stage where the in-house department and the ICG got into a bidding war against each other for the rights to Zadie Smith's novel *White Teeth*, with both losing out to Channel 4.

Such competition was not limited to being between the BBC departments and independent producers. Georgina Born, who made a close study of the BBC Drama Group during this period for her book *Uncertain Vision*, records that in 1996 the in-house Drama Serials and Drama Singles departments were discovered to have both been developing adaptations of *Mansfield Park* and *Jane Eyre* at the same time. In an entry from her diary reproduced in the book, Born wrote that: "It seems interdepartmental rivalry is so strong it prevents the kind of routine coordination that would avoid duplication."

All of this may sound somewhat complicated and confusing, but in fact, it was even worse than that. In 1996, the BBC Drama Group was seemingly at such a low ebb that the Corporation couldn't find anybody who actually wanted to run the department. As Born wrote: "It was rumoured every leading figure in television drama approached by the BBC refused the job, which was seen as a poisoned chalice."

The last Head of Drama at the BBC during the time of *Doctor Who*'s original run had been Mark Shivas, who held the post from 1988 to 1993. Shivas left to run BBC Films, and was succeeded as Head of Drama by Charles Denton; he had been the founder and chief executive of Zenith Productions which, among other programmes, made the highly successful detective drama *Inspector Morse* for ITV. Denton remained in charge of BBC Drama until the beginning of May 1996 – the month of the TV Movie's broadcast on BBC One – according to media reports lamenting as he left that the BBC had become an "Orwellian nightmare". While Denton didn't have a great deal to do with the TV Movie himself, anyone who has studied the history of its complicated path to the screen probably has some sympathy for this statement.

As the dust settled on the TV Movie, who then was left at the BBC to have any say on whether or not the Corporation might like to have a crack at carrying on with *Doctor Who* under its own steam?

There was still Alan Yentob – the man who many fans at the time saw as perhaps *Doctor Who*'s strongest supporter in the upper echelons of BBC management, even though as we've heard he was not particularly enamoured with the movie. But even if Yentob's enthusiasm had been fired by it, he was not to be the Controller of BBC One for very much longer. In June 1996, the month after the TV Movie was shown, Yentob moved to a new role as Director of Programmes at BBC Production.

The Director-General of the BBC, John Birt, was implementing a great deal of reform and restructuring across the organisation, in an attempt to modernise it. As part of this, he had effectively split BBC Television into two halves. One of them was BBC Broadcast, which would control the channels and scheduling and commission the programmes from both independent companies and the BBC's own in-house departments. The other was BBC Production, which would be the new home for those in-house programme-makers. So while Yentob was now in charge of the BBC's own production teams, he didn't actually have the final say on which shows would make it to air, instead having to pitch ideas to BBC Broadcast to get the go-ahead. The commissioning job had gone to Michael Jackson, Yentob's successor as Controller of BBC One and also installed as the overall Director of Television at BBC Broadcast.

Given the upheavals ongoing at the time and the labyrinthine structure of the commissioning process, it's unlikely that *Doctor Who* was even a vague consideration for anybody at the top of BBC Television towards the end of 1996. Jackson confirms that by the time he had taken over that summer, *Doctor Who* was very much off the table as far as BBC One was concerned. "The film was not considered a success creatively," he explains. "I don't remember it ever being discussed in my time at BBC One. As such it left the field clear for the huge success that was to come."

The split between BBC Broadcast and BBC Production created a frustrating situation for the in-house teams; while Broadcast could commission from either independent companies or the BBC's own departments, Production were not allowed to make programmes for other channels. 20 years later, when the in-house production arm was spun-off into a merger with BBC Worldwide to create a commercial subsidiary called BBC Studios, this was finally allowed to happen. But in the late 1990s, BBC Production were stuck with BBC Broadcast as their one and only customer; albeit they were of course by far and away Broadcast's biggest supplier of programmes.

"If my department developed something and Michael Jackson didn't like it, then it had nowhere else to go," says Jo Wright. "There was no way of turning anything around quickly, and no way of saying if they didn't say yes to it we'd take it somewhere else. Which is how you always sell something. There was nothing you could do."

Meanwhile, with Denton gone, it took over a year for the Corporation to find a new Head of Drama. The former Head of Drama at BBC Wales, Ruth Caleb, initially took over the position on an acting basis. Then from November 1996, Alan Yentob was directly overseeing the work of the department, with assistance from BBC North's former Head of Broadcasting Colin Adams. Adams had joined BBC Production in the autumn of 1996 as overall Production Controller. With no Head of Drama appointed, Adams had been helping Yentob to run the department on an administrative level, though he had no actual drama experience.

It was therefore something of a surprise when, in June 1997, it was announced that Adams had been given the full-time job, now retooled as 'Controller of Drama Production'. "His appointment effectively formalises what many BBC Drama insiders have said for some time," wrote *Broadcast* magazine of the news; "that the head of department job has become a managerial rather than a creative role."

The American trade paper *Variety* also reported on the long search to find someone to head up BBC Drama:

> "It's taken more than a year, but the BBC has finally found somebody to fill the embarrassing vacancy at the head of its Drama department. Or rather, after the job was turned down by every senior drama exec in British TV, its specification has been downgraded until finally the pubcaster [public broadcaster] could find somebody to fit it... The BBC's extended failure to attract a heavy hitter to the post reflects the fact that its creative reputation has been compromised by the widespread impression that the bureaucrats have taken the upper hand at the pubcaster in recent years."

The Guardian had been equally scathing, with Maggie Brown writing before Adams was appointed that:

> "To the industry's mounting amazement, the BBC has been without a permanent Head of Drama for a year... The BBC's chairman, Sir Christopher Bland, is perturbed no one seems to want the job; as he remarked last week, it is surely one of the best in the industry... Nobody of real stature wants the job because what power would they have in Yentob's shadow? And in a BBC where the links between the channel controllers and the programme makers are dissolving under Birt's latest reorganisation? A wedge has been driven between the two wings of the BBC."

"R.I.P. DOCTOR WHO"

There was speculation in the trade press in the summer of 1997 that BBC Broadcast might set up a parallel drama position; a drama commissioner to work with the channel controllers in deciding which shows to take from both BBC Production and from the independent companies. ITV's drama boss Nick Elliott was spoken of as a target to try and tempt back to the BBC to fill such a role. This set-up was something which did happen with other areas of programming – a commissioner at BBC Broadcast, and a head of the in-house department at BBC Production – but Elliott could not be tempted over, and in the end, no such drama commissioning job was created at this point.

In May 1997, the month before Adams was given the full-time job as Controller of Drama Production, *The Guardian* had speculated that another name might be in the frame for the position, writing that: "Wooing someone back in to run the emptying Drama department proved impossible despite last year's search (in-house producer David Thompson is expected to be anointed shortly)."

David Thompson had at this point been working at the BBC for over 20 years, mostly producing documentaries and one-off dramas. Latterly he had been overseeing much of the output of the *Screen One* and *Screen Two* anthology strands, but he denies ever having been a contender to run the whole Drama department.

"I never read that article," he says. "No, I wouldn't have wanted it! I liked doing what I was doing. I liked being nearer to the content. We were very hands-on with all the productions, actually producing as well as commissioning."

It's possible that *The Guardian* simply had their wires crossed, as Thompson was about to take one of the other top jobs in the department. However, he agrees that at this point BBC Drama was facing a number of issues.

"The headlines were as often about the crisis in the BBC's Drama department as about the dramas!" he remembers. "It was partly because there were a lot of maverick people working there, who were quite difficult to control. It was fraught with challenges and was very difficult to manage. There were lots of different departments who weren't necessarily all working in harmony and weren't very good at doing what they were told. There were also significant problems with some departments overspending each year, at that time.

"There was lots of hand-wringing and head-in-hands. It was too baronial; feudal. Too divided up into separate divisions. It was too much internal competition, and it probably wasn't sufficiently audience-focused either, to be absolutely honest."

Alan Yentob is guarded when asked about his view of the Drama department during this time, but he does admit that it was in some difficulty. "I think it's fair to say that it wasn't at its best at that moment. I don't want to criticise people, and actually, there was some very good stuff that came out of that era. But yes, the London Drama department wasn't really delivering in the way that one would have hoped."

Jo Wright is much franker in her recollections. "They'd done *terrible* decision-making in Drama. Nobody wanted to run Drama. They had a lot of quite difficult people in Drama, and they were used to doing whatever they wanted. It just wasn't run very well.

"There was a bureaucracy and a 'can't-do' attitude. I'd come in with lots of new ideas and they'd tell me I couldn't do them. They would find loads of ways of trying to stop you doing anything. One of the worst ones was actually trying to employ somebody. Say you were trying to employ a director, you'd have to go through a department that would say you couldn't possibly pay them that much, because when they last worked for the BBC 20 years ago, they only got so much. You'd point out that although they hadn't worked for the BBC, they'd worked at ITV and they were the best director and they've earned this amount. But they'd come back and say no, the last time they were at the BBC they earned two pence, so they could only have three pence now. It was ridiculous!

"I don't want to sound like I'm moaning about the BBC, because I love the BBC. But the management was the appalling side of it, because nobody was managing! There was a real lack of personal management."

Along with the internal problems, the external reputation of the BBC's drama output had taken something of a bruising from

"R.I.P. DOCTOR WHO"

critical and popular failures such as the epic, expensive historical drama *Rhodes* and the Joseph Conrad adaptation *Nostromo*. Neither of these serials, both made for the BBC by independent companies, had managed to find much favour with reviewers – or more importantly, with viewers. While popular in-house staples such as *EastEnders* and *Casualty* remained ratings favourites, BBC Drama was not at one of its high points as Colin Adams took full-time command of the department in the summer of 1997.

So it's easy to see where *Doctor Who* simply got lost in all of this. After all, its most recent outing in the TV Movie had been confusing in and of itself. Had it been an independent production? An acquisition? Or a co-production? Where did it fit into all of this new-look BBC structure? Who was even left to fly the flag for it, anyway? This version of *Doctor Who* had arrived at the end of an era for a mid-1990s BBC hierarchy who had all now moved on.

The only real development with *Doctor Who* during this time came at the end of 1996 when Universal Television's option on the series was about to expire. After the failure of the TV Movie to do the business in the US, they'd been unable to interest Fox in picking up either a series or further movies – but surprisingly, it seems that at least someone at Universal was keen to keep trying with other broadcasters.

In January 1997, *Doctor Who Magazine* reported on a press release from BBC Worldwide, which stated that Universal had:

> "...negotiated an extension to its option on further *Doctor Who* films or episodes with BBC Worldwide. The option was originally due to expire at the end of 1996... If BBC Worldwide and Universal wish to develop a new film before the end of 1997, they will have to find the support of another US broadcaster... The fact that Universal has chosen to signal its continued interest in *Doctor Who* indicates that all is not lost, and that both it and Worldwide are keen to produce more material. The hunt must now be on for new network support."

THE LONG GAME

Three issues later, the magazine reported comments from TV Movie producer Philip Segal, made at the annual Gallifrey One convention in Los Angeles in February, stating that Universal's new option actually expired at the end of April 1997, rather than at the end of the year. However, it seems that Segal was mistaken and that the end of December report was correct, as in July 1997 the BBC's beeb.com website posted the following report:

> "Thank you for all the messages relating to *Doctor Who*. We sent your queries to BBC Viewer and Listener Correspondence, and they responded with the following statement...
>
> "It now seems unlikely that a series will be made from the last year's movie pilot starring Paul McGann, as Fox TV have decided not to proceed with the project. However, Universal TV still have options on making a series until the end of 1997. Therefore they will continue to attempt to interest US backers until then, whereupon the rights revert back to the BBC and the series will be in the same position it was in 1989 when it ceased production. Paul McGann's option to play the Doctor for a period of five years expired at the end of 1996 – this could, however, be renegotiated should another movie transpire."

This was, though, no great new insight which the website had uncovered – the BBC's Viewer and Listener Correspondence unit had been sending the same form statement to fans who had written to enquire about the future of *Doctor Who* since at least April that year. Universal never did manage to achieve the unlikely feat of interesting another US broadcaster in the series, and their rights option eventually lapsed.

"I think it took about a year for most fans to accept the fact that the TV Movie wasn't going to spawn any sequels," says Shannon Patrick Sullivan. "The period from 1997 to 1999 was probably the bleakest, most pessimistic time for *Doctor Who* fandom."

"R.I.P. DOCTOR WHO"

But unlikely as it may have seemed to Sullivan and other fans at this point, the outlook was not, in fact, totally bleak. Controller of Drama Production Colin Adams was not to be the only important BBC appointee of 1997 – and more than one of those gaining other senior positions at the Corporation that year had affection and even enthusiasm for *Doctor Who*, and would play key roles in eventually bringing the series back.

2
THE CLASS OF '97

"WITHIN THE BBC, A SINGLE, CONSTANT VOICE had been nagging about *Doctor Who* for years – and that was Mal Young."

So Russell T Davies told *Doctor Who Magazine* in 2013. But to fandom, Young's name had never really been associated with *Doctor Who* at all; not until the very day that the show's revival was officially announced in September 2003.

Throughout the 1990s, *Doctor Who* fans had often played the game of attempting to guess or to find out whether or not various BBC executives were sympathetic to the show – "Is this person good for us, or bad? Does his or her appointment to this or that position make bringing back *Doctor Who* more likely, or less?"

Alan Yentob, for example, was always seen as being one of 'the good guys', as it were; but Mal Young's name went pretty much under the radar as far as *Doctor Who* fans were concerned. Conversely, in the late 1990s and early 2000s, Young was actually one of the best-known television executives in the country – in so far as television executives can ever be said to be 'well-known'. He was responsible for overseeing the likes of *EastEnders* and *Casualty*, two of the most popular programmes on British television, and he was often prepared to go into bat to defend those series publicly in times of trouble.

Young, however, did not outwardly seem to be the type of executive who might be interested in reviving something from television's past. For example, when he delivered the Huw Wheldon Lecture to the Royal Television Society in September 1999, he protested about the snobbery that existed in certain quarters towards the soap genre in comparison to long-gone drama classics such as *Play for Today*, telling the audience that: "When soaps are good, they can be brilliant, iconic telly... They have become the *Play for Today*... Miss it, miss out."

This was not the sort of comment that would have indicated to a slightly cynical 1990s fandom that here was the type of person likely to have any desire to bring back a show of similar antiquity such as *Doctor Who*. Yet after the noise had died down following the TV Movie, Mal Young was one of the first senior BBC executives to have the desire to see whether it was worth perhaps having another go.

Born in Liverpool in January 1957, Young had trained as a graphic designer. His initial involvement with the television industry was on-screen, working as an extra, and it wasn't until the age of 27 that he began working full-time in TV. This came about during an assignment as an extra on the Channel 4 soap opera *Brookside* – which was made in his home city – where he spotted an advert for a vacancy in the design department at the show's production company Mersey Television; a position which he applied for and ended up getting.

The job ended up being three weeks of holiday cover as a props runner, but over the next decade Young stayed with the company and with *Brookside*; by 1991 he had worked his way up to become the show's producer.

Young oversaw *Brookside* for five years, guiding the soap through one of its successful eras, and in 1994 masterminded one of its most famous moments – the first pre-watershed lesbian kiss seen on British television. This was a scene so notable it was even included in the montage of memorable British television moments shown during the opening ceremony for London's 2012 Olympic Games.

Young also produced *And the Beat Goes On*, Mersey Television's drama about the early 1960s rock and roll scene in Liverpool for Channel 4. But up until this point the majority of his TV production career had been tied to *Brookside*. This all changed in October 1996, when Greg Dyke tempted Young to London.

Dyke was a future Director-General of the BBC and the man who helped bring about many of the changes within the Corporation which were instrumental to *Doctor Who*'s return. But at this point, he was the chairman and chief executive of Pearson Television. Pearson owned the former ITV franchise holder Thames Television, which still made programmes for various channels, and were also part of the consortium which had won the rights to launch the UK's fifth national terrestrial television network, Channel 5, due to go on-air in 1997.

Young became Pearson's Head of Drama, overseeing the production of Thames Television's police series *The Bill*, which had been running since 1984 on ITV and had grown into one of that network's cornerstones. He was also in charge of setting up a brand-new soap opera which became *Family Affairs*, one of the main offerings of Channel 5's launch schedule.

Young's time at Pearson proved to be short, however. In the autumn of 1997, after just a year in the post, it was announced that he was leaving the company to take up the offer of a job with the BBC. He hadn't been certain about the idea of leaving, especially so soon – but it was actually Dyke who persuaded him that he should take the chance, on the basis that everyone in television should work for the BBC at some point in their career. Dyke himself, of course, would follow a couple of years later.

"I didn't think I was a BBC person, and I'd heard it was very bureaucratic and that there were a lot of comings and goings, and I wasn't sure," remembers Young of first being approached by the BBC. "I told them I didn't even own a tie! They all had their ties on, and it was all white, middle-class guys and they didn't sound like me. But they all took their ties off, bless them, and said they wanted me to change them, not them to change me.

"They said they wanted someone like me to come along and do something different. Because it wasn't working. They knew they weren't reflecting the audiences. They were too middle-class, too Southern and too middle-aged.

"So that attracted me, and that's when I said I'd do it. I told Greg that I felt really bad because I'd only been there a year and he'd moved me to London. But he said I should do it, that it was a great opportunity, and to never worry about moving on and pissing people off. Always do what you should do next for your career. He was great for that."

So Young made the move to Centre House, a utilitarian office block across the road from Television Centre, where the BBC's Drama department had been based since the early 1990s. He was there to take up a job that had lately been something of a revolving door – Head of Drama Series. When Young was given the role, he was the sixth person to hold the post in just four-and-a-half years.

After being united as the Series and Serials Department within the BBC Drama Group throughout the 1980s, in 1989 the two had been split back apart by new Drama Group boss Mark Shivas. Peter Cregeen was appointed as Head of Series early that year, and it had been he – along with the then BBC One Controller Jonathan Powell – who had taken the decision to finally bring *Doctor Who* to an end; the series having come under his responsibility after the separation, rather than going back to its old home of Serials.

Meanwhile, with Cregeen having been given the Series job, Michael Wearing moved to London from his post as Head of Drama at BBC Birmingham to become Head of Serials. Cregeen stayed as Head of Drama Series until 1993, when he left the job and the departments were briefly brought back together again under Michael Wearing's control.

The following year they split in two once more, with Wearing going back to being in charge of Drama Serials only and a new face being brought in for Drama Series. This was Nick Elliott, who had spent much of his career at the ITV company LWT, where he had overseen the launch of the highly successful Sunday night dramas *London's Burning* and *Poirot*. This was not an entirely smooth transition, however – Wearing was upset at having Drama Series suddenly taken from him and tendered his resignation, although he was eventually persuaded to stay.

The BBC were hoping that Nick Elliott would bring his popular touch and nose for high-quality, returning hits to their drama department. But although he was able to commission at least one series which proved to be a long-lasting success – the pathology drama *Silent Witness*, launched in 1996 and still running over 25 years later – Elliott resigned from the BBC in 1995, after just ten months in the job.

Elliott had rapidly tired of the internal bureaucracy of the Corporation, telling *The Guardian* newspaper that there were "too many people in the room at those crucial decision-making moments." He quickly moved on to become Controller of Drama at the ITV Network Centre until his retirement in 2007, in charge of many popular hits that would be regular thorns in the BBC's side – to such a degree that the BBC later allegedly tried, unsuccessfully, to tempt him back as their overall Head of Drama. The fact that they didn't is another one of those accidents of fate that was to eventually allow for the return of *Doctor Who*.

After Elliott's brief time as Head of Drama Series, Chris Parr was brought in from being Head of Drama at BBC Birmingham to take up the job in 1995. However, he was to last for little longer than Elliott had done – in June 1996, Parr was forced to step down from the Drama Series role after a controversy over a loan he had been given by a friend who was involved with an independent production company, from which Parr might potentially have been able to commission programmes. The BBC told *The Guardian* that:

> "Chris Parr did receive a personal loan from a personal friend who is also a director of an independent company. The BBC is satisfied there was no intention to advantage the independent supplier, but Chris Parr has potentially compromised his role as Head of Drama Series... He has therefore stepped down as Head of Drama Series, but will continue to work for Television Drama Group as an executive producer."

So once again the game of musical chairs had to be played, and this time Jo Wright came in as Head of Drama Series – initially on an acting basis after Parr's demotion, but then taking on the job full-time from October 1996. Previously working in the Drama

Serials department under Michael Wearing, it was in this capacity that Wright had served as the BBC's executive producer on the *Doctor Who* TV Movie. Indeed, Wright thinks that it was her work on the film's somewhat fraught path to the screen which convinced BBC Production boss Alan Yentob to give her the job running Drama Series.

"Alan and I got on really well," says Wright. "He knew that I was working incredibly hard to make it work, and therefore I think that was why in the end I got the Head of Series job. Because he could see that I worked every hour to get it to be as good as it could be."

However, Wright immediately found that the department had big problems. "I was announced, and everybody came up to me as if I'd died! I remember that more than anything. They came up to me after the meeting where it was announced and said, 'You poor thing, what a poisoned chalice!' Not one person in the department said congratulations! Now, I think that said a lot about what that job was like!

"I remember thinking, 'What have I done?' Everybody was not very nice to me – there was lots of backbiting. I remember taking all the team out to go bowling, to try and make them feel better and somebody from the other department went, 'Who do you think you are, head girl?' That's how bad it was. It was a nasty, nasty place in lots of ways, when you were at the top."

Departmental politics aside, the work itself was no less fraught. "There weren't enough hours in the day to do that job," says Wright. "It was really badly run and organised with no Head of Drama to help you out. Basically, what I was doing the whole time was just trying to sort all the problems that were already there. Now, if I look back on it, I'd have probably been better off just ignoring the problems and just trying to get some new stuff going. But you can't! It was impossible to ignore the fact that *Casualty* was in a terrible state, all the real long-runners. *EastEnders* was actually alright, thank God.

"I was looking after all the series from the regions, all the series from the indies. So I was running hundreds and hundreds of hours of drama. I didn't see any family, any friends; I worked every weekend, I was getting terrible migraines. I was getting [BBC One Controller] Michael Jackson ringing up asking where all the new series were, when it takes at least 18 months to develop a show. The cupboard was bare when I came in. So the pressure of it was just horrendous."

Perhaps unsurprisingly given this atmosphere, Wright also didn't stay for long as Head of Drama Series. Like Nick Elliott, she departed to take up a position as a part of the ITV network; in August 1997 it was announced that she was leaving to join LWT, where she became the company's Controller of Drama.

"I didn't decide to leave, I got headhunted. I probably would have stayed a bit longer, even though I wasn't enjoying it. But Andrea Wonfor rang me up, invited me for dinner, and said here was a lovely job. That was a fantastic offer, and I'd started off in ITV at Yorkshire, I love ITV. So it was impossible to say no to, and I adored being at LWT. It was just great.

"When I left, somebody from the department forced some of the people not to come to my leaving do. Oh God, I can't tell you, there were some pretty grim people in there! They'd had it their own way rather too long, I think. So it wasn't a pleasant place to be. A lot of people were lovely, and I had a great time at the BBC – until I got that job!"

It was after this parade of departmental heads had come and gone in rapid succession that the BBC recruited Mal Young, with his move to the Corporation announced at the end of October 1997. When he then arrived to take up the job a couple of months later, he found similar problems to those which had confronted Wright – although his remit was slightly smaller, as the department no longer had to oversee the independently produced series.

"I got in there and I found a department very deflated," Young remembers. "I walked down the corridor in the Drama department and all the doors were closed. Everyone was hiding, and it was a horrible atmosphere. You could have been mistaken for thinking it was a solicitors' office or an insurance firm. It didn't feel like show business.

"I don't want to sound like a luvvie, but what we do is we entertain people. So if you're creating or developing those shows, the place should be fun. When I was at Mersey TV it was fun. We were all new to television and it felt different. It felt like we were the punks. So I tried to inject a bit of that into it."

Young pinpoints the legacy of one particular series as the cause for much of the department's malaise. "I realised that they were still suffering from what we called the 'E syndrome'. Which was *Eldorado*. It was such a high-profile disaster that people didn't recover from it. People had lost their jobs and been moved sideways or out. It had been in the papers and in the media – and this was pre-social media. Imagine what it would be like today!"

Eldorado was an ill-fated soap opera about the lives of British ex-pats in Spain, initiated under the watch of Jonathan Powell and Peter Cregeen. It was launched in 1992 with three episodes a week, in an attempt to capture a larger slice of the early evening audience for BBC One. It also helped with the BBC's new need to fulfil their 25 percent quota of programming made by independent companies, as it was a production of Verity Lambert's Cinema Verity. *Eldorado* was conceived by *EastEnders* creators Tony Holland and Julia Smith, and much was hoped for from the programme. Millions of pounds were spent on the outdoor set and dedicated production facility in Spain, and the show was greatly hyped by a high-profile advertising campaign in the run-up to its launch.

Eldorado ended up as a disaster, suffering from various behind-the-scenes issues and never finding a large enough audience to justify its slot and expenditure, despite all the talent behind it. After only a year, the show was cancelled in 1993 by the incoming Controller of BBC One Alan Yentob. The very title *Eldorado* became a byword for television failure in the UK – with the BBC's own website admitting in 2013 that, "Critics still describe it as the biggest disaster in the Corporation's history, a £10 million embarrassment."

Young felt that this chastening experience had made the Drama Series department very cautious, even nearly five years later when he arrived. "I met a lot of people who'd lost their confidence," says Young. "Everyone was made to feel guilty for past sins."

His predecessor Jo Wright, however, disagrees with Young's assessment of *Eldorado*'s aftermath. "I didn't feel that. I mean, Mal's a soap person so that's what he would think. I felt they were demoralised because there'd been such appalling decision-making for so long. There'd been terrible, really bad decisions on hiring. I inherited an *unbelievable* mess of people who just didn't care. I think the biggest problem in the BBC at that point was they didn't deal with any emotional or personal problems with the people that were running any of those things. So you're talking about a very demoralised department, where people knew that their bosses were just not doing the slog."

Either way, it's clear that the Drama Series department had its fair share of problems when Mal Young arrived to take command. "I inherited all this mess, and it *felt* like a bit of a mess," he says. "I brought in Patrick Spence, who I had met when I went to Pearson. He'd already been in a development role and we just clicked. He was very different from me – very different background. He knew every writer in the UK, he knew every up-and-coming writer in the UK. He knew so much about drama. I've never met anyone like him. Fantastic guy.

"When I moved over I thought I was going to need as many allies there as possible to pull it off. Patrick was the only person I knew in development in London at the time, because I'd only been in London a year and all my contacts and relationships were via *Brookside*. So I brought Patrick over and it clicked. I told him he'd run development, and I'd run the department. We'd come up with a strategy to put out as many big, popular shows as possible."

One of the reasons why Young had been keen to bring Patrick Spence over to the BBC with him as his Head of Development was that Spence had previous experience of working in BBC Drama Series. Two years earlier he had been script editor on the first series of *Silent Witness* but had not enjoyed the atmosphere of the department at the time.

"I had absolutely *hated* it," says Spence. "The drama department felt badly run, full of fear, full of indecision. I was quite angry, so I went out into what we would now call the independent sector. I wanted to be anywhere else but the BBC. I went to work for Thames Television, which was then owned by Pearson and merged whilst I was there.

"Then Mal came in, and asked about my time at the BBC, and I told him how badly-run it was, and how it needed somebody with strength and determination and a bit of enthusiasm – the hunger to make good work. About eight weeks later Mal walked in and said they'd offered him the job and told me he was only going to do it if I went with him, because I knew the BBC.

"He promoted me from being a script editor – I was quite lowly at the BBC when I left *Silent Witness* – and brought me in as his Number Two – Head of Development and executive producer. It was a massive promotion. But he wanted me to watch his back, because he didn't know who to trust. So we went in together, and it felt quite exciting. Mal was determined that if *all* he achieved was that he would stay for five years, that would be better than any of his predecessors.

"So he made a commitment on his first day to the team. He said, 'I don't know whether you're going to like me or not, but I promise you one thing – I'm going to stay. I'm not going to leave like everyone else did.' I think we then discovered why people left quite quickly! It was frightening. The stakes were quite high, the politics were high."

The immediate challenge was the department's morale. "There was no love of series in those days," says Spence. "It feels very glamorous now, making TV series, but in those days it was not. The top of the pile was single film. Then the next level down was serials, and then we at the bottom were the people who made the soaps and the series. In those days you would be desperate to get off series and do 'proper' television like serials or single films. And we just had to try and bring enthusiasm and pride back into that department."

Young drew upon the BBC's rich history as he began the unenviable task of motivating his team. "I used to talk about this being the department that made *All Creatures Great and Small*,

Bergerac, all the greats," he explains. "I was trying to give them their confidence back and say, 'This is what we do'. We invented popular drama. ITV had taken it and made it ITV's, but actually, the BBC created that genre of popular drama – that was our heritage and our legacy, and we had to lean into that.

"Very early on, we knew that *Doctor Who* was one of our crown jewels. I remember talking about it when I talked about *Play for Today* and all the iconic pieces."

One of the ways in which Young attempted to connect the staff working under him with the BBC's heritage in such shows was to hang on the walls framed copies of covers their programmes had earned down the years from the *Radio Times* listings magazine. Included among these was the edition that had marked the *Doctor Who* TV Movie's broadcast in 1996.

This is slightly cheeky when you consider that for the majority of its original run, *Doctor Who* had actually belonged to Drama Serials – apart from when Series and Serials were merged. On the other hand, however, it *had* ended up in Drama Series for its final season in 1989, and were *Doctor Who* ever to come back after the TV Movie it seemed clear that its old 'series of serials' format would have to be abandoned in favour of mostly standalone episodes. So, if the BBC ever *did* want to resume in-house production, Drama Series was always likely to be its home; although in the event, when the time came this wasn't quite how it turned out.

Young was no dyed-in-the-wool *Doctor Who* fan, having been keener on the likes of *Batman* and Gerry Anderson's shows when he was growing up in the 1960s. However, he had observed with interest the way in which his two nephews had gone through stages of being fanatical *Doctor Who* fans, purely on the basis of watching videos of the show, and felt that a programme which could engender such enthusiasm even when it was no longer a going concern had to have some special pulling power to it. But Young was not the only person recruited by the BBC in 1997 who believed that *Doctor Who* still held some value.

In May 1997 BBC One had lost its controller, when Michael

Jackson decided to jump ship after less than a year in the job to succeed Michael Grade as the chief executive of Channel 4. Given how conspicuous by its absence *Doctor Who* was from BBC One's schedules during the 1990s, it's curious to note just how much of the decade the channel spent under the control of men who were actually interested in reviving it. Alan Yentob was involved in attempts to get *Doctor Who* back onto the screen in one form or another almost all the way through his tenure. And in 1997, the job went to another man who also tried to get new *Doctor Who* off the ground – Peter Salmon.

After working as a government press officer and then a local newspaper reporter, Salmon had joined the BBC as a general trainee in 1981. Later in the decade, he had made his way up to become a producer, working on the BBC's monthly witness-appeal programme *Crimewatch*, before in 1989 moving away from London to become the Head of Television Features at BBC Bristol. Bristol was mostly known for its factual output, notably the work of the BBC Natural History Unit. But Salmon was also responsible for helping to establish the corporation's relationship with the city's Aardman Animations for their *Wallace & Gromit* productions, on which he was an executive producer.

Salmon left the BBC in 1993 to become Controller of Factual Programmes at Channel 4, and by January 1996 had joined Granada Television as Director of Programmes. Granada was the oldest and, arguably, the most prominent company within the ITV network. Its flagship offering was the long-running soap opera *Coronation Street*, which Michael Grade and Jonathan Powell had pitted *Doctor Who* in hopeless competition against in the late 1980s.

Granada held the ITV franchise for broadcasting in the north-west of England, but also made many of the channel's nationally-networked shows. Following the deregulation of the ownership of commercial television companies in the 1990 Broadcasting Act, Granada and fellow ITV company Carlton began a process of buying up most of the other regional franchise holders; this would eventually culminate in Carlton and Granada's merger, and the formation of ITV PLC, in the early 2000s.

At this point, however, Granada was still an independent entity, producing programmes, not just for ITV but also for the BBC and Channel 4.

After Peter Salmon had been at Granada for less than eighteen months, Jackson's departure opened up the BBC One controller's job, and Salmon was tempted back to Television Centre to fill it - actually applying for the job rather than being approached or headhunted. Mal Young believes that Salmon's arrival paved the way for his own recruitment by the BBC.

"Peter Salmon was a good friend of mine from our Channel 4 days," explains Young. "So he was instrumental in supporting me coming to the BBC. I was part of one of his first ideas to shake things up. I think he must have said to them, 'I tell you who you should try...' Because they'd tried everyone! It worked because we trusted each other, we had great respect for each other, we knew what we wanted to do.

"We wanted to get rid of the old fusty-dusty stuff. I inherited *Hetty Wainthropp Investigates* and some developments that were going into production because we had nothing else. But we knew that they weren't great. His job and mine, we agreed, would be to revitalise BBC One and make it much younger, much more popular and much more entertaining."

When Salmon took up the job as Controller of BBC One in September 1997, *The Guardian* reported that when asked what he wanted to do with drama on the channel, he replied that he was "looking for the next big series, a bit of derring-do, a bit of ambition."

Ultimately Salmon would be thwarted in his attempts to make *Doctor Who* that Next Big Series, and it would be his successor who finally recommissioned it. He declined an invitation to contribute to this book, on the basis that his involvement "was some time ago." But there's no doubt that if events had gone only slightly differently, it could have been under his watch that a Russell T Davies-written *Doctor Who* came to be launched.

Another BBC returnee who would be key to that eventual revival also came back on board at the Corporation in 1997,

THE LONG GAME

although her arrival was less noted at the time than either Young's or Salmon's in more prominent jobs. Jane Tranter was another one of those BBC executives, like Mal Young, who *Doctor Who* fans monitoring the BBC hierarchy for any sign of a sympathetic voice never saw coming. But unlike any of the others involved in *Doctor Who*'s revival, she had actually worked on the show before, albeit in a peripheral role.

Born – like *Doctor Who* itself – in 1963, Tranter had joined the BBC as a secretary in the Radio Drama department in the mid-1980s, before moving across to a similar job in television drama's Series and Serials department. She told a 2013 DVD documentary:

> "There were all sorts of amazing things happening [in Drama], and the only thing I could really, really get excited about was the fact that I was working in the same building that *Doctor Who* was being made in. *Doctor Who* wasn't regarded by everybody in the same way that I saw it, which was really the most glamorous show that the BBC could be making... [*Doctor Who* producer] John Nathan-Turner was a man who would whirl through the BBC, followed by an entourage, and the rest of us all looked a bit dowdy or a bit earnest... I would just hang around until some assistant floor manager who was working on *Doctor Who* would let me go in and do their job for a weekend."

Tranter tells me that her persistence eventually paid off. In the dying days of television drama still being rehearsed and then recorded in multi-camera studios, she found herself marking up the rehearsal space for *Doctor Who* one weekend at the BBC's North Acton rehearsal rooms.

"The BBC ran this amazing training scheme where you would become a trainee assistant floor manager, or a trainee production manager, or trainee location manager, or trainee continuity," she explains. "I had really wanted to be a trainee assistant floor manager and there were very, very few secretaries moved up to do that. It was normally people who came in from the outside, from theatre – more male than female. You really had to put your homework in, and I was incredibly fortunate.

"I had a good friend and assistant floor manager called Julie Edwards – she's a director now – and she explained how I needed to get experience of doing what was called the mark-up. These things were absolutely bamboozling! You would have this coloured tape and the designer would give you a floor plan for the rehearsal and you had to mark out all the different floor things and the doors and how they opened and place the tables and all the props that you were given.

"I did it on a Saturday, on behalf of another assistant floor manager, which meant they could have a Saturday off and I got the experience of doing it. I marked up the whole thing and then I looked at it – it was on this thin sort of paper – and realised that I'd done it the wrong way round! So everything was back-to-front. I had to pull up all the tape and do it all over again! But it was a great privilege. I loved it. I just couldn't believe it... there I was, all on my own – *bloody* dusty floor, I remember – marking up the TARDIS for this show that I had just loved and loved and loved growing up."

Tranter was not crawling around in the Acton dust for long. By the end of the decade she had moved full-time into the production side of drama, working as assistant script editor on the fourth series of *Casualty* in 1989 – just missing crossing paths with *Doctor Who* script editor Andrew Cartmel, who took over as the show's script editor for the following series. Tranter then became a script editor on the BBC's *Screen One* and *Screen Two* anthology strands, before leaving to join Carlton Television in 1992.

Carlton had just won the ITV franchise for London weekdays, which they took up at the start of 1993. That year, Tranter quickly earned a promotion to become their Head of Drama, aged just 30. One of the series she was involved in bringing to ITV during her time at Carlton was *Bramwell* – the Victorian medical drama which had been the TV Movie's competition for its BBC One broadcast, and which starred future *Doctor Who* guest star Jemma Redgrave.

Tranter returned to the BBC in July 1997, during a period when many were leaving the Corporation's Drama department. *Broadcast* magazine later recorded her thoughts of that time:

> "'It wasn't the calmest time,' says Tranter. 'I felt like I was driving in the wrong direction on a motorway in bank holiday traffic.' Nevertheless, the exodus afforded her plenty of opportunity. As she herself acknowledges: 'I was incredibly lucky; in a way, I could only go up.'"

When I put this quote to Tranter today, and suggest it does seem like an odd time to have chosen to go back to a department clearly in turmoil, she explains why she was so keen to do it.

"I'm not saying that the late 1990s weren't a great time for TV," she insists. "If you look back you'll find *Our Friends in the North*, you'll find *This Life*. But it was interesting that both those shows were on BBC Two. I think it was really BBC One that was suffering. BBC Two always did these great things and at the time actually had quite a decent budget, but BBC One had a lot less money to spend than ITV. ITV had all the stars, they had *Prime Suspect* and *Cracker* and everything else, it was just really going for it. I think as well there was just a sense of slight snobbery about seriously popular television."

Tranter also observed the same hierarchical divisions within BBC Drama that Patrick Spence had encountered. She explains how she felt the different departments were then perceived.

"The BBC at that time was still divided into the Series Department, which is where you went to work if you weren't very good; the Serials Department, where you went to work if you were Oxbridge-educated; and the Single Films Department, where you went to work if you were really lucky! It just was all wrong.

"It was the time when independent production companies were starting. There used to be a time when those producers who were really ambitious all worked for the BBC. When I started my career at the BBC, Television Centre was crammed with all these huge names and big personalities, and it just wasn't the same. They were all leaving to go and start indies and be rich. By the time I got there, it was all a bit limping.

"I had worked at ITV since 1992, so had seen the rebirth of ITV, but I wanted to do something that was different. I wanted to make drama that didn't have an ad break in it, and to use everything I had learned – about where you find the pulse of entertaining drama that's also got something to say. I never want to make anything that hasn't got something to say, but I like it to be entertaining as well – if the subject matter allows for it.

"I just thought the BBC was the place to do it. It's more fun to go somewhere that needs some work done to it than somewhere that's all ready. I'd never buy a show-house, for example. I don't want someone else's good taste. I want to go and sort it out and say what I want."

Like her fellow 1997 recruit Mal Young, Tranter also chose to illustrate her office with markers of the BBC's past, as she told the 2006 book *Doctor Who: The Inside Story*:

> "When I first came to work at BBC Drama, I put up in the office an enormous black-and-white photograph of a Dalek, alongside one of Carol White in *Cathy Come Home* and one of *Dixon of Dock Green*, to remind everyone working in BBC Drama of our roots and our history."

"Jane Tranter literally loved the show," Russell T Davies told *SFX* magazine in 2009. "She worked on it as an AFM, and she watched it when she was a kid, and that's not just a BBC exec doing their job, she genuinely is a proper fan."

Tranter's love of *Doctor Who* would remain unknown to the wider world for the time being. For now, she was working as an executive producer in the Drama Singles department, overseeing one-off productions for BBC One.

Young, Spence, Salmon and Tranter would all in their various ways in the coming years attempt to get *Doctor Who* off the ground again, with Tranter and Young eventually succeeding in that ambition. But it was another appointee at the corporation in 1997, the man who had brought Jane Tranter back to the Drama department, who would actually be the first BBC executive since the TV Movie's transmission to talk publicly about the possibility of reviving *Doctor Who*.

This was David Thompson, an experienced producer of one-off dramas, who at this point was promoted to take over what had previously been two different jobs. In the spring of 1997, he succeeded both Mark Shivas, who had been running BBC Films, and George Faber, who had been running television's Drama Singles department until leaving in December 1996, to become the BBC's first Head of Film and Single Drama. This combination came about – at least partly – to try and eliminate the competition for scripts that had previously existed between the two units.

"It was fraught with competition and internecine difficulties, and it made no sense," Thompson explains. "There weren't really two separate jobs. The film department was too small to be viable, it needed to be part of an entity. Although it was kind of difficult running both, because they were such different things."

David Thompson was to occupy this job for the next ten years, carving out a notable niche for both himself and for the BBC within the British film industry.

And it was Thompson who, at the Cannes Film Festival in May 1998, took *Doctor Who* fandom by surprise when he announced that the BBC were looking to bring the Doctor back – but to cinema, rather than to television.

3

SET THE CONTROLS FOR THE SILVER SCREEN

NOT A DECADE HAS PASSED in *Doctor Who*'s history without someone trying to make the show into a big-screen feature film.

However, only in the show's earliest years did anybody actually succeed in this ambition. Producers Milton Subotsky and Max J. Rosenberg put later efforts to shame by succeeding twice, in quick succession, turning out the Peter Cushing-starring *Dr. Who and the Daleks* and *Daleks' Invasion Earth 2150 AD* in 1965 and 1966.

In the late 1970s, Tom Baker himself unsuccessfully attempted to finance his *Doctor Who Meets Scratchman* film idea, created with co-star Ian Marter and director James Hill. A company variously known as Green Light, Coast-to-Coast and Daltenreys then purchased feature film rights for the show from the BBC in the late 1980s, promoting their *Doctor Who* film for several years without ever progressing to filming.

The fall-out from this particular project continued into the late 1990s, with the team behind it launching legal action against the BBC in February 1997, claiming that the TV Movie had infringed the rights deal they had with the Corporation to make *Doctor Who* cinema films. Despite gaining coverage in various newspapers, nothing ever came of this and they never won the case.

Following the success of the eventual television comeback of *Doctor Who*, the 2010s saw *Harry Potter* director David Yates talk about taking the Time Lord into cinemas again. But before this, before the show was even revived on television, in the late 1990s and early 2000s the ball seemed to be firmly in the BBC's court – although they were never actually able to put together a deal to bring *Doctor Who* back to the big screen.

There had been feature film versions of BBC television dramas going back to the 1950s, when Hammer Film Productions remade the likes of Nigel Kneale's *The Quatermass Experiment* and *The Creature* for theatrical release. In the following decades, adaptations of other BBC dramas and comedies had similarly been made by outside parties who had simply bought the film rights, rather than the BBC becoming actively involved in their own movie-making.

That all changed at the turn of the 1990s, with the setting-up of the BBC Films unit within the Drama department. The initial driving force behind this was Mark Shivas, who became Head of Drama in 1988 and was keen for the BBC to emulate Channel 4's successes in investing in cinema. David Thompson was a part of that process, producing BBC films for both television and general release, before taking charge when he became Head of Film and Single Drama in 1997.

"It was driven by loads of factors," says Thompson, recalling the BBC's move into cinema. "The individual desire of people working at the BBC at the time to make movies was one factor. We had a very strong single drama tradition, but single drama television films are very hard to finance, whereas for movies you could raise other co-production [funding]. So it made a lot of commercial sense – you could pull in a lot of co-production money, with the right project.

"Secondly – although the BBC was slow to recognise this – you also obtained a great deal of rights. You could show the films many times. A classic example is *Billy Elliot*, or *Mrs Brown*, which are wheeled out every year at Christmas because the rights deals were fantastic. You had the rights to show them 'x' number of times every year, whereas with television drama you had to pay repeat fees to everybody each time.

"There was always a tension between BBC Television and BBC

SET THE CONTROLS FOR THE SILVER SCREEN

Films – understandably, because it's a television company – and a lot of suspicion and hostility towards making films. But ultimately this argument did bear some sway and have some weight. Because if you'd got a film that worked you could keep showing it and pull in audiences a lot of times.

"The other key reason was the talent ambitions. We wanted to nurture and hang on to our talent, and our talent naturally had aspirations to move into feature films. Over the years I worked with, for example, Armando Iannucci on his first feature film. We gave feature film opportunities to numerous first-time directors, including Stephen Daldry and Paul Greengrass and Tom Hooper, all kinds of people. Writers and directors, and actors too. So it was a talent magnet thing as much as anything else, and it was a successful talent magnet. There were dozens of people whose first feature films we did in that way. Everybody was exploding with ideas, and single television drama couldn't contain these ideas adequately."

With this 'explosion of ideas' on BBC Films' slate, Thompson headed to the 1998 Cannes Film Festival.

Cannes is one of the great annual get-togethers of the film-making world, held every May in the south of France. At this glamorous event, new releases are promoted to high-heaven, the stars are out in force, prizes are awarded, deals are done, projects are announced and the great and the good of the movie-making business generally network and schmooze.

Thompson was there in 1998 with a big project to unveil. Acclaimed television writer Jimmy McGovern, by then well-known for his ITV dramas *Cracker* and *Hillsborough*, had been recruited to write the screenplay for BBC Films' most expensive production yet – a multi-million-pound historical epic, telling the story of Mary, Queen of Scots.

As it turned out, this film never reached the cinemas, with the script eventually emerging as one half of McGovern's two-part television drama *Gunpowder, Treason & Plot* in 2004. But even back in May 1998, it found itself overshadowed in the press by another project – one which didn't yet have a script or even a rough outline... and appeared to amount to nothing more than a vague idea.

BBC Films apparently wanted to bring back *Doctor Who* as a big-budget, big-screen movie. The question was, why?

"We made lots of 'indie' kind of films, lower-budget films, some of which had done very well, and some of which hadn't done so well," says Thompson. "There was a feeling amongst certain people that we should be taking on Hollywood. Because we'd had quite a lot of success and presence at the Academy Awards with a number of films, there was a feeling that we ought to be doing bigger international films.

"I was very conscious that it was going to be hard to do that, and I did always feel that our audience were probably more in independent cinema, and that's where we were more likely to succeed. But there was a constant push to see what we could do that was bigger and more brash. It was all sensible, looking at our own intellectual property and thinking what we could make some money out of and make a splash with."

The idea certainly *did* make a splash after Thompson mentioned it to the press at Cannes, and most of the British newspapers hoovered up the story. *The Sun*, for example, suggested that the Doctor could be played by a woman in any resulting film. "We have not cast the lead role yet nor do we have any scripts," Thompson was quoted by them as having said. "But who knows, Doctor Who might even turn into a female."

The *Daily Mail* went even further, stating that such casting was definitely going to be the case, and suggesting that Daniela Nardini, who had recently starred in the highly-successful BBC Two drama series *This Life*, might be a contender for the role:

> "The Scots actress is strongly tipped to become the first female Dr Who battling those malevolent dustbins known as the Daleks. The BBC recently announced plans for a £10million film in which the timelord will be revived as a female. Last week Miss Nardini won a BAFTA for *This Life*. But before she can step into the

TARDIS, she will have to fend off a strong challenge from English star Helen Baxendale who is currently appearing in the US sitcom, *Friends*."

David Thompson admits that, while the idea of making a *Doctor Who* film was genuine, there was a degree of mischief that went on when it came to dealing with media coverage at Cannes.

"It was good fun to see who would write what," he confesses. "It was all total speculation, and they just loved it. If you didn't answer people's questions at every Cannes about this stuff, they'd get pissed off. So it was a sort of game that we played, and the press still play that game. It was all a bit insubstantial – that's the truth of it."

So how did he feel about this insubstantial bit of nonsense knocking his main announcement, the Mary, Queen of Scots film, out of many of the column inches covering the 1998 festival?

"We were philosophical about it. There was an imperative to get the announcements into the national papers. BBC management wanted BBC Films being written about – for people to be aware of what we were doing. So it was part of my mission to get noticed and get written about; not in the trade, but in the nationals. We were usually very successful at that. You had to play that game, so you needed something juicy – even if it wasn't 100 percent concrete.

"There was a slightly mad, heightened imperative to announce things before they were ready. This is not about the BBC, this is about the industry generally at those festivals – people showing off and trying to impress with what they were doing."

If there was no great substance behind the talk of a *Doctor Who* film, then the way in which it was so eagerly seized upon by the British press did at least show there was still an interest and excitement about the series.

"Every time we made an announcement at Cannes or anywhere else, the one thing everybody went on and on and *on* about was *Doctor Who*," recalls Thompson. "There was a furious interest. People were absolutely fascinated by it."

"There is obviously a great movie to be made from *Doctor Who*," was what Thompson was reported as having told journalists at the time by *Doctor Who Magazine* Issue 266, published in June 1998. However, when the magazine contacted the BBC for more detail, they were told that there were "absolutely no concrete plans for a *Doctor Who* movie."

By the following month, though, things appeared to have changed slightly. *Doctor Who Magazine* Issue 267 reported that *Variety* had named HAL Films and Miramax as the BBC's potential partners in the *Doctor Who* movie venture.

The American film company Miramax had been established in 1979 and bought by Disney in 1993, where it continued to operate as a quasi-autonomous subsidiary of the powerful corporation until being sold again seventeen years later.

A tie-up with the BBC did make a certain amount of sense, as Miramax – particularly in its pre-Disney days – had a track record for backing feature films made by British television companies, such as Granada's *My Left Foot* and LWT's *The Tall Guy*, along with several previous collaborations with BBC Films. The company had also recently distributed Anthony Minghella's *The English Patient*, which had won nine Academy Awards in 1997 including Best Picture, so certainly had the cachet the BBC might seek in a production partner.

HAL Films, on the other hand, was a new company, formed in London in October 1997 by former Channel 4 executives David Aukin and Colin Leventhal (the 'A' and 'L' of the name), and one former Miramax one, Petrea Hoving (the 'H'). The company was bankrolled by Miramax, and its founding trio was described by the American company as "the European dream team."

Doctor Who Magazine reported that discussions between the BBC and Miramax regarding a potential *Doctor Who* film had taken place "four months ago" – so in early 1998. They did also relate, however, a contradictory claim by David Thompson to *Variety* that the subject had only come up a week before it was mentioned at Cannes.

At the end of July, *Doctor Who Magazine* Issue 268 followed this up with a brief report from "well-connected fan Tim Collins", then a serving member of Parliament for the Conservative Party. Collins had contacted David Thompson directly, and was told at the beginning of June that "together with co-production partners, we are examining the possibility of a feature film... but there are, as yet, no definite plans to go into production."

Looking back now, Thompson only vaguely recalls the involvement of Miramax in the venture and thinks that the reports may have been due to that company overstating how far the process had got.

"I'm sure they had no formal involvement in it at that stage," he says. "But that's what happened with Miramax a lot. They would attach themselves to things. On the first film I did with them, *The Hour of the Pig*, they announced themselves as the co-producers before anything was signed. I think that was more talk."

Little more was heard about the idea for most of the rest of 1998. But it was actually a comparatively busy year for *Doctor Who* film projects – or reports of them, anyway. At least two other parties also looked at trying to bring the Doctor back to the big screen that year... but from slightly different angles.

Before the intrigue generated by David Thompson's comments at Cannes, *Doctor Who Magazine* had reported that TV Movie producer Philip Segal had met with the BBC early in February 1998, with *Doctor Who* one of the topics under discussion – including the question of the feature film rights. It later transpired that Segal had been informed by Alan Yentob that there was some possibility of the rights being available to remake the two Dalek films of the 1960s.

Segal eventually decided that this option wasn't really worth exploring. But it turned out that someone else had noticed that there might be something to be exploited in the residual rights to those films. In *Doctor Who Magazine* 267, the very same issue where they had featured the proposed deal with HAL Films and Miramax, the magazine ran a small news story immediately below, reporting that a company called Chaos Films were looking to take advantage of an option which producer Milton Subotsky had held onto, to make a third *Doctor Who* film, and that they had allegedly approached an actor to star in such a venture.

Rather improbably, said actor was apparently Michael Sheard.

Sheard himself had reported the news during an appearance at a convention in May. While he'd enjoyed a long and successful career – including half-a-dozen supporting roles in various *Doctor Who* stories, small parts in the *Star Wars* and *Indiana Jones* film series and was known to a generation of British viewers as Mr Bronson in the BBC's school drama *Grange Hill* – Sheard hardly seemed the sort of name that might be attached to the starring role in such a project.

Subotsky, who had tried to get a third *Doctor Who* film made in the 1980s, had died in 1991, and what rights he may or may not have held – or the status of these rights by 1998 – wasn't clear. Nor was it clear whether Chaos Films had ever actually had any contact with Subotsky's family. Chaos had been established in Devon in May 1998 by producers Mitchell Henderson and Martin Cahill, but nothing more ever came of them or their supposed involvement with whatever rights Milton Subotsky may once have held.

Even at the time, doing anything with *Doctor Who* based on rights left over from a decades-old project – perhaps in the manner of the 'unofficial' 1980s James Bond film *Never Say Never Again* – never seemed particularly plausible. Indeed, it says something that the BBC effort always appeared to be the more realistic project, even though it was a film that never even got anywhere close to production.

Nonetheless, in an article published on the BBC News website to tie in with *Doctor Who*'s 35th anniversary in November 1998, an indication was given that the idea of a big-screen outing was moving forward in some form. There was no mention of Miramax, HAL or any other details, but an unidentified 'BBC spokesman' did tell the website that: "We're in talks about a possible feature film for the cinema. Scripts have been prepared, but the film will be at least two or three years away if we decide to go ahead with it."

The idea that a script or scripts actually existed was a new one. If a full script or even a treatment was ever written for BBC Films at this point, then it's never surfaced, and nor has the name of any writer who might have worked on it. Certainly, David Thompson has no memory of ever having seen a script. But whoever may or may not have been approached to write it, by the spring of 1999 the film did at least suddenly seem to have one thing that made it seem like a slightly likelier proposition – a director.

One year on from Thompson's apparently casual remarks at the Cannes Film Festival, in May 1999 *Total Film* magazine carried an interview with British director Paul Anderson – who later credited himself as Paul WS Anderson to avoid confusion with an American director of the same name. Anderson had helmed the 1995 video game adaptation *Mortal Kombat* and the 1997 science-fiction film *Event Horizon*, and *Total Film* reported that his next feature was likely to be a big-screen version of *Doctor Who*.

It was only a small mention at the end of an interview but, as the first solid piece of information to emerge regarding any *Doctor Who* film for some time, it immediately launched another summer of speculation and rumour. *Doctor Who Magazine* 282, published at the end of August, reported that Impact Films, a company run by Anderson and producer Jeremy Bolt, was now another partner in the proposed deal behind any film. The magazine also relayed speculation that names as disparate as Hollywood star Denzel Washington and former *Coronation Street* actor Linus Roache could be possible candidates to play the Doctor.

On August 29, the *Independent on Sunday* ran a feature by journalist Matthew Sweet about *Doctor Who*'s potential future. Sweet was a fan who, fourteen years later, would go on to make the BBC's 50th anniversary documentary *Me, You and Doctor Who*. For the article, he spoke to Mike Phillips of BBC Worldwide, who confirmed to him that, "Paul wrote an interesting treatment, and we thought he had a good take on the material, and that it might be a saleable mainstream film. So we made a deal with Paul and Jeremy, and they're in LA talking to studios about making a *Doctor Who* movie."

Mike Phillips had joined BBC Worldwide from Thames Television in 1996, and by 1998 he was Worldwide's Managing

Director of International Television. Despite this quote from the time, he now claims to have no memory of the discussions with Anderson and Bolt.

But it certainly *does* seem to be the case that at around this point, BBC Worldwide became much more involved in the *Doctor Who* film idea – as indeed they were becoming more heavily involved with BBC Films generally. By late 1999 they had entered into a deal to invest £40 million into BBC Films projects over five years – that £8 million-a-year sum representing a doubling of BBC Films' annual budget.

Rupert Gavin was then the chief executive of BBC Worldwide, having joined the organisation in the summer of 1998. "BBC Television and David's unit was very, very keen for Worldwide to get more involved in their film projects," Gavin says.

"David was looking for ways to be able to do more projects and bring more money to the table. So they came to us, and I found a way of making it possible. We thought we had a good model to at least be able to cover our investments, through distribution advances, and be a good corporate citizen and help the BBC say that they were more present in the sector."

When asked about why he thought a *Doctor Who* film, in particular, might be a viable option, Gavin echoes David Thompson's comments. "We were looking around for something more substantial," Gavin explains. "Because BBC Films were all a bit too art-house, a little too obscure and under-cast. So from the Worldwide side – and Mike was leading on this – we said maybe we should throw in something that's got more commercial appeal.

"We came up with various ideas to balance the portfolio, one of which was *Doctor Who*. About which BBC TV production was very excited – at that stage there weren't really any firm plans for what to do with *Doctor Who*. We were able to persuade them that this could be the way of giving more commercial effectiveness to the film activity that we were embarked upon."

David Thompson thinks that it ended up being BBC Worldwide, more than his own department, who were providing the main impetus behind the *Doctor Who* feature film project.

SET THE CONTROLS FOR THE SILVER SCREEN

"It was more driven by Worldwide, that's certainly true," he says. "I was really keen for it to happen, I bought into the idea it could be a big international film. But I was sceptical. How you set up the whole world view in one single movie? I was also a little more wary of this idea that the BBC needed to be making big, international, blockbuster-y kind of films. I was somewhat sceptical that we were going to take on Hollywood at their own game. I thought it was a punt worth taking, but it wasn't primarily driven by me."

For his *Independent on Sunday* article in August 1999, Matthew Sweet also spoke to the mooted film's producer:

> "'*Doctor Who* needs to be reinvented for a global audience,' argues Jeremy Bolt. 'That means casting an international name in the lead role.' He won't confirm or deny Washington's involvement, but it's clear that the 45-year-old Oscar nominee would be a smart choice. And there are other actors under consideration. 'What about Laurence Fishburne?' he suggests. 'Or Anthony Hopkins?'"

The following month, yet another new name was added to the list of potential partners involved with backing the proposed film – Artisan Entertainment. Artisan were hot property at the time, as they were the distributors of one of 1999's most talked-about films – *The Blair Witch Project*, a horror movie shot as 'found footage' on camcorders, which had become something of a cultural phenomenon. Eventually earning nearly $250 million worldwide at the box office, after being made on a budget of only a few hundred thousand, it's little surprise that BBC Films or BBC Worldwide might have been interested in doing business with *Blair Witch*'s backers.

In an article published on September 19 1999, *The Sunday Times* claimed that Artisan were now being lined up as partners for the notional *Doctor Who* film – although whether this was in place of or alongside Miramax wasn't stated. The article claimed that

THE LONG GAME

David Thompson had been in negotiation with Artisan at the Toronto International Film Festival, which came to a close that weekend, and that an official announcement was expected to coincide with BBC Two's planned *Doctor Who* theme night in November. Once again there were quotes from producer Jeremy Bolt, who seemed to have become the venture's principal spokesman. "We intend, with the BBC, to make this bigger than Bond," Bolt told the paper.

Subsequent issues of *Doctor Who Magazine* related that the plot of the movie involved the Doctor battling the Master, "in one form or another," and quoted Bolt as saying that, "There will be a large time travel element to it. And it will have an edge... There won't be as much gore as in *Event Horizon*, but we do want to scare people."

The Sunday Times piece in September 1999 had reported that the film was due to start shooting the following year, with a budget of £14 million. In another piece in the same newspaper the following month, a report on Worldwide's new investment into BBC Films, it was said that a £12 million *Doctor Who* film would be, "the basis of a long-running film franchise."

Either sum would be pretty paltry by big-screen sci-fi standards, but Artisan had shown that you didn't need a massive budget to make a blockbuster hit.

However, there was certainly to be no multi-million-pound budget for this particular project. Within six weeks of the *Sunday Times* report on Artisan's involvement, it was all over; the deal with Impact Films had fallen through.

SFX magazine broke the story on its website on November 4 1999, with a disappointed Bolt telling them:

> "Artisan Entertainment and ourselves have parted company with the BBC. They decided not to go with it – what can you do? I worked for five, no, six months on this, brought the BBC the most exciting film company in the world, the people who have the internet success – which is where the fans are – and the BBC

decided not to go with it. It'll take the BBC God knows how long to sort something else out."

Today, David Thompson only vaguely recalls Anderson and Bolt having been attached to the project.

"There was a conversation with them," he confirms, making it sound somewhat less substantial than Bolt was claiming at the time. "I don't remember the year of it. That was never very concrete, it was just a very vague conversation. Somebody else, Jeremy Bolt, may remember it differently. BBC Worldwide were also trying to drive this themselves; there was this desire to set up a kind of rival operation, in a way. To the best of my knowledge I was across all of the various discussions that were going on, but it always seemed a bit speculative."

Jeremy Bolt did not respond to requests for an interview for this book, so his side of the story remains unknown. It's possible that HAL Films may have also continued to be involved in the project throughout the Bolt and Anderson negotiations. In a November 1999 piece about what any potential future for *Doctor Who* might hold, the *Radio Times* reported that "a spokesman" for the BBC had told them: "We are talking to HAL Films in an attempt to get a *Doctor Who* feature film made."

However, HAL's involvement or otherwise quickly became a moot point: in February 2000, *Variety* reported that Miramax would be withdrawing its support for the company after just four films, with the founders all leaving and Miramax taking over HAL's London offices under their own name. "HAL's much-vaunted autonomy in creative decision-making from its New York-based paymasters proved, in the end, to be an illusion," *Variety* stated.

With all its partners having now left the deal or gone out of business, the BBC – whichever part of the Corporation was actually driving the project – were back where they had started with the *Doctor Who* film; nothing other than a vague desire to perhaps make one at some point.

However, after deciding not to pursue the venture with

THE LONG GAME

Anderson, Bolt and Artisan, BBC Worldwide did move on to find a new partner in the new Millennium. In May 2000, *Variety* reported that the BBC were in discussions with the Mutual Film Company, which had been one of the partners behind the Oscar-winning *Saving Private Ryan*, about a *Doctor Who* feature film. In November of that year, *The Sunday Times* claimed that a *Doctor Who* film would be used to help launch BBC Director-General Greg Dyke's plans for a "full-scale Hollywood-style film studio," and even that "sequels are already being prepared."

It's the tie-up with Mutual which BBC Worldwide's Mike Phillips most strongly recalls from his time trying to get the film off the ground. He had come to know Mutual's co-founder, South African film producer Gary Levinsohn, through other projects that he and the BBC had been involved in together.

"Gary had an existing relationship with the BBC's film acquisition department," Phillips explains. "He was experienced in raising international finance and had partnered with Mark Gordon, a top Hollywood film producer with a long list of studio credits, to form Mutual Film. We started talking about *Doctor Who*, and we got quite excited about the idea of doing a mainstream, big-time Hollywood movie. So that's how it started, completely outside the public service BBC.

"We talked about *Doctor Who* and we felt that some of the later series had got a bit wacky and moved a long way from the original premise. We thought that something closer to the original William Hartnell series would be more saleable – we saw a great part for an older actor alongside the young characters. The next step was for Gary to try to find a writer who would be credible to a major Hollywood studio. He duly came up with someone who I thought was a terrific guy, a screenwriter called Ed Solomon, who had written the original *Men in Black* movie. He had both studio credibility and the experience of creating a hit fantasy movie.

"We got together with Ed, and he completely got *Doctor Who* – he was married to an Englishwoman and had spent quite a bit of time in the UK. He also agreed with our take on the story. I assumed that the next step would be for Ed to write a treatment,

SET THE CONTROLS FOR THE SILVER SCREEN

but he said that we should just go around and do a pitch directly to the studios.

"Ed's reputation enabled us to get quick meetings with the key players. Our main focus was on Universal, both because Ed had good relationships there, but mostly because the then Senior Vice-President of Production was a lady called Donna Langley, who was a Brit. She subsequently rose to be chair of Universal Pictures. She knew *Doctor Who* and was excited to listen to Ed's ideas."

The irony of a potential second *Doctor Who* team-up between the BBC and Universal, the same company that had backed the TV Movie, appears to have been a coincidence rather than any lingering connection from the Paul McGann project. "It was just a different level," according to Phillips, and this was Universal's feature film wing, rather than its television division.

Donna Langley had joined Universal Pictures in June 2001, moving from a similar role at New Line Cinema, so the *Doctor Who* negotiations must have taken place after that point. When approached for this book, however, Langley had no memory of the *Doctor Who* discussions. Scriptwriter Ed Solomon declined to comment on whether he remembered the project or not – although his involvement is also recalled by both Rupert Gavin and David Thompson.

"Ed Solomon *really* fell in love with the idea and started to say he was excited about doing it," Gavin remembers.

"I remember vividly a meeting in the Four Seasons Hotel with Ed Solomon and probably another producer to discuss this, but we never got very far," is Thompson's memory. "I'm not aware that a script was commissioned – if there was, I don't remember. Certainly not by me. It's possible that somebody in BBC Worldwide did it. I think it's unlikely."

Mike Phillips, however, doesn't just strongly remember Solomon's involvement with the *Doctor Who* idea. He also recalls how the writer's actual pitch to Universal went.

"The pitch was incredibly simple. When we discussed it beforehand, one of the other reasons that Ed had felt that it might ring a bell there was that it had strong connections to *Back to the*

Future, which was one of Universal's greatest ever franchise movies. This had some similar elements and the potential for a multi-picture franchise.

"Briefly, Ed's pitch was: we open with a very young couple, they're seventeen or something like that. And they're at a romantic location, either at the beach or on a hillside, and we go in and we hear them talking, and it's clear that they're madly in love with each other but devastated because for various reasons the parents are *absolutely* against the relationship and determined that they should split up.

"So you had this conversation and then out of the blue, this strange figure arrives. We had talked about Anthony Hopkins as our ideal Doctor. He says to them something like, 'Not only is it important to you that you get together, but if your offspring isn't born then the whole future of the world will be imperilled.'

"That was it! No other plot was pitched. Ed rightly judged that it was enough to get them interested. Working out the story would come later in development – let's try and get them excited about the idea.

"At the time, most Hollywood studio people had probably never heard of *Doctor Who*. For those who had, the perception was that it was a British children's sci-fi show with relatively low production values. Hardly any British television shows were seen in the US except on public television. But Donna Langley could see the potential.

"So we thanked the group and said that we would engage with their Business Affairs folks. I then briefed a lawyer from one of the top LA entertainment firms and we started the negotiations. Business negotiations on big movies take forever. These are huge companies, with all sorts of layers of executive responsibility, and all the divisions are determined to grab their share. So this was going to take a long time."

In May 2002, the *Financial Times* claimed that the BBC Worldwide had recently committed "a six-figure sum" in developing the *Doctor Who* project with Mutual. "These things take years to develop," a BBC Films spokesman pointed out to the official *Doctor*

Who website at the time; although they did confirm that *Doctor Who* was indeed an ongoing project for them.

But if Universal's Donna Langley was indeed so enthusiastic, why wasn't BBC Worldwide ever able to get that film made, or even started?

"One of the particular problems we ran into – pretty much immediately – was merchandising," remembers Mike Phillips. "My proposition was quite simple. That the BBC should continue to retain and exploit the worldwide rights on all of the characters and series that they owned. For the movie, there would be a completely different cast, different graphics, poster art, et cetera, and that would be all for Universal to market worldwide. The BBC would participate in all revenues as the intellectual property owner. But that didn't go down well either with Universal or with the BBC. So that alone took up a lot of lawyerly discussion.

"Universal is a giant company. Every big movie is a huge investment and a huge risk. They think about their global marketing spend on the picture, theme parks, toys, video games and so on. The BBC has been very successful in exploiting the *Doctor Who* rights, but the potential revenue on a major hit movie would be on a different scale."

David Thompson's view on why the film never happened is slightly different.

"No one ever really had a good enough concept for it – at least not that I'm aware of," he says. "It seemed like a nice idea but – when you actually put it into practice – very, very difficult to pull off in a single movie. It would have to be the most amazing movie. So a lot of it was just rather overblown talk.

"But the positive side of it is that, in terms of BBC Films, we did need to get attention and be written about, otherwise people would wonder what the point of it was. There was always going to be a healthy tension within the BBC about whether feature films should exist or not, and I'm sure that still goes on."

Given the complications and difficulties that any attempt to get a *Doctor Who* film for the big screen made would inevitably present, it begs the question of just why BBC Worldwide seemed so keen to pursue the idea in the late 1990s and early 2000s. For their then-chief executive Rupert Gavin, the answer was in the underlying appeal of *Doctor Who* itself.

"It had always occurred to us that there was an absolute, underlying passion for this brand," he insists. "That it had an extraordinary history, and that all it would take was the right execution and the right creative treatment to really ignite that passion. So I'd always found it very odd that it had ever been cancelled in the first place."

Mike Phillips, who led BBC Worldwide's efforts to make a *Doctor Who* film during those years, holds a similar view to his former boss.

"I thought it was a great title and I think that, essentially, time travel – if you can get it right – is just a classic storyline. I thought that, with what eventually became Ed's take on it, *Doctor Who* could have been a terrific movie. It would have had all of the expertise and the cash that a major studio can throw at a property to really make it come alive."

Unlike the proposal with Paul Anderson and Jeremy Bolt in 1999, the later effort between the Mutual Film Company, Universal and Ed Solomon had never been anywhere near as publicly-discussed and didn't have as definitive an announcement when it ended. When it emerged that the Anderson and Bolt film deal had collapsed in the autumn of 1999, though, it has to be said that there wasn't exactly unrestrained wailing and gnashing of teeth from *Doctor Who* fandom; not because of any great animosity towards Anderson and Bolt or their previous work, but because there has never really been unbridled enthusiasm among *Doctor Who* fans for the idea of the show becoming a film franchise.

Doctor Who fandom, on the whole, generally seems to prefer the idea of a regular series of several adventures every year, rather than one extended outing every two or three years at best, no matter how hugely budgeted or spectacular that outing may be.

There was also, perhaps – consciously or otherwise – a feeling among some fans that the show might be 'safer', less mucked-about-with, were it to return as a television series rather than on the big screen – a concern that the format might be bent out of shape to suit the whims of Hollywood paymasters.

This was an attitude encapsulated by a correspondent to the letters page of *Doctor Who Magazine* at the time, who wrote despairingly: "Has the BBC completely lost the plot? Presumably [the film will] be a mangled mish-mash designed for another market in much the same vein as the McGann TV Movie. Is that what they think we really want? Do they really think we would prefer some clueless epic to an ongoing commitment to a new series? It is typical of their short-sighted, short-term attitude, and smacks of nothing but greed."

The greatest frustration for *Doctor Who* fans in the autumn of 1999, then, wasn't the news that an attempt to put together a film deal for the show had gone to pieces. Rather, it was the fact that this film proposal had, while it was still active, resulted in the abandonment of a very tentative attempt to bring the show back to television; as an in-house BBC series, to be broadcast on BBC One.

The person with whom the BBC had briefly discussed this, with a view to perhaps writing the revival, was a television scriptwriter with a rapidly burgeoning reputation. Someone who was also known to be a dyed-in-the-wool *Doctor Who* fan, who had adored the series for as long as he could remember.

His name was Russell T Davies.

4
"I THINK THAT'S DEAD"

AT THE BEGINNING OF 1999, the career of television scriptwriter Russell T Davies was about to shift up a gear.

Born in Swansea in April 1963, Stephen Russell Davies was always known by family and friends by his middle name; he added the 'T' to his credits in the early 1990s to distinguish himself from the established writer and broadcaster Russell Davies. In 1984 he graduated from the University of Oxford's Worcester College with a degree in English Literature, before returning home to South Wales where he initially worked in the theatre.

In 1985 he gained his first television job, when he was taken on for part-time casual employment by BBC Wales, to work on the production of the children's series *Why Don't You?* This was a programme typically broadcast during the school holidays, presented by different groups of young people and showcasing ideas for games and activities with which children could entertain themselves.

Davies gained experience in various different roles while working on *Why Don't You?*, including writing his first television scripts. His increasing work for the BBC's children's television output also led to a brief foray in front of the cameras. In June 1987, he was given a one-episode trial run as a storytelling cartoonist on the BBC's long-running young children's series *Play School* – the rehearsals for which took place at the BBC's North Acton Rehearsal Rooms at the same time as the *Doctor Who* serial *Paradise Towers* was being rehearsed there, which pleased Davies.

He had been a huge fan of *Doctor Who* from childhood and had carried this passion for the show into his adult life.

Davies' performance on *Play School* was judged to have gone well and he was offered the chance to take part in further episodes, but he had found the experience not to be for him. Concentrating his efforts on working behind the cameras, in 1988 his career was given a boost when he was recruited by Ed Pugh, in charge of children's programmes at BBC Manchester, to come and work on *Why Don't You?* there.

Throughout most of its history, *Why Don't You?* had been produced on a rotating schedule by various different regional branches of the BBC, but it had now been decided that in future all series of the show would be made at BBC Manchester. Pugh had been impressed with Davies' work after meeting him during a visit to BBC Wales, and Davies took up the offer to go and live and work in Manchester.

Being on the staff at the BBC Manchester children's department gave Davies the chance to experience the full gamut of studio and location production skills – not just writing, but also producing, directing and editing. He ended up being responsible for moving the format of *Why Don't You?* from a magazine programme into more of a scripted drama, with the gang of young presenters becoming involved in an ongoing narrative storyline.

Davies was keen to make the move into fully-fledged drama scriptwriting, and after writing, producing and directing the Saturday morning comedy series *Breakfast Serials* in 1990, he got his break writing drama the following year. He had scripted the first episode of an adventure serial on spec, provisionally titled *The Adventuresome Three* and, with a covering letter from Pugh, sent it to Anna Home, the overall BBC Head of Children's Programmes in London.

Home liked the script and commissioned Davies to write a second episode to see how it developed. Home then found that she had an impending gap in her schedules as writer and actor Tony Robinson had decided to take a year's break from making his popular children's sitcom *Maid Marian and Her Merry Men*. Davies was subsequently commissioned to write the full six-part serial, which became *Dark Season*. Broadcast in November and December 1991, this science fiction thriller about a threat to a school from a mysterious organisation distributing free computers also featured one of the first starring roles for a young Kate Winslet.

Davies later wrote *Century Falls*, a more fantasy-based serial for the same production team, which was screened in 1993. By this time, however, he had left the BBC and was now working for another Manchester-based broadcaster; the ITV network's northwest of England regional franchise holder Granada Television. Davies became the producer of their children's medical drama *Children's Ward*, also writing several episodes for the series.

Davies' love for *Doctor Who* meant that he was aware of the BBC's apparent desire in the early 1990s to find an outside company to make the series for them. He suggested at one point to his bosses at Granada that they should bid to make it for the BBC as an independent production, and later recalled to *Doctor Who Magazine* that he was "laughed out of the room."

In 1994 Davies left his production job at Granada to concentrate on a full-time freelance writing career. He still worked on several Granada programmes, while hoping to get a chance to work on their flagship soap opera *Coronation Street*. He co-created and wrote the late-night soap *Revelations*, and also contributed scripts for the supernatural soap *Springhill*.

Davies did eventually get to briefly work as a storyliner on *Coronation Street* and, perhaps less prestigiously, wrote the straight-to-video spin-off *Viva Las Vegas!*, featuring some of the show's characters on a trip to the USA. However, his career suddenly accelerated when he found himself working on a new prime-time drama series.

However, just before this in 1996, Davies had his first professional brush with *Doctor Who*, writing the novel *Damaged Goods* for Virgin Publishing. Virgin had been producing a licensed range of *Doctor Who* novels called *The New Adventures* since 1991, continuing the story of the show from the point at which the TV series had ended.

Davies had intended to take three months off from his TV work to complete the novel, which was published in October 1996. However, in the event, his schedule became somewhat more frantic when he was asked by Granada to take over the writing duties on a new ITV drama series.

This was *The Grand*, a period drama set in the early 1920s, telling the stories of the staff and guests of the eponymous fictional hotel in Manchester. The writer who had created the project had left the production, so Davies was given the job instead. He wrote all eight episodes of the first series, which was broadcast from early April to late May 1997 – with the first two episodes helmed by future *Doctor Who* director Douglas Mackinnon. There was a *Doctor Who* name from the past involved too, with Granada's then-Head of Drama, Antony Root, serving as executive producer; Root had briefly been the script editor of *Doctor Who* in the early 1980s.

Davies himself later criticised his work on *The Grand*, feeling that it was too dark and miserable, although he also admitted to having learned a great deal from the experience. The series did well enough with audiences to be recommissioned for a second run – having benefitted from being broadcast in the midst of the 1997 general election campaign, for which BBC One ran extended hour-long editions of the *Nine O'Clock News*; five of *The Grand*'s eight episodes faced the news as their main opposition.

During this time, Davies also wrote an episode of Paul Abbott's detective series *Touching Evil*, which was also screened on ITV in May 1997.

At the time when *The Grand*'s first series was made and shown, the Director of Programmes at Granada had been Peter Salmon. Salmon would have been well aware of who was making their new ITV period drama, and who was writing it. However, by the time the second series came to be broadcast, Salmon had left the company – having gone south to Television Centre to become Controller of BBC One in September 1997.

Like Salmon, Russell T Davies politely declined an invitation to contribute to this book, but fortunately, Davies has given several interviews down the years, from which the story of what happened next can be pieced together. "When he went to BBC One, I said 'If you ever want to bring back *Doctor Who*, give it to me!'" Davies told *Cult Times* magazine in the summer of 2000.

The Grand returned for its second run in January 1998, this time consisting of ten episodes, with Davies again taking on the majority of the writing duties. Here he was able to put into practice some of the lessons he'd learned from the first series. Not only did he infuse his scripts with a greater degree of humour, but he also found himself writing one particular episode which would come to be a defining moment in his career.

The sixth episode of *The Grand*'s second series focused on one of the show's supporting characters, Clive the barman. Davies recalled in an article for *The Guardian* in 2003:

> "Clive was a working-class lad struggling to express his sexuality in a time when the proper adjectives and nouns barely even existed. And by focusing on Clive's sexuality instead of sub-plotting it, I wrote better... The Granada executives, Gub Neal and Catriona MacKenzie, were then appointed as heads of drama at Channel 4. Catriona pointed out that the Clive script was better than anything else I'd written. In essence, she was saying, 'Go gay!', but a lot more elegantly than that. The idea was enough. Go gay."

With *The Grand* now over, Davies parted company with Granada and teamed up with another former employee of theirs, producer Nicola Shindler. Shindler had formed her own production company, Red, and its very first commission was to be a Channel 4 drama series written by Davies, telling the story of a group of young gay men living in modern-day Manchester – *Queer as Folk*.

The series created something of a sensation, lauded by many but also criticised by certain sections of the media, with Davies finding himself becoming an increasingly public face for the programme. *Queer as Folk* was also the first drama series of Davies' where he had a degree of control beyond simply being the scriptwriter. He also served as the programme's co-producer, taking on the authorial control and showrunning responsibility that would follow through with all of his subsequent work.

Davies remembered in that 2003 *Guardian* piece:

> "If you happened to be at the centre of that small *Queer as Folk* world, then that world was mad. The first indication of what was to come was at the press launch. Normally, they are attended by 20 jaded journalists, 30 if you're providing wine. We had 200. All with teeth and knives bared. Then, as transmission started, so did the papers. But here's a fact. Everyone now talks about the 'tabloid storm'. In fact, that amounted to one page in the *Daily Mail*. Every other article then referred to that article, so a thousand references make it look as though there were a thousand original condemnations. As for the broadsheets, *The Guardian*'s telly page didn't review the first episode, and I presumed we'd been ignored, until someone pointed out that the review was on page three of the News section. News!"

One of the characters in *Queer as Folk* – Vince Tyler, played by Craig Kelly – was even a card-carrying *Doctor Who* fan. Clips from *Pyramids of Mars* and *Genesis of the Daleks* featured in the programme, a K9 prop made an appearance in one episode, and the set dressers even cheekily included a copy of Davies' *Damaged Goods* in Vince's flat. Oddly, however, when Davies spoke to the BBC *Doctor Who* website about the show at the time of *Queer as Folk*'s transmission in early 1999, he seemed to want to downplay his fan affection:

> "I'm not a huge *Doctor Who* fan, but I really love television. I'll stay up to five o'clock if something like *The Vanessa Show* is on. I thought if I'm going to write a character who's obsessed with television it might as well be a *Doctor Who* fan, partly because the character is true-to-life, and partly because it meant that I didn't

have to do much research! If he'd been a *Juliet Bravo* fan, I'd have had to go and watch loads of episodes of that!"

Whatever the reason for Davies having made this claim, something else happened around this time which confirmed that he was more of a fan than he was letting on.

And it all began with a series called *Harbour Lights*.

Harbour Lights concerned the activities of a harbourmaster on the English south coast and starred Nick Berry, who had just spent several years as the lead in *Heartbeat*, one of ITV's most successful dramas of the 1990s. Debuting on BBC One in February 1999, *Harbour Lights* was made independently for the BBC by Valentine Productions, a company Berry himself co-owned with producer Steve Lanning – which is where the problems had started.

When *Harbour Lights* was going into pre-production in the spring of 1998, Patrick Spence had only been in his job as Head of Development at the BBC's Drama Series department for a few months. "Steve Lanning had sold to Peter Salmon direct – without going through any drama commissioners – the idea of a show starring Nick Berry, set in a harbour in the south of England," Spence explains. "Peter Salmon greenlit it, without any scripts.

"About eight to twelve weeks before filming began, Steve Lanning sent the first two scripts to Peter Salmon. Not that they had been requested, because there was no drama commissioner on board. And Peter read them and went, 'Oh God, I think we've got a problem!'

"He called up Mal Young and said he'd done something in secret. Because Nick, at that stage, was just coming to the end of his deal with ITV, we were not allowed to begin working with him until after that deal ended. So it was all perfectly legal, but the conversations with him up until that point had been on the quiet. Peter admitted that he'd commissioned a show without talking to us – without talking to anyone – and that he'd just read the first few scripts and thought they were rather poor."

"That's absolutely right," says Mal Young. "Peter Salmon did a deal with Nick Berry's production company to get him away from ITV. It was a big deal because he was huge on ITV, but what ITV had failed to point out was that he'd stopped being huge. *Heartbeat* was a big hit for him, but he'd left that and they'd put him on a deal and they shot all these pilots, all of which failed. They were all disastrous because he was just Nick Berry. Nick would even say to us – very nice guy – 'I don't have much range. I'm just me. I'm just Nick Berry.' And we went, 'Oh dear!'

"So Patrick and I inherited *Harbour Lights*. It was an independent production, and we didn't do indies, but we were told we had to take it over and run it with the indie company. But that created a problem because you've got the guys who own it at the indie company, and that company is half-owned by Nick. Then you've got us at the BBC trying to think how to make it better, because the scripts weren't very good. The only idea was a harbourmaster. I mean, who's going to rush home to watch that?"

Patrick Spence takes up the story: "Mal was sent the scripts to *Harbour Lights*, and they were indeed ghastly. He came into my office and said we had a serious problem. We had a show going into production, we'd just been handed responsibility for it. He said to think of ourselves as Red Adairs, to try and rescue it. We needed to find a writer very quickly to put this ship back upright. But we needed someone who could start writing tomorrow.

"I called Tony Wood, who was in the same department and a very good friend of mine, and explained that the only solution I could see would be if we could pull one of the good writers off the soaps. Did he know anyone? Tony replied that he thought he could do better than that, and told me to read a script called *Queer as Fuck* – as it was then titled – by a man called Russell T Davies. Who, if you had worked at Granada, you would have known. I did not know him at that stage. I'd heard his name, but I'd never read his work, I'm embarrassed to admit."

Tony Wood had been the producer of *Children's Ward* when Davies had first written for that show in 1992. Later, he and Davies had worked together on creating *Revelations*, and Wood had produced *The Grand*. They had remained friends since, with Wood now working under Mal Young in the Drama Series department at the BBC.

Spence continues: "Tony said I should consider him because he thought he was the best writer out there and *Queer as Fuck* was waiting for a green light at Channel 4. He thought Russell was kicking his heels, and whilst he might not be remotely interested in writing a show for Nick Berry, that I should at least read the work. So I read *Queer as Fuck* with that aim, to try and find a writer for *Harbour Lights*, and I called up Russell immediately. It was one of the best scripts I've ever read. I said, 'Oh my god, I've just discovered your work. I have a job that I'm looking to fill that I don't think for a second you're going to be interested in, but I'm going to try and pitch it to you anyway.'

"On the phone, Russell said he wasn't remotely interested in trying to rescue *Harbour Lights* but thank you for inviting him, that it was very flattering. I asked him what *did* he want to do, because I was now desperate to work with him, and he said, 'I want to do *Doctor Who*.'

"The thought of this writer reinvigorating *Doctor Who*, which had been on a shelf for a while, felt like the most exciting thing on Earth. Suddenly it became my obsession."

In recounting these events in assorted interviews down the years, Davies has never mentioned an invitation to try and rescue *Harbour Lights* – perhaps to spare the blushes of the writers of that series. When telling the story to *Doctor Who Magazine* in 2003, he attributed the approach to Tony Wood having had existing knowledge of BBC Drama Series already being interested in bringing back *Doctor Who*.

"He knew that Mal Young's department was very keen on resurrecting the Doctor," Davies told the magazine. "So a meeting was arranged, and I met with Mal's development producer, Patrick Spence. It was just an ordinary, inconclusive getting-to-know-you meeting. Nothing was written down, nothing was decided beyond a general agreement that the programme could be great again."

THE LONG GAME

The meeting lasted, by Davies' later reckoning, no longer than about 20 minutes – and came to something of an abrupt end when Wood turned up drunk, having resigned from the staff of the BBC that day, and took his friend off to a bar.

However, when speaking about what had happened to *Cult Times* in 2000, Davies felt that the overall tone had seemed very positive. "They were literally going, 'Off you go and write the script'," he told the magazine.

When exactly this meeting took place is not entirely clear. Davies has given various non-specific timings for it at various points – in December 2003, he told *Doctor Who Magazine* that had been in "late 1998"; in June 2000 he suggested to *Cult Times* it had been "in the winter of 1999"; and in *Doctor Who Magazine* again in July 2005 he hedged his bets and went for "late 1998 or early 1999, after *Queer as Folk* was made, but before it went out."

When approached for this book, Tony Wood was unable to remember when exactly he had left the BBC – although he had certainly done so by the beginning of February 1999, with *Broadcast* magazine reporting early that month that he was setting up an independent production company with support from Channel 4.

Spence, however, is insistent that the meeting must have taken place much earlier than Davies recalls: "I'm pretty sure it was as *Harbour Lights* was hurtling into production," he says. "I'm going to say it was earlier in the year than that, in the summer I reckon. If you'd asked me, I would have guessed that those meetings took place in May or June."

Harbour Lights was announced in May 1998 and, according to a July piece in *The Sun* newspaper, it was due to go into production in August. All of which would make May or June correct if Spence's estimate of it having been eight-to-twelve weeks before the series went in front of the cameras is also accurate.

Tony Wood, however, was certainly still at the BBC in September 1998 when a drama he oversaw called *Sunburn* was announced. So it's possible that Spence's first contact on the phone with Davies about *Harbour Lights* was earlier in the year, but their actual face-to-face meeting about *Doctor Who* didn't take place until

"I THINK THAT'S DEAD"

some months later, sometime between September 1998 and February 1999 - more in line with Davies' recollection. In 2016, the official partwork *Doctor Who: The Complete History* stated that it had been in December 1998. But whenever it happened, and however enthusiastic Spence might have been about the idea, there was a problem.

"Of course, I'm an old *Doctor Who* fan," Davies explained in the DVD documentary *Doctor Forever: The Unquiet Dead* in 2013. "So I know some of the details and stuff. So I said 'Do you know there might be a problem with the rights? With Universal? With the film?' I wasn't sure what it was, but 'I think there's a problem with the rights.' 'Noooooooo!' they said, 'We're the BBC, we can do anything...'"

It quickly turned out that there was indeed a problem - but not to do with any lingering rights issues from the TV Movie. It was to do with another part of the BBC itself.

"Two weeks later, Patrick discovered that BBC Films was developing a script, and therefore a TV version would have to wait in line," Davies recalled in *Doctor Who Magazine* 338 in 2003. "Then Patrick moved on to another job, I had other ideas to write for other people, and the whole thing just seemed to slide away."

Patrick Spence agrees with Davies' recollection of the initial enthusiasm for the idea: "I spoke to Peter Salmon, who obviously knew Russell better than I did, and immediately he said that was such a good idea, let's do it! I then very quickly discovered that a man called David Thompson, who ran BBC Film and Single Drama, had the rights. I went to David and said we have this amazing writer who's desperate to do it, please could we have the rights? But David said no, and that was pretty much as far as the conversation went.

"That would have been one of the most exciting moments in my career. Teaming this writer with that underlying material. David, not unreasonably, had the rights himself, and he had other plans, it ground to a halt and we moved on. David's a decent friend of mine and a well-respected colleague. I'm not blaming him at all. I think I was told David controlled the rights and that he said we couldn't have them. Peter Salmon got involved, so I'd imagine that conversations took place between Peter and David. At my level, I was told we couldn't have it, and to back off."

When I spoke to David Thompson, he did not remember stopping any BBC Drama Series effort to bring back *Doctor Who* in 1998 or 1999. His memory is that it was BBC Worldwide who wanted to prevent any new television version from being made while film negotiations were ongoing.

"That was idiotic," says Thompson. "It was one of the reasons the film never happened, because I think that people thought it would damage the television thing."

Mal Young's recollection is that it may have been a mixture of pressure from both BBC Films and BBC Worldwide. "David Thompson was a great guy, we got on very well," says Young. "He was very ambitious, and he was really going after titles hard, but ring-fencing his area. But because David's a nice guy, he wouldn't maybe say it directly. But we were told, very clearly, that Worldwide didn't want us to make this as a TV series.

"So they essentially *did* stop us. I know we were stopped, because I got quite grumpy about this, because I'd started to really get into the idea. Patrick and I both pursued it internally at the BBC. We met with Alan Yentob about it, who was our direct-line boss. He knew that we wanted to do it, that we could get Russell, that it would work. So I had a lot of support, I'd got Peter Salmon onside, a big supporter. I'd got Alan. But, everyone's going to have their reason for why they did what they did."

All this was happening less than three years since the TV Movie had come and gone and failed. So it seems incredible to think that people in more than one part of the BBC now wanted to bring *Doctor Who* back. For Patrick Spence, however, it was less about the show itself than it was the man who was so keen to write it.

"I am a very writer-led executive, and if I get excited about a writer I sort of don't care what they want to write," Spence explains. "I just want to support that vision. The idea that the writer of *Queer as Folk* wanted to bring *Doctor Who* to life, that's what was exciting. *That's* what made *Doctor Who* feel alive again, not whether the last film was successful or not. I just thought *Doctor Who* could be electrifying in this writer's hands.

"*Queer as Folk* is still one of the five best scripts I've ever read. All I cared about was that this writer wanted to work on *Doctor Who*. I'm not saying that it wasn't a courageous decision to go and make it later. I'm saying it became much easier and much less scary when you had a writer that in control of his craft, and with that much voice and talent, who wanted to tackle that kind of lumbering beast of a brand. That's what our meeting was about, him talking through what he'd do with *Doctor Who*. It was just thrilling – it was so obviously a brilliant idea. But it wasn't to be."

As for why Peter Salmon might have been so keen on resurrecting the show as Controller of BBC One, an interview given by Mal Young to *Broadcast* in September 1998 perhaps offers a clue. When asked by the magazine what sorts of drama series Salmon wanted, Young answered: "He wants bums on seats... Popular, contemporary drama, fewer frocks [period dramas]; weekends and pre-watershed are the priorities."

On that list of criteria, *Doctor Who* was certainly a series which could tick the boxes for both 'pre-watershed' (before 9.00pm, the time after which more adult content was allowed) and possible weekend fare. *Doctor Who: The Complete History* claims that there was further contact between Salmon and Davies about the series in early 1999. But by the time Patrick Spence left the BBC at the end of that year, no further progress had been made on the idea, with the feature film proposal evidently still taking precedence... and yet as ever still stuck in limbo.

"I only stayed for two years," he says. "I promised to stay for longer, but I then fell in love with an American and we moved to America. So I left that department behind, and I can't really speak to what happened thereafter. But I think at the time there was a real sense of energy and enthusiasm. We overhauled the department and I think mostly did some stuff. But *Doctor Who* would have been the jewel in the crown. There's just no doubt. It would have been our finest hour. It was the kind of mainstream series that we were looking for, that had a proper author's voice and vision behind it, and I was very sad to watch it slip away.

"You know what the final thing that I'd like to say about this is? I'm not sure it's a bad thing, actually, that it had to wait another few years. Because the ability, the post-production technology, the CGI, all of that, the special effects stuff that was available to us... I'm not sure that waiting another three or four years didn't help *Doctor Who* become even more successful, because they had access to CGI and VFX technology that we just didn't have in 1999."

There it might have rested, an unknown curio perhaps not discussed until years later when Davies eventually did get the job of reviving the series. But in August 1999, journalist and *Doctor Who* fan Matthew Sweet revealed a few scant details of what had happened in a piece about the then-proposed *Doctor Who* movie idea for the *Independent on Sunday* newspaper:

> "Interestingly, the fast progress on *Doctor Who: The Movie* has scuppered plans by the BBC's drama department for a domestic, small screen revival of the series. Only a few months ago, Russell T Davies... was invited to develop a new series for broadcast on BBC One. Davies is a long-time fan of the programme – the romantic climax of *Queer as Folk* involved the *Who*-obsessed hero choosing between suitors on the basis that anyone who could name all the actors to play the Time Lord must be his one true love. Channel Four even altered the production schedule for an imminent *Queer as Folk* special to allow Davies time to set up the series, tentatively titled *Doctor Who 2000*. Now that Impact is poised to take the Doctor into the cinema, however, these plans have been abandoned."

A particularly interesting aspect of what Sweet wrote is that it gives the sense of Davies' discussions with the BBC about *Doctor Who* having been in 1999, and not 1998 as Spence recalled. Either way, in 2003 Davies denied to *Doctor Who Magazine* that the title

"I THINK THAT'S DEAD"

Doctor Who 2000 had ever been given to the idea. But the thrust of Sweet's report was true, and this was the first time that fans had heard they might have missed out on a whole new series because of the possible film deal. Many of them were not at all happy.

One comment on the rec.arts.drwho discussion group, made the day of the *Independent on Sunday*'s revelation, summed up the mood: "Bloody Paul Anderson and his bloody one-off Hollywood film, scuppering the prospect of Russell T Davies-produced *Who* on TV. Bastards, all."

Doctor Who Magazine reported the news in Issue 283, published in September 1999.

> "One side effect of the movie's development has been to temporarily sideline a mooted new television series of *Doctor Who*, which BBC One controller Peter Salmon had approached... Russell T Davies to write."

The magazine also included a quote from Davies, who assured them that:

> "Readers certainly shouldn't see these projects as having been in competition at all. They should take heart from the fact that *Doctor Who* has a lot of friends and supporters at the BBC, and I'm sure the time for a new TV series will come soon, whether the film is made or not."

By early November, it was apparent that the film was not going to happen – at least, not with the Paul Anderson and Jeremy Bolt team behind it. Understandably, this led fans to wonder whether Davies' series could now be made. This was still a question left hanging in the air when Davies spoke to Issue 57 of *Cult Times*, published in May 2000.

"The television people are waiting for the film people to stop development and then they will come back to me," he told the magazine. "I get an e-mail every six months saying 'We haven't forgotten you', so it might happen."

That same month, Davies became linked to the *Doctor Who* film rumours himself, when wildly speculative reports emerged that he was writing the screenplay for a movie to be directed by Russell Mulcahy. The director was probably best known for the original 1980s *Highlander* film, as well as for his work on various pop videos, but Davies was quick to reveal there was no truth to the rumour of them working together on a *Doctor Who* film, explaining to *SFX* magazine that: "Russell Mulcahy is actually directing the first three hours of the *Queer as Folk* American remake. So that's how the two Russells have come to be linked!"

Interestingly, when viewed with hindsight, Davies was very firm at the time of the *Cult Times* interview that were a new *Doctor Who* series to get off the ground, he would only want to write for it and not be involved in its production. "I wouldn't produce it," he insisted to the magazine. "I would never produce for the BBC. I would rather die." Perhaps a reflection of how the experience of working for the troubled BBC Drama department of recent years was then seen by outsiders in the industry.

Davies also gave *Cult Times* a brief insight into some of the thoughts he had about how such a relaunch would need to be done to capture the audience:

> "It would be set now, but with a huge amount of science fiction... If we are trying to do BBC One primetime and the opening scene is a red planet with pink moons and someone in a cape, you've had it. You could not get people to watch that on primetime now. You've got to start in a city - in Manchester, in London - with ordinary people."

The prospect of Davies getting his chance to put these ideas into practice, however, seemed to diminish in September 2000. That month, the BBC announced that Peter Salmon was to move from his job as Controller of BBC One, after a rocky period in the ratings for the channel, to become the BBC's Director of Sport.

This move of someone who was now known to the fans as a supporter of *Doctor Who* did not go unnoticed.

"Peter Salmon loses BBC1 Controller position!" was the slightly panicked-sounding title given to a discussion thread on the rec.arts.drwho group towards the end of August, responding to rumours of Salmon's impending removal from the role. The thread's starter, Gareth Parker, pondered: "Does his departure now mean that the project will be abandoned completely by his successor, or remain 'on ice', as if it were?"

One person who did certainly seem to think that Salmon's change of jobs meant the end for the *Doctor Who* idea was Russell T Davies himself. In November 2000 he was interviewed by Scott Matthewman for the website Gay.com UK, principally about the forthcoming American version of *Queer as Folk*. But at the end of the interview, Matthewman asked Davies about his involvement with *Doctor Who*, and whether he thought anything might yet come of it. Davies answered:

> "That was Peter Salmon wanting that, bless him, and now he's no longer Controller of BBC One I expect that's dead. I haven't heard anything for about six months. Apparently, there's a film deal still ticking away, which would stop any television versions, so I think it just had the support of Peter Salmon and I don't know who to talk to now. Lorraine Heggessey [the new Controller] I don't know at all, wouldn't know her to look at her, so I think that's dead."

Davies would come to know Lorraine Heggessey, and her arrival as the new Controller of BBC One didn't mark the end of the road for *Doctor Who* – instead, it was the beginning.

Heggessey's appointment was one of a raft of changes taking place at the BBC under its new Director-General, Greg Dyke. These changes would see BBC One and the BBC Drama department enter a well-funded and confident new era, overcoming some of the setbacks of the 1990s and eventually providing the right combination of people, place and timing for the return of *Doctor Who*.

But there was still a little way to go.

5
COTTAGE INDUSTRY

EVER SINCE THE DAY IN JUNE 1963 when Verity Lambert first stepped into her new office in room 5014 at BBC Television Centre in London, there has always been *someone* at any given moment whose full-time, paid, professional employment has been entirely concerned with *Doctor Who*. Always, at least one person through all of those years, who has relied exclusively on *Doctor Who* to pay the bills, put food on the table and keep a roof over their head.

This has been the case even during the long periods when the programme itself has been off the air. It might, at times, have been down to just one single person; often someone who didn't even work for the BBC. Whoever was then the current editor of *Doctor Who Magazine*, for example.

But there has always been someone.

In the late 1990s, it wasn't just down to the *Doctor Who Magazine* team. There was someone else – and someone who worked for the BBC, too. His name was Steve Cole, and he was employed by the Corporation's commercial subsidiary, BBC Worldwide.

"I had started at BBC Enterprises, as it then was, back in January 1993," Cole explains. "I was working in the Children's Magazines department. My counterpart in BBC Children's Books was Nuala Buffini. We both had bosses who were slightly spiky and didn't really get along. So when it was the case that we needed stuff from each other, as we periodically did, Nuala and I would tend to deal together and cut our bosses out of it. That worked fine for things like *Pingu* and *Noddy* and *Playdays* and all the rest. But then, imagine my surprise when Nuala starts saying that they're taking back the *Doctor Who* licence."

At the time of the *Doctor Who* TV Movie, when it had seemed possible that the show might come back permanently in a blaze of high-profile glory, BBC Worldwide had decided to bring the licence for full-length, original *Doctor Who* novels back in-house. This was not the only way in which the BBC's commercial activities were spurred into action by the TV Movie. The *Radio Times* listings magazine, then still owned by the BBC, launched a weekly *Doctor Who* comic strip in the issue following the film's UK broadcast. With no series or follow-up on the horizon, however, this was ended by a new editorial team at the magazine in March 1997.

BBC Books' efforts were to last for rather longer, but their decision to launch their own novel ranges meant not renewing their contract with the existing rights holder for *Doctor Who* fiction. This was Virgin Publishing, which had been responsible for the vast majority of *Doctor Who* books of all types released throughout the 1990s, under their '*Doctor Who* Books' imprint.

In 1989 Virgin had purchased Target Books, whose main stock-in-trade was novelisations of televised *Doctor Who* stories. With few serials left to be novelised at that point, and the television series then having come to an end, Virgin were able to agree a contract with the BBC which allowed them to publish full-length, original *Doctor Who* novels written directly for print.

Their first such series of these, *The New Adventures*, began in 1991, carrying on the journeys of the seventh Doctor and Ace from the point at which the television series had come to an end. As they were primarily selling to established fans who had grown up with the series rather than to a new audience, they tended to be more adult in flavour than the television programme had been. They also developed their own overarching storylines, introduced their own companions, and were successful enough to see a sister range telling new stories of previous Doctors, *The Missing Adventures*, launched by Virgin in 1994.

Virgin's licence with the BBC was not exclusive, however, and if the BBC wanted to do something themselves in-house, they could. BBC Books took advantage of this fact in the publicity drive

COTTAGE INDUSTRY

around the TV Movie in May 1996, publishing under their own banner both a novelisation of the film by Gary Russell and a script book. The following month, the BBC confirmed that they would not be renewing Virgin's *Doctor Who* licence; this therefore, expired at the end of May 1997, after which BBC Books launched their own new ranges of *Doctor Who* novels.

"It was nothing to do with Virgin's performance," says Cole. "It was simply the fact that *Doctor Who*, along with *Top Gear*, is one of the two big BBC properties they own outright, rather than having to get permissions from other people. Anticipating that the McGann movie would be a massive success, they decided that it would be good for one publisher to be in control of all media for the first time – books, video, audio. The whole package, really. That was what the plan was."

So the job of being in charge of the new BBC *Doctor Who* novels was bundled with overseeing the programme's range of VHS releases and other merchandise and licensing around the show. *Doctor Who* became a full-time job for one person at BBC Worldwide, and towards the end of 1997 that job became Steve Cole's. As he put it to *Doctor Who Magazine*, looking back at this period in the run-up to the new series' launch in 2005, "If I was taking a leak or picking my nose, *Doctor Who* ground to a halt!"

"Nuala didn't know anything about *Doctor Who*, and didn't know that I knew anything about *Doctor Who* either," Cole explains. "She asked me if I'd be interested in reading through the submissions slush pile for a bit of extra consideration, which I agreed to do. But then she said that BBC Books wanted a full-time editor. It was too much work for her because she was still expected to do the actual children's stuff at the Children's department. She said that they were going to be recruiting somebody, so at that point I had to come clean and confess that I was somewhat knowledgeable about *Doctor Who*!

"This was no news to the licensing department at the BBC because they already knew me as the person they would go to for *Doctor Who* information. In those pre-internet days, it would be a choice between wading through lots of books to find out who owned the rights to the Morbius creature, for example, or they could just phone internally to me downstairs and be told that was Robin Bland, but actually Terrance Dicks under a pseudonym. So they were well aware of that.

"It was not seen as a great career move for me because, at that point, I was the group editor of preschool magazines, I was managing a team of twelve people. I was 24, and miserable because I didn't want to be a manager, I wanted to be an editor.

"Obviously the prospect of being in charge of *Doctor Who* across all media was an appealing one, but it did mean that I would have to take a pay cut. The biggest problem I had was convincing Rona Selby, the publisher, that I was happy with that. Because they thought I was going to become disaffected and discouraged. They pointed out that I was dropping down the career ladder, and wondered why I wanted to do it.

"So I just had to say that I felt promoted into a corner, I wanted experience of different media, and it was *Doctor Who*! Having shown them that I did know about *Doctor Who*, they appointed me as 'Project Editor, Science Fiction Titles'. That was my official job title. Which meant, in theory, they had the right to chuck *Red Dwarf* at me as well. That was what they were aiming to do."

However, having taken on the *Doctor Who* brand, Cole recalls that BBC Worldwide then didn't really know what to do with it. The TV Movie had come and gone and, although there was vague talk of a feature film, nothing ever seemed likely to come of it any time soon.

"For the BBC, the whole thing was a slightly problematic aberration. It seemed like a good idea when the McGann movie was in development. But, as things developed, it turned out to be less of a good idea, perhaps.

"I think the publisher realised the writing was on the wall. That led to the issue whereby a profitable *Doctor Who* line looks great on paper, and a boost to a department's bottom line because they're great turnover. They get you more money in, but to be releasing that much product and not getting huge returns back - because you're selling everything to the same three or four

COTTAGE INDUSTRY

thousand people – meant that Children's Books didn't really want *Doctor Who* on their bottom line anymore.

"All this led to a slightly odd situation where, although I was based in the corner of the Children's office, *Doctor Who* became part of the Sports, Motoring and Entertainment Group – or 'SMEG' as it was known. Because they had [sci-fi sitcom] *Red Dwarf*, their thinking seemed to be that *Red Dwarf* is science fiction, so clearly *Doctor Who* and *Red Dwarf* were the same thing.

"But then, when *they* didn't really want us on their bottom line we ended up in Factual, which made me laugh! The BBC Factual Books department! We were making *Doctor Who*! This isn't factual! Everyone just passed it around. It was desperately unloved, the poor thing, and I felt fairly unloved as well."

Doctor Who may have been unloved at BBC Worldwide, but outside of the Corporation, there was still some evidence in the late 1990s that such an attitude wasn't universal. There were signs, just every now and again, that *Doctor Who* was fondly remembered by a much wider audience than its hardcore fans.

A few months after the TV Movie was broadcast, BBC Television marked its 60th anniversary with a special awards ceremony celebrating the best of its programmes from down the decades. Shortlists for various genres were presented to the public in special preview programmes on BBC One and put to a vote. The results were broadcast in a gala ceremony to mark the culmination of this 'TV 60' season on November 3 1996. Titled *Auntie's All-Time Greats* – 'Auntie' being a common nickname for the Corporation – the programme saw awards given out in various categories in front of an audience of stars spanning the history of BBC Television.

Doctor Who was nominated in the 'Best Popular Drama' category, alongside *All Creatures Great and Small, Ballykissangel, Bergerac, Casualty, Colditz, EastEnders, The Onedin Line, When the Boat Comes In* and *Z Cars*. And among all these favourites from down the years, *Doctor Who* went and won.

The presenter of this particular award, the television host Noel Edmonds, read the result with a nod and in a tone of voice which suggested, 'Of course! Of course, it's *Doctor Who*, what else?'

Past Doctors Peter Davison and Sylvester McCoy then took to the stage to accept the accolade, with both using it as a platform to call for the BBC to resurrect the series.

"I hope there are a few more years in *Doctor Who*," Davison said. "I don't think it's had its life, really. And maybe this vote of confidence will make everyone think again!"

"And the BBC might bring it back!" McCoy added. This got a laugh from the audience, who presumably did not take the idea particularly seriously – even though it was less than six months after the first crack at doing so.

There were some suggestions afterwards that the category had been somehow 'rigged' by *Doctor Who* fans organising mass voting, although there seems to have been no evidence of this. The three weeks between the announcements of the nominations and the awards ceremony itself didn't allow time for *Doctor Who Magazine* or any of the printed fanzines devoted to the show to try and push fans to vote, and there's no sign of any great collusion in the archives of the most popular method of fan discussion online at the time, the rec.arts.drwho newsgroup. It seems that those who voted simply did so in greater numbers for *Doctor Who* than for any other series – fair and square.

In any case, no such accusations of bias were made about other polls in which *Doctor Who* also performed well around the turn of the century. In October 2000, the British Film Institute unveiled its 'TV 100' list to much publicity – a poll of industry professionals to find the 100 greatest British television programmes. In the dizzy heights of third place – behind the hard-hitting 1960s drama *Cathy Come Home* and the classic 1970s sitcom *Fawlty Towers* – was *Doctor Who*.

Doctor Who fans often enjoy results such as this, in the same way that fans of a football club celebrate their team winning trophies. The fans may have had absolutely nothing to do with the outcome, but it makes them feel good about their passion. Especially when it seems like a victory against the odds, or validation in the eyes of the general public or those with a knowledge of the industry.

There were other such victories, too – for example, in the

COTTAGE INDUSTRY

edition of the *Radio Times* published on September 23 2003. This contained the results of a poll of readers carried out to mark the magazine's 80th anniversary. One of the categories asked which defunct TV show readers would most like to see revived – and the winner, with 31 percent of the 12,000 votes cast, was *Doctor Who*. This result, however, was rather overshadowed by the fact that a mere three days after the issue was published, the BBC announced that they were bringing *Doctor Who* back – which must have seemed like quick work to some of those who'd voted!

One interesting aspect of the 1996 TV 60 awards didn't just come from the nomination and the win for *Doctor Who*, though. The opening title sequence for the star-studded awards ceremony had featured an animated living room changing to represent different decades, with an emblematic image or clip on a television in the corner for each period. Representing the 1960s in this line-up of the BBC's best-known images were the Daleks, plotting away in one of the few surviving clips from *The Power of the Daleks*.

This sense of *Doctor Who*, and particularly the Daleks, being used by the BBC as totems of its history and heritage would become increasingly common in the late 1990s.

In 1998, the BBC created a trailer celebrating their children's programming, shown frequently at junctions between programmes, which included an appearance from the Daleks. Another trail that same year publicised the launch of the new digital television channel BBC Choice, featuring actress Pauline Quirke emerging from a Dalek in an approximation of a Tom Baker hat and scarf to suggest that viewers might get whole evenings dedicated to their favourite programmes.

True to Pauline Quirke's word, a themed *Doctor Who* night was broadcast on BBC Choice on Sunday November 22 1998. This led into a week of repeats of various episodes on the channel, celebrating *Doctor Who*'s 35th anniversary.

While 35 years is not generally regarded as a significant landmark, there were various other efforts to celebrate it elsewhere, such as special releases from BBC Books, and a mammoth poll in *Doctor Who Magazine* to establish the readers' ranking of all *Doctor*

Who stories. Even Channel 4, one of the BBC's rivals, broadcast an item about the programme and the prospects of it ever coming back in their *Right to Reply* programme. The show dealt with viewers' thoughts and complaints about programmes seen on all channels, and *Doctor Who* fan Will Hadcroft presented a five-minute feature questioning the BBC's attitude towards the series.

The launch of BBC Choice had prompted Hadcroft to contact *Right to Reply*. "I knew it was the 35th anniversary of *Doctor Who* and I was hoping that there would, at the very least, be a run of repeats on BBC Two, like the old *Five Faces* season," he explains. "If the BBC felt that 35 wasn't a standout and didn't do anything, then fair enough."

However, the BBC then announced that, although they were going to run some special anniversary programmes and repeats of *Doctor Who*, it would all be on BBC Choice. This new channel had technically been launched on September 23 1998, although at that point hardly anybody had the equipment at home with which to receive it. It was then part of the package when Britain's dominant satellite television provider Sky launched their digital service on October 1, and again when digital terrestrial transmissions received through an aerial began on November 15.

The *Doctor Who* night on BBC Choice followed one week later, but any fans wanting to watch it either needed to have taken out a subscription to one of the new services, or bought a digital box or integrated digital television. The latter option, however - even just to pick up the 'free' channels such as the BBC's - cost several hundred pounds, as the digital receivers were at this point largely subsidised by the subscription companies.

"If you didn't have digital television then you just didn't see those channels," Hadcroft continues. "It angered me that the BBC couldn't give a monkey's about the fans - in terms of giving the series repeats on BBC Two - but they were very happy to use the fanaticism as bait to get us to sign up to BBC Choice. So I wrote to *Right to Reply* - that was the thrust of my argument."

As well as touching on the fact that *Doctor Who* was being used to promote BBC Choice and discussing the reasons for the show's

COTTAGE INDUSTRY

enduring popularity with then *Doctor Who Magazine* editor Gary Gillatt, Hadcroft's item asked whether or not the series could ever possibly return?

Representing the BBC in the piece was Steve Cole, who found himself exterminated by a Dalek at the end of the segment. As now often seemed to be the case, when the Corporation needed a *Doctor Who* spokesperson, Cole was pressed into service.

Cole's love of *Doctor Who* was of course no secret to fandom. Will Hadcroft was surprised to see him effectively presenting the opposition for the *Right to Reply* piece: "All right, he works with BBC Worldwide, he is their employee, but it just seemed strange to me that the editor of the BBC Books range - who clearly was as obsessed with *Doctor Who* as me - was the man to answer the questions."

Cole was resigned to performing these chores. "No one really wanted to be the face of *Doctor Who*, because it was perceived as a failure," he explains. "But it was one of those irritating failures that attracts attention and mail and interest and phone calls. So someone had to take them."

For BBC Worldwide, their in-house ambitions for *Doctor Who* merchandise had faded fast. "It was a pain in the arse, because it didn't actually fit into anything that BBC Worldwide was based upon," says Cole. "Worldwide was not a fiction publisher, and yet it was producing 22 fiction titles a year. The videos had always been going on, so they were on happy ground, BBC Video were there doing that."

Cole's workload had rapidly expanded beyond editing the BBC's novel range: "I was expected to take on the video titles, so that meant that I would have to write the blurbs for the back covers and order up the tapes from the archive. At the same time, with the audios, I'd be expected to suggest titles and pull those together - commission those, edit those, book the studios, book the producer, *and* do the music for nothing, because we didn't have any budget but I wanted to have some music on the releases!"

Tasked with single-handedly maintaining this conveyor belt of products, Cole's workload was gruelling: "It wasn't a job you could do in office hours," he explains. "I could do everything except the editing. But the editing was what the job was meant to be. So editing always happened in the evenings or at weekends, on the Tube into town, or on the way back again.

"When I said it was too much work for one person, they gave me one freelance assistant one day a fortnight! That was the lovely Lesley Levene, who was great and knew nothing about *Doctor Who* but was very keen and enthusiastic and found it all quite amusing, and we got along well. So Lesley came in one day a fortnight, and I had two freelancers doing copy-editing and proofreading as well, so I didn't have to do that, just the structure edit and the back-and-forth on each book until it was a workable manuscript.

"But of course, you're doing two of those a month apart from December, and you're doing non-fiction, and you're doing the audios, and you're doing the videos. That's how it was for nearly two years before I was totally burnt out. I cared *so* much about *Doctor Who*. That was the trouble."

However much he loved it, Cole eventually did end up leaving BBC Worldwide in 1999. Rather than being replaced, he found that the combination of roles he'd had to shoulder was split up between various different people.

"Jac Rayner came in to help me out, free of charge initially," he remembers. "She just wanted work experience. I knew that she knew her stuff, and she just got better and better and more able. Jac was still able to turn up and help out there, physically running between the different editors. I'd appointed Justin Richards as my replacement – you have to appoint your own replacement before you leave, otherwise, you stay there forever. But he wasn't in the BBC, he was freelance.

"But they divided it up. All the stuff I'd been saying, that it was too much for one person, they finally accepted when I left! It's the age-old thing, they'll listen to you moan, but they'll keep you there until you physically walk and then they'll say they'd better do something about it!

"But it was a good time. I made some great friends from it, and I didn't really leave. I still carried on doing the typesetting for the

COTTAGE INDUSTRY

books, and I was still brought in to do copy edits and proofreads and things. Then of course it wasn't that much longer until we were looking at books for the new series, and I was lucky enough to do one of those. So yeah, it was good to have been there for a while in that time."

During Cole's period editing the *Doctor Who* range, the main rumours concerning any possible return for *Doctor Who* centred around the idea of a feature film version – although as we've seen, the Drama Series department at BBC Television were also looking into it. Were these efforts anything that ever filtered down to Cole, as the one person at the BBC who was actually paid to fully concern himself with *Doctor Who*?

"Yeah, I knew that stuff was happening, but you tuned it out. I remember meeting with Gary Gillatt, who was editing *Doctor Who Magazine* at the time, and the two of us confessing to each other, 'Can't they just leave it alone? We don't have to get our hopes up, we're minding the store'. You actually realised that starting to think that way is probably not the best thing. But it was just a sense of wanting it to be done right, wanting it to be done well. There'd been so much letting down."

In the spring of 1999, however, there was actually a new *Doctor Who* production on television, which garnered a great deal of attention, and it was on BBC One, too.

It had already been a good start to the year for fans, with the announcement in January that the 1965 episode *The Lion*, part one of *The Crusade*, had been discovered in New Zealand. This was the first missing episode return for seven years, and it was rush-released onto video that summer.

Then in February, rumours began to spread of a possible *Doctor Who* project being made for the BBC's Comic Relief charity telethon. Comic Relief had been set up in the mid-1980s to support underprivileged people in the UK and in Africa, and since 1988 had benefitted from a special appeal night on BBC One – from 1989 onwards this had taken place biennially, in the spring of odd-numbered years.

Parodies and special episodes of popular series from both the

THE LONG GAME

BBC and their commercial rivals were traditionally used as showpiece features of the night. The rumour in early 1999 was that a *Doctor Who* episode was being made with big-name actors such as Alan Rickman and Kate Winslet, with suggestions that some of the original Doctors might even be appearing.

Little of this turned out to be accurate, but the finished production was impressive enough in and of itself. *Blackadder* and *Mr Bean* star Rowan Atkinson played the main Ninth Doctor seen in the story, called *The Curse of Fatal Death*, before regenerating through a host of other star names in the final episode – Richard E. Grant, Jim Broadbent, Hugh Grant and finally Joanna Lumley, a name who had more than once been mentioned in the press down the years as a candidate to be the first female Doctor. There was a new companion played by Julia Sawalha, a Master played by Jonathan Pryce, and plenty of Daleks to battle – as well as a script which mostly laughed *with* the series rather than at it.

The idea had come from producer Sue Vertue, one of those responsible for putting together the 1999 Comic Relief features. Vertue was married to writer Steven Moffat, a lifelong *Doctor Who* fan, and suggested that he could perhaps write a *Doctor Who* sketch for the evening. Moffat had previously contributed a short story to one of the *Decalog* anthologies Virgin Publishing had put out when they held the *Doctor Who* fiction licence, and was an active poster on the rec.arts.drwho newsgroup online – as well as being a successful television scriptwriter.

When *Doctor Who Magazine* published their behind-the-scenes feature on *The Curse of Fatal Death* a couple of months after the broadcast, Moffat explained how the project had quickly become more ambitious than just a short sketch.

> "They all got very enthusiastic 'cos they realised that it still has quite a following, and it's a following that tends to spend quite a bit of money on it, so that's useful for Comic Relief. And it's got sufficient comedic overtones. It was known that Rowan was quite interested in playing it – I wouldn't overstress that, but

he was quite interested in playing the part of the Doctor, so that was immediately an interesting thing 'cos they were looking for something for Rowan to do. So we did it. I didn't quite expect it to be the size of the job it's become."

Moffat, of course, would later go on to play a much greater role in the series' history after its revival – but the whole of *The Curse of Fatal Death* represents something of a halfway house between *Doctor Who*'s past and its future. In production terms, it was shot on a soundstage but with the live 'video look' of old *Doctor Who* and made at a breakneck schedule. Most of the incidental music and sound effects came from previous *Doctor Who* serials, but as well as the script by Moffat the digital effects also showed a sign of things to come; they were provided by The Mill, the company which went on to create the CGI for the early years of the show's 21st-Century return. One of the episode's final Doctors, Richard E. Grant, would have a prominent guest role in Moffat's era of *Doctor Who* proper – but before that, would portray another alternative version of the Doctor in a production which ended up playing an unexpected role in the show's return.

Along with Moffat, there was also another future *Doctor Who* writer involved too – executive producer Richard Curtis. Curtis was a co-founder of Comic Relief and would write the episode *Vincent and the Doctor* for Steven Moffat's first year in charge of the series in 2010. Back in 1999, he told *Doctor Who Magazine* that the production was a good thing for Comic Relief for three main reasons.

"One, Comic Relief needs something that your famous people are going to want to do – and I know that Rowan, for instance, actually wanted to do *Doctor Who*. Two, it's episodic and exciting, therefore we can have a cliffhanger and two ten-minute halves. Three, it's immensely trailable – Comic Relief is not only to entertain people once they're there, but to make them watch in the first place, because the more viewers there are, the more money they'll call in and the more change we'll make in the world."

In the event, the finished production ended up being edited into four mini-episodes totalling just over 20 minutes of material, broadcast throughout the appeal night on BBC One on Friday March 12 1999. Curtis was certainly right about it bringing attention to the evening; although most of the guest star Doctors were not revealed in advance, Atkinson's casting as the main Doctor gained a good deal of publicity for the charity. *Radio Times*, for instance, made "the ever-popular *Doctor Who*" the subject of their weekly *Everybody's Talking About...* feature in their issue covering Comic Relief night, commissioning a special photo shoot of Atkinson in costume.

The production was also generally very well-received by fans and did its job in helping to raise money for Comic Relief – even more so when it was released on VHS later in the year. It also led *Doctor Who Magazine*, in their behind-the-scenes feature in Issue 278, to beg the question; could this be a good sign for the eventual return of *Doctor Who* proper? Steven Moffat offered an answer.

> "It's probably now possible to make it relatively cheaply and not look like rubbish. There is no resistance to it – I think the fan notion that there is a thing called the BBC which is inimical to *Doctor Who* is... well, for a start, there is no such place as the BBC, just an awful lot of people, many of whom are rabid *Doctor Who* fans. It's just, 'How can we make a version of *Doctor Who* which lots of people will watch, that doesn't cost an awful lot of money?'"

Moffat's words about the BBC not being as anti-*Doctor Who* as some fans liked to imagine were perhaps borne out in November, with the broadcast of a dedicated *Doctor Who* theme night. This was the second *Doctor Who* night the BBC had put together in a year, following the 35th-anniversary celebration on BBC Choice. This outing, however, was much more prominent, since it was on BBC Two.

Broadcast on Saturday November 13 1999, the *Doctor Who* night even received a *Radio Times* cover, featuring a picture of a Dalek by esteemed photographer Lord Snowdon. The picture was originally taken for a Royal Mail postage stamp, one of a set put out in 1999 celebrating popular British entertainment, to mark the impending millennium celebrations.

The night itself was presented by Tom Baker, appearing in pre-recorded inserts, and included a brand new documentary; a repeat showing of the TV Movie; an edited version of an episode from the first Dalek serial; and various other items – including three sketches produced by and starring well-known fan Mark Gatiss, a member of the popular *League of Gentlemen* comedy troupe and author of various *Doctor Who* novels. Gatiss took the opportunity to play the Doctor himself in one of the sketches and was duly awarded a cover by *Doctor Who Magazine*. One of the other sketches gently mocked fans and fandom with a guest appearance from Peter Davison; another told a comedy version of the show's origins. This latter sketch contained an offensive remark about some of the 1980s Doctors, about which Gatiss later expressed his regret.

While the BBC Choice *Doctor Who* evening in 1998 had led into a week of repeats on that channel, BBC Two's *Doctor Who* night was initially intended as the launchpad for a dedicated repeat run. The following Tuesday, the first two colour episodes of *Doctor Who* – the opening instalments of *Spearhead from Space* – were run back-to-back from 6.00pm on BBC Two, in one of the channel's established 'cult' slots.

The idea – or, at least, the apparent hope – was that these repeats would span the entire run of colour *Doctor Who* at two episodes per week – by far the most ambitious series of *Doctor Who* repeats the BBC had ever put out on one of its own channels. However, despite being heavily promoted, the viewing figures were not as high as hoped and after the first two Pertwee serials, BBC Two skipped ahead to Tom Baker's *Genesis of the Daleks* –

the most-repeated *Doctor Who* story on BBC television, which had last been broadcast on BBC Two in 1993. After *Genesis* had finished its run, the repeats then disappeared altogether in early 2000.

All of this had at least helped to keep *Doctor Who* in the public eye to some degree. But there was also news for fans during 1999 which, while not so prominent, certainly generated a deal of excitement among many of those who still cared about *Doctor Who*. Because someone was finally going to be producing new, official *Doctor Who* – albeit in audio form.

Through the 1990s, various companies run by fans had started producing their own professional audio and video projects related in some way to *Doctor Who*, for direct-to-video sale; or on CD and cassette in the case of the audio products. These usually took one of two forms; they might use characters such as *Doctor Who* enemies or companions who could be licensed from the writers who had created them or their estates without needing the rights to actually make the show itself. Or they were *Doctor Who*-like projects which featured familiar actors in roles not a million miles removed from those they had played in the series.

One of the companies in this market was Big Finish Productions, who in 1998 began releasing full-cast, radio drama-style adaptations of novels featuring the character of Bernice Summerfield. Bernice had originally been created for Virgin Publishing's *New Adventures* novels, and although the dramas couldn't feature any *Doctor Who* elements, they did achieve their goal of demonstrating that Big Finish was a credible, professional outfit.

This was necessary because Big Finish boss Jason Haigh-Ellery and producer Gary Russell had another target in their sights – *Doctor Who* itself.

By the end of 1998, they had signed a deal with the BBC to produce and sell fully-licensed *Doctor Who* audio dramas, and had signed up Peter Davison, Colin Baker and Sylvester McCoy – the fifth, sixth and seventh Doctors – to reprise their roles, along with several original companion actors.

The first Big Finish *Doctor Who* production was released in July 1999, and the range was immediately successful; the following year they announced that eighth Doctor Paul McGann had signed up too, allowing them to produce an ongoing series of adventures for the then-current Doctor.

"I was the one who guided it through the BBC," says Steve Cole of Big Finish gaining the *Doctor Who* audio licence. "BBC Audio was just around the corner on the third floor from me. They were a good source of advice for when I was getting in single readers for our in-house audio projects, and we'd always pool information.

"Big Finish had come in, and the BBC were impressed. Here was a company which, rather than just using the show's stars and making their own product, without seeking to reimburse the BBC - basically infringing copyright - were prepared to pay a royalty and do it all officially. So that appealed. But BBC Audio were saying these were audio dramas, and shouldn't we be doing them in-house? I had to say to them that these were not going to be commercially viable for BBC Worldwide to do. Because I knew that Big Finish had a good system of fans in place. They could get access to the right people to make them, and make them to high-quality. The Benny audios that they gave us had proved that.

"I also knew that they, as a small outfit, would have way lower overheads than the BBC would. We'd have to be booking studios in Soho and hiring people in. I thought if I could convince the BBC to concentrate on the TV soundtracks - because we had an awful lot of soundtracks we could exploit, and that wasn't so expensive - we could also get an income stream from Big Finish. They'd do monthly releases without us having to do any work. I could exec that and make sure that it was in line with BBC quality and guidelines and all the rest of it.

"I was employed on that first set of releases as the executive producer - basically making sure that there was nothing in there that was going to cause offence - but also just making sure that we weren't duplicating ideas and stuff. It was just common sense. So yeah, that's how I came to do those early Big Finishes, I think the first five or six. Then I left the BBC, and they'd proved they knew what they were doing by then, so there was no need to have someone at the BBC overseeing them. Someone would still be approving it all, but they didn't need an exec producer doing that."

For many fans, Big Finish's output scratched a *Doctor Who* itch. Between books and audio, there was now a steady stream of new stories serving a small, dedicated audience. Perhaps the goal of returning *Doctor Who* to television wasn't so important after all?

Steve Cole mentioned how he and *Doctor Who Magazine* editor Gary Gillatt shared this feeling of wanting the series to be left alone, given the ultimate disappointments of raised hopes in the past. So did he ever believe during his time 'minding the store' that *Doctor Who* would eventually be brought back?

"As I said on *Right to Reply* before being exterminated by a Dalek, 'It's inevitable that it will come back,'" he points out. "I was always certain that it would. But you knew it would have to come back in an entirely different form. It couldn't just be 25 minutes of slightly shoddy fun, as it had been in my time growing up.

"I didn't know *when* it would happen, but I did feel very certain that it would, which is why I put so much work into trying to make everything as good as it could be – to try to find every opportunity we could to make it work. When I had to go to sales conferences, people knew that it was the same old stuff coming out. There was not a new programme being made or a new opportunity to exploit – it was basically raiding the back catalogue for the best stuff, whilst generating new books and audios. They didn't read or follow the books or anything. So I would try to make it fun, and try to send it up a little bit – but fondly so – reading out some of the letters that I'd received. I remember one of my publishers, Stuart Snaith, head of all the SMEG group, said to me that I needed to be careful sending it up. Because you don't want people thinking it's a joke.

"I think that was the first time someone had said something kind about *Doctor Who* in the entire time I was there. I said, 'I think people realise that I love this show to death, which is why I'm still here, and why I'm working till forever o'clock every single day. But I also know that you get more people to like it if you can poke a little bit of fun at it, then people will find it less scary, less alienating.' I think that's what Russell did when he brought it back; he allowed people to see that this show is actually massive fun – escapist action-adventure in space. Which is kind of what you want. Even if it seemed like that would never happen."

6

THE VELVET WEB

SINCE THE 1970S, the news sections of fanzines and then later, more prominently, *Doctor Who Magazine* had been the main means through which most of those with an interest had learned what was going on in the world of *Doctor Who*. But towards the end of the 1990s, the breaking of news stories related to the series – and the vast majority of the discussion taking place around them – was increasingly happening online rather than in print.

Shannon Patrick Sullivan, a Canadian *Doctor Who* fan from Newfoundland, was behind one of the most prominent fan sites of the late nineties – the *Doctor Who* News Page. He'd initially set it up as a way of keeping track of news relating to the production of the TV Movie in early 1996 but found there was still plenty to report on, even after the film had come and gone.

"In late 1995, I challenged myself to learn HTML and create my first web page," he explains. "The result was '*Doctor Who*: A Brief History of Time Travel', which was basically just a capsule episode guide. Soon, I was casting about looking for ideas about what else I could do with the site.

"At the same time, I was very active on the rec.arts.drwho Usenet newsgroup. News that the *Doctor Who* TV Movie had entered production prompted a real explosion of traffic on rec.arts, with many people asking the same questions again and again, and the responses they received were not always consistent or accurate. Pretty much every Usenet newsgroup had a 'Frequently Asked Questions' entry, but the rec.arts.drwho FAQ wasn't really set up to be updated in a focussed and timely manner. So that suggested that an FAQ specific to the TV Movie would be useful. Since I knew there were online *Doctor Who* communities beyond rec.arts, a web-based FAQ seemed like the best way to go.

"Around the same time, I took over a dynamic rankings resource for the *Doctor Who* novels which had been created a few years earlier by Steve Traylen. Steve had always included a few news items as part of his monthly rankings posts, and I continued that tradition. Again, though, the rankings were a largely rec.arts entity, and I thought that the information deserved a wider audience. So that prompted me to marry the TV Movie FAQ and the book-related news into an expanded website that would cover all emerging *Doctor Who* news of interest to the global internet community. Thus the *Doctor Who* News Page was born."

Around the same time that Sullivan was setting up his site, another North American fan was also creating what would go on to be a prominent online *Doctor Who* destination. California resident Shaun Lyon was a long-time member of the Time Meddlers of Los Angeles fan group and organiser of the city's popular Gallifrey One convention, which had run annually since 1990. Lyon's website became perhaps the best-known and most widely-visited *Doctor Who* fan site of its era – Outpost Gallifrey.

"The website began during the Christmas break in late 1995 as an experiment since the web was very new," Lyon recalls. "It was designed simply to advertise two things; our convention and our local fan club. At the time, I was one of the senior moderators of the SF Media Forum on CompuServe, so I used my personal homepage space CompuServe provided to experiment.

"Since I was editing our newsletter for the Time Meddlers club, some of the members suggested I add the *Doctor Who* news I was compiling to the website. But it was a wonderful chap named George Brickner, better remembered by so many CompuServers as 'Dupa T. Parrot', who came up with the moniker Outpost Gallifrey, sometime in early 1996, in light of the convention's name, and it stuck. Over the next few years, I added episode guides, a crude web store for our local vendor Ambrosia Books who sold *Doctor Who* merchandise, a few more things, and it started to take off."

THE VELVET WEB

The late 1990s saw a vast increase in both the number of places to go for the latest news about *Doctor Who* and the speed at which it could be distributed. But given the show was no longer in production, how much was there for these sites to actually report?

"The first year of the News Page's operation, 1996, remains a great big blur of activity in my mind," says Shannon Patrick Sullivan. "Between the TV Movie, the end of Virgin's *Doctor Who* ranges, the start of the BBC Books series... all the questions about what these developments would mean for things like *Doctor Who Magazine*."

Lyon agrees that the book and, later, the audio ranges were an important focus.

"By the late 1990s *Doctor Who* fandom – at least online and at conventions – was all about two things; Virgin Publishing and BBC Books, and a bit later, Big Finish Productions," he says. "I genuinely think by 1999, ten years after the final cancellation of the original series, people were giving up expecting the show to come back – the TV Movie was our one great hope. But those books and audios gave a lot of people happiness, and the news was largely about those releases, fan events and happenings, and keeping up with the actors and celebs who'd been involved with the show – and sometimes those vague rumours."

Despite being fan websites, however, both Lyon and Sullivan had high editorial standards for their news pages and were keen not to simply publish unsubstantiated rumours. This helped to enhance their popularity and credibility as news sites, and they became trusted sources in the online fan community.

"The website meant a lot to me, and though we would occasionally publish rumours, I was very careful to ensure that they were noted as such," says Lyon. "While I'm in the US, many of our readers were in the UK, so I'd get a lot of links to what was being reported in *The Times*, *The Mirror*, *The Sun* and the *Daily Mail*."

The integrity of the sites in turn meant that they would often be trusted with insider information, as Sullivan recalls.

"I usually had a lot of advance warning about book-related news, in particular. I'd also get occasional updates from folks with

BBC connections about prospects for a TV or film revival. Perhaps most notably, when Russell T Davies was briefly attached to a TV comeback in 1999, I was tipped off by none other than Russell himself! I hope he won't mind me revealing that, all these years after the fact."

In November 1999, however, Sullivan decided that he no longer had the time or the same enthusiasm to devote to the news site, and passed on the *Doctor Who* News Page title to Mark Phippen of Logopolis.com. The following year, Phippen in turn passed the title on to Shaun Lyon to use for the news page on Outpost Gallifrey, which became the dominant fan-run news site for the show over the next decade.

"I will say that there were multiple news pages during those years," Lyon points out. "Not just mine and Shannon's, but many others. When Mark was ready to give it up, he let me have it and I added it to my established news site, so they all basically came from different places but eventually melded together into one."

By the end of the 1990s, though, fan sites like Outpost Gallifrey and the *Doctor Who* News Page were not the only places on the web dedicated to the series. For a short while, there were also two completely different, 'official' BBC *Doctor Who* websites – both of them with equally valid claims to holding that status.

The BBC had made its first tentative steps into the online world in the early 1990s, with the bbc.co.uk domain being registered by one of the corporation's engineers, Brandon Butterworth, in 1991. By the middle of the decade, individual websites were being created to tie in with certain programmes or services; the very first being for the BBC Two series *The Net*, which began broadcasting in April 1994. The corporation also put up some sites linked to specific events – the 1996 Olympic Games, for example, and the 1997 general election. But there was not yet an overall BBC website as such.

It's fair to say that at this point, the potential power and importance of the internet was not yet fully appreciated by many people within the BBC. Several of these early sites had been popular in terms of the still-growing UK online user base of the

THE VELVET WEB

time, but some in the BBC saw the internet as closer to publishing than to broadcasting.

Magazines related to BBC programmes had grown to become a big part of BBC Worldwide's business, published as commercial products and carrying adverts. This was, on the whole, uncontroversial and for a while, it seemed that the Corporation's web presence was going to go the same way – rather than being a licence fee-funded, non-commercial public service like the BBC's television channels and radio stations.

The Director-General of the BBC at this point was John Birt. He explained the dominant thinking around this time to *The Register* computing website in 2012.

> "It felt like the kind of medium you'd use to send academic papers to a foreign university. This is a medium in which you can transmit news – but in what form – and to what market – these were things we didn't know the answer [to]. The early but faulty insight was that the internet was an extension of the world of publishing. What part of the BBC published magazines? That was BBC Worldwide. And we couldn't see, at that point, any real prospect of utilising the technology. That plainly was a mistake."

As the BBC website was initially conceived as a commercial endeavour, a commercial partner was sought. In September 1996 it was announced that the BBC had signed a deal with a technology company called International Computers Limited, or ICL. Originally an independent British computer firm, by the time of the BBC deal ICL was part of the Japanese technology giant Fujitsu. In a deal that was reported to have been worth £50 million, ICL partnered with BBC Worldwide to publish BBC-branded news and sports content and sites related to assorted BBC programmes on a commercial domain called beeb.com – 'the Beeb' being a common nickname for the Corporation.

Then, in December 1996, Birt suddenly changed his mind.

THE LONG GAME

Fifteen years later, he told *The Register*:

> "In life sometimes you make a decision instantly. I saw we had made a big mistake and that we needed to do a U-turn – and it was unthinkable you could put that service like that out with advertisements. All of those thoughts occurred to me in half a second – all of those things became instantly apparent. That was really bad news for ICL in some ways although they still had the ability to participate."

Rupert Gavin joined BBC Worldwide as its chief executive in the summer of 1998. Although the deal was done before he arrived, Gavin ended up having to pick up some of the pieces from this sudden change-of-heart from the public service side of the organisation.

"For the BBC Worldwide development, we had – at John's encouragement – got external funding, a huge amount of money, to set up the BBC's internet presence as a commercial activity," he explains. "Then, the BBC decided that they'd made a mistake. That this couldn't be a commercial activity, and there was a period of a slightly odd overlap. The boundary kept moving inch by inch. You can understand that ICL were not exactly best-pleased when they woke up and discovered that what they were investing in something that was being competed against, with public money from essentially the same organisation."

Beeb.com still launched, in June 1997, providing official tie-in web-pages for popular BBC programmes such as *Top Gear* and *Top of the Pops*. As the idea had spun out of printed publishing, it's no surprise that a website for the *Radio Times* listings magazine was also included. Another important aspect of beeb.com was the ability to link through to the BBC Shop website, to buy merchandise associated with BBC programmes; and, of course, unlike BBC radio or television services – but like BBC-published magazines already did – beeb.com carried adverts.

Even though Birt had decided that the public service part of the

THE VELVET WEB

BBC should have its own web service, beeb.com was still promoted and supported by the BBC on-air. There were references to particular sites during certain relevant shows and promotional announcements during junctions between programmes. But Birt's decision meant that it was never to be the home of the BBC's news coverage.

BBC News Online was launched on the bbc.co.uk domain in November 1997, with the rest of the broader BBC Online site joining it there the following month. This contained no advertising on its pages and was a public service funded out of the BBC licence fee, as opposed to the commercially-based beeb.com. But it quickly became apparent that there was some confusion, and a great deal of overlap, between the two services – which were rapidly butting heads by operating separate 'official' sites for the same BBC programmes.

Even though it was a dead property as far as television was concerned, in 1998 this doubling-up between beeb.com and BBC Online resulted in each of them launching sites for *Doctor Who*.

Beeb.com had featured *Doctor Who*-related content from very early on, via its *Radio Times* website. In July 1997 the site hosted a vote in its 'Have Your Say' section asking users if they wanted to see *Doctor Who* return, and the same month they also posted the latest update from BBC Viewer and Listener Correspondence about what the future might hold for the programme.

The very first dedicated BBC *Doctor Who* website appears to have been launched at beeb.com/drwho at the beginning of December 1997, although this was not a full-blown site covering the series generally. Instead, it was purely designed to promote the PC CD-ROM game *Destiny of the Doctors* – which had been released in the UK by BBC Worldwide in November. The site contained basic information about the game, a link to where it could be purchased via the BBC Shop, a page of screen captures and a mini-game that visitors could play on the site itself.

Curiously, this small site seems to have remained at that address for much of beeb.com's existence; meaning that their main *Doctor Who* website never sat at the user-friendly /drwho link. Instead, when it did launch in September 1998, it was at the rather unwieldy twplus.beeb.com/html/doctorwho. This was because the 'webzine', as they called it, was part of beeb.com's *Tomorrow's World Plus* – a spin-off from the BBC One science series *Tomorrow's World*.

Like *Doctor Who*, *Tomorrow's World* had launched in the 1960s – but unlike *Doctor Who*, at this point in the late 1990s, it was still a going concern. The *Tomorrow's World Plus* site was just one example of the duplication that came to arise between the BBC's commercial and public service websites, as *Tomorrow's World* – which was, by its very nature, engaged with the latest online advances – had a standalone site long before either beeb.com or BBC Online had launched; this site then continued to exist on the bbc.co.uk domain in parallel with the commercial version.

Beeb.com made a conscious decision that science fact and science fiction should sit together on the *Tomorrow's World Plus* site, as it also hosted their pages for 1998's brand new BBC One serial *Invasion: Earth* and for the corporation's US import *The X-Files*. This certainly pleased the person in charge of overseeing the *Tomorrow's World Plus* site from the BBC Television side of things – Saul Nassé, who at the time was the editor of the main *Tomorrow's World* programme and, as he puts it, "brand guardian." Nassé also happened to be a long-term fan of *Doctor Who*.

"*Tomorrow's World* had its own website on bbc.co.uk, but beeb.com were keen to launch their own site," Nassé explains. "*Tomorrow's World Plus* was a name BBC Worldwide already had, as we made *Tomorrow's World Plus* for their UKTV Horizons channel. The proposition was for a site that blended science and science fiction. Having a *Doctor Who* section was very much Worldwide's idea, although of course, it was something I was enthusiastic about!"

Andrew Mark Sewell was the producer of the *Tomorrow's World Plus* website, and thus in charge of its *Doctor Who* section. Sewell was no stranger to the series – in 1991, he had been one of those behind production company Naked Eye's unsuccessful proposal to win the rights to make *Doctor Who* independently for the BBC.

"There was *Doctor Who* content scattered around various sites," says Sewell. "Which prompted a desire to promote the commercial aspects of *Doctor Who* – books, videos and DVDs – across a more uniformed platform.

"We had a news column called 'Gallifrey Times', which had information on forthcoming books and videos, features such as looking at the Comic Relief special, interactive games, and regular prize competitions. We also ran a short story competition – with 150 entries – judged by Saul Nassé, Colin Baker, Terrance Dicks, BBC Books editor Ben Dunn and myself.

"The site was essentially conceived as a mini-webzine – like an interactive convention to celebrate the 35th anniversary. There was a hope – and intention – that it would continue, but that wasn't to be."

The *Doctor Who* site had evidently been proposed and planned for some months, as in May 1998 it was referred to by one fan in a rec.arts.drwho discussion thread as something that beeb.com had "been talking about forever". It finally went live in mid-September 1998, a couple of months before the show's anniversary in November. By the time that anniversary came around, however, the BBC Online public service operation on bbc.co.uk had created their own *Doctor Who* offering. This was officially launched three days before the big date, on November 20 1998, although it was already live and had been trailed on BBC Two the previous evening after an episode of *Star Trek: Deep Space Nine*.

By this point, BBC Online was already far outstripping beeb.com in popularity. In March 1998, only three months into its existence, BBC Online as a whole recorded just over 900,000 users and 21 million page impressions. This compared to 147,000 users and 3.51 million page impressions for beeb.com in the same period, despite the commercial site's advantage of having set up shop several months earlier.

In February 1998, the month before those statistics were recorded, BBC Online had launched a 'Cult' section. This was dedicated to imported programmes which were being shown on BBC Two, such as *The Simpsons*, *Space: Above and Beyond*, *3rd Rock From the Sun* and assorted *Star Trek* series. The decision to add a home-grown programme to the mix – albeit a dead one – came from one of the site's commissioning editors, Mark Rogers.

"I was really interested in what people wanted from the BBC online," Rogers explains. "Because clearly, that should have a big impact on what we then built in terms of the website. It was obvious that for the early adopters, *Doctor Who* was a pretty important touchstone.

"We got a lot of e-mails – probably the second biggest topic ever, always, at any stage of the BBC's existence, was *Doctor Who*. There's this thing called the Duty Log that came in, and when people e-mailed in, more-or-less the second biggest topic, ever, in any given week was, 'When are you going to bring back *Doctor Who*?'

"You realised that it absolutely had this hardcore of fans. The bit of the online service that I worked for was the bit that essentially created websites for programmes. So the question was what we would do first, whether it would be *EastEnders*, for example, or something else. *Doctor Who* was an early idea because we knew it had this incredible following, and we knew the following was very frustrated by the fact there wasn't much else out there.

"There was a little bit of calculation about it, in that we knew because the *Doctor Who* fans were so enthusiastic and engaged, they would amplify the fact that the BBC was doing this. So they'd like it, but also they'd talk about it, which we thought would be good for validating what we were doing and giving us a good jumping-off point."

The man actually put in charge of building the new site was Damian Rafferty, one of the producers working under Rogers in the commissioning area of BBC Online. "I joined in January 1998," Rafferty remembers. "By the time the *Doctor Who* site launched in November, I'd made about 20 websites for the BBC, which just doesn't happen anymore, thankfully!"

Rafferty was already running the existing BBC Cult section – something his department wasn't actually designed to do: "Our job was to create the websites; build them; figure out how to keep them up to date, and then hand them over to production. So I'd done sites for *Watchdog* and other things, and there you would make it and design it and everything else, and then they would hand it over to a production assistant or something like that, and they would be responsible for putting in new content every week; that kind of thing.

"But the difference with Cult TV was there was no one to hand it to. Those shows, things like *The Simpsons* or *Star Trek: Deep Space Nine* weren't made by the BBC. So I couldn't just make a site and hand it over to a production assistant, because they'd be in LA and they'd be like, 'Who are you? What is the BBC?'

"So I just borrowed a bit of money and would go down to [London science fiction store] Forbidden Planet and buy stuff for giveaways. I would research content, because I had a content background anyway, and I would make these sites. We'd have quizzes and different things like that, and sometimes I would persuade the announcers to say something like, 'If you've enjoyed *The Simpsons*, go to bbc.co.uk/thesimpsons and you could win something'. The stats would go through the roof! So it was a good wheeze, and probably on a budget of about 50 quid per show."

Mark Rogers explains that there were some benefits to the web team having to maintain the sites for imported shows themselves.

"The TV production folk, they weren't digital natives," he recalls. "They didn't know how to upload images or had to be taught quite a lot of stuff. They weren't necessarily writers either. The TV productions, in particular, would often assign it to quite a junior person – which sometimes works, because junior people were often more technically literate than senior people. But sometimes you'd just get the person who was a bit of a duffer. So it wasn't entirely a bad thing that we did it in-house."

Where Rogers' and Rafferty's recollections differ comes in the motivation behind adding a *Doctor Who* site to the Cult section. Rafferty remembers it being a slightly more cynical process, as explained to him by Rogers when he was called into the latter's office at Bush House – the building at the time best-known as the home of the BBC World Service, but where the BBC Online commissioning team was then also based.

"He called me in and asked me what was the most popular

letter – not e-mail, it was 1998 – that we received at the BBC. I said I had no idea, and he said it was people asking for *Doctor Who* to come back. I asked why didn't we do that, then? Why don't we have *Doctor Who* back if people wanted it? He looked at me with his patrician eyes and kindly explained that those days, those budgets, were well gone. There was just no way the BBC would ever have the budget to do anything in the sci-fi realm that was vaguely credible. But, he explained, the high-ups at BBC TV broadcasting would like to get these letter-writers off their backs. They would like to have something to offer them. So could we do a website?

"So I said yeah, sure, okay, let's do that! It was an attempt to kick it into the long grass, I think. That wasn't *my* intention, it was *their* intention. Because I wasn't given a team, or a budget, or anything. My intention was that if I was going to do this, I was going to do it as well as I could. If there was a group of people who were very well-organised writing letters to the BBC, I was pretty sure they existed online too, and I wanted them not to think poorly of me!"

Neither Rafferty nor Rogers recall any particular problem with the fact that the commercial site at beeb.com had already got its *Doctor Who* 'webzine' up-and-running. But they do both remember the broader issues with duplication between the two different BBC web services.

"It was moderately uncomfortable, but only moderately," says Rogers. "They were perfectly affable people. It was fairly clear that this wasn't going to be a long-term option. The BBC Worldwide remit was fairly 'un-thought-through' – I think that's a good way of thinking about it.

"They couldn't do as much as they wanted. But fundamentally, it was the tie-ins and the other licensing rights they were supposed to be running. But I have to say it was fairly chaotic, the way it worked. We didn't get into any serious rows with them over *Doctor Who* because there wasn't much to argue about."

"It was a right mess!" is Rafferty's appraisal of the general situation between BBC Online and beeb.com. "It was an absolute mess! We'd come up against it again and again. We'd be thinking about doing a motoring site, for example, and they'd say we couldn't because of *Top Gear* or something. 'Oh no, you can't do that, Beeb's got some rights to this, that and the other.'

"I don't remember a single conversation or *anything* about the *Doctor Who* site. This wasn't one of those. I don't think we had anything to do with Worldwide for *Doctor Who*. We did for other things, but *Doctor Who*? No, they didn't seem to have any interest."

Rafferty's effective opposite number at beeb.com, the producer of their *Doctor Who* site Andrew Mark Sewell, thought that the two different offerings were not necessarily rivals.

"Essentially our site was dedicated to providing new material rather than a retrospective of the classic series," he explains. "In that respect, we always saw ourselves as complementary to, rather than in competition with, the BBC's public service *Doctor Who* site."

Sewell's boss at the beeb.com site, Saul Nassé, is more blunt.

"To be honest it was a bit of a car crash, the disconnect between beeb.com and bbc.co.uk. The Worldwide proposition had been cooked up when it seemed like digital extensions of BBC brands would be similar to magazines, a purely commercial proposition. But once bbc.co.uk had been set up and resourced there was bound to be a conflict. I loved *Tomorrow's World Plus*, but it was a real confusion for viewers having two sites, and it was the same for *Doctor Who*."

Quizzes were a popular element of the early days of the BBC Online *Doctor Who* site. Damian Rafferty says they were also an effective tool to help boost the site's traffic figures in the eyes of management.

"BBC Online used to have this meeting with the producers and the commissioning editors every week. At that meeting, they would discuss those sites with the highest number of page views. So it was kind of a game really, to get as many of my sites in there as possible. The *Doctor Who* site was me, working on about twelve other sites at the same time, and a really lovely HTML coder who, I'm ashamed to say, I can't remember his name now. That was it.

"Every now and then I'd go to Forbidden Planet and buy a toy or something like that to use as a prize in a quiz. In order to get the most page views – which is not a metric that's used anymore, possibly because I abused it so much, as did other people – I thought if I created a JavaScript quiz that reloaded a page every time you went to a new question, when you did the quiz it was going to be twelve page impressions. I'm not sure the visitor numbers were enormous, but certainly, the number of page impressions meant that every week I was up there telling them about the amazing success of *Doctor Who*!

"It was very, very cheap. Apart from part of our time, two of us, it was probably a couple of hundred quid. But it was out-performing Radio 1 and things like that! Part of that is because it wasn't too bad, and part of it was because I managed to get TV announcers to announce that there was now a *Doctor Who* website, at the end of *Buffy* or one of those shows.

"Those who were in the know would groan a bit, because it was getting all these page views. But those people were very much the minority, and they were not the senior management. They were real figures. That's what they chose to measure, and there they were!"

"Lots of things like that would happen," agrees Mark Rogers. "They didn't have a very sophisticated understanding of page impressions, that's for sure. I used to do something like that on *Tomorrow's World* where we had a webcam that used reload all the time – a good way of spoofing the numbers! Well, not spoofing the numbers... But because you counted them as if they were individual page views, it bumped up your numbers."

The success of the BBC Online *Doctor Who* site eventually saw it change hands within the Corporation, as the bbc.co.uk web presence continued to grow and expand. Damian Rafferty explains what happened.

"Here was something that we did for all the wrong reasons – or at least the BBC did for all the wrong reasons. My reasons were noble, I think, but the BBC's weren't great – and people loved it! It didn't cost much money, and it didn't get any backlash from the community of people who were really invested in *Doctor Who*.

"Suddenly there were a bunch of sites – *Doctor Who*, *Buffy*, *Simpsons* – with really good traffic, that were there for the taking. We were commissioners, so we didn't really have a leg to stand on and say we were going to keep them. BBC Entertainment – who had no interest in it, and nothing to do with its creation, at all – were suddenly very keen to take it on. They were, in fact, keen to take on all of the BBC Cult TV websites that I'd created, and that was fine.

"They took them on because they were doing well and were getting attention. I remember going to BBC Entertainment, which was in White City just opposite TV Centre, and I went up to the Online floor. The first thing I saw was this giant, life-size Dalek, and I thought, wow, they've really bought into this, big time!"

It was in this change of location that BBC Online's Cult section, including the *Doctor Who* site, then came under the management of Martin Trickey.

"I joined the BBC in 2000 as the entertainment editor," Trickey explains. "Basically, there was bbc.co.uk/entertainment, and my job was to update that website. I don't quite know how, but there were all these other websites kicking around the place, and at that point, they tried to pull them all together. I think because I was doing entertainment, and that was all-encompassing, I somehow found myself suddenly managing these websites like *EastEnders* and *Top of the Pops* and *Doctor Who* and the Cult website. I didn't know any of these people, and then we all came together and started working in Centre House, the horrendous monstrosity building opposite Television Centre. The good thing about working in Centre House was that you didn't have to look at it!"

Centre House was also the same building where the BBC's in-house television Drama department was based.

"That became serendipitous later down the line," says Trickey. "We were part of a thing called Fictionlab. It started off being run by a guy called Richard Fell, and he was doing drama stuff and interactive, trying to take new narrative forms forward.

"Then Sophie Walpole came on to run that, and there was

myself and a bloke called Jamie Cason, and we ran that department and all the websites. So there was *EastEnders*, comedy, drama, entertainment, *Doctor Who*, Cult. Loads and loads of websites, and Red Button stuff as well.

"The Cult team – which was James Goss, Rob Francis, Daniel Judd, and Anne Kelly – were all incredibly passionate and talented. The thing about the Cult website was it wasn't just about BBC content, which would, later on, become its downfall. When I started, James was very much leading that and doing it. They were fans of cult TV, so *Doctor Who*, *Buffy*, *X-Files*, *Star Trek*. Also, nostalgia stuff like *I Love the 70s* and *I Love the 80s*. There was generally just a love of television.

"The sites were incredibly popular, they'd found a niche and they'd got a really big audience. *Doctor Who* as a legacy brand obviously had a fanbase, which meant that when you were comparing it to other sites it would always do really well – despite the fact that didn't really have a show on-air, or have any calls to action off the back of stuff. There was always a demand for it.

"I think we even ran an *Angel* site, and that was on Channel 4! It didn't seem to matter, because the point was that we were serving an audience. I'd loved *Doctor Who* as a kid, but I wasn't a big fan. I'd chat to the team and see how they were getting on, and they sort of indoctrinated me! I became more knowledgeable about it than perhaps I needed to be! But it was definitely an infectious passion that came from the team."

Two of the members of that team, Daniel Judd and Rob Francis, are both quick to praise the man who was directly running the *Doctor Who* site in the early 2000s, James Goss.

"It was very innovative, and James took risks," says Judd. "We had a member of the team, Anne Kelly, who used to work in the rights department. So she'd often be asked questions about what we could or couldn't do, and one of them was about those *Rock and Roll Years*-type clips which we put online. If you put music into the context of a documentary, you should really pay rights, but I don't think we did! So he'd take risks. It was a very supportive and very 'can-do' department at the time, trying to do new things. We did things like e-books before you had e-book readers!"

"James was, and continues to be, an endless source of ideas, so it was great to put those into practice," says Francis. "My first job was to head down to the BBC Written Archives at Caversham, armed with a portable document scanner and a ZIP drive, to scan the holy of holies – John Cura's telesnaps. They were in two scrapbooks, badly stuck in with paper glue, which meant hours of painstaking Photoshop work back at the office to get them looking their best."

The site's 'photo-novel' recreations of lost *Doctor Who* episodes using the 'telesnap' photos taken off-screen at the time of transmission proved extremely popular, as did their e-book releases of long out-of-print novels from the old Virgin Publishing range. There were also the requisite episode guides, photo galleries, games and quizzes, and a regular stream of special features and interviews. So how did all of this productivity go down with others in the BBC, with so much effort being put into a website which didn't even have a programme?

"Because there was no show, and therefore no internal politics or a bigger creative vision to adhere to, we pretty much had free rein," says Rob Francis. "Certainly, within the BBC it felt like there was a lot of love for it, and a great willingness to bend a few rules – if need be to get things done – because it was *Doctor Who*. For every Russell T Davies, Steven Moffat or Mark Gatiss rising through the industry ranks, there were dozens more within the BBC willing to help get things done because of their pride in the show and the BBC – people like Mike Tucker, who went to extraordinary lengths with his beautiful TARDISCam model shots, for example. Other people, like James Dundas in the rights department, moved Heaven and Earth to get things done for us when we decided to go all-out with original fiction, and effectively became the *Doctor Who* production team for a couple of years."

Despite being the two biggest beasts of the *Doctor Who* online jungle at this point, it was clear that there was also a good relationship between the BBC Cult team on the official site and Shaun Lyon's Outpost Gallifrey at gallifreyone.com. In January

2001, for example, the BBC site even took time to praise Outpost Gallifrey in a news story dismissing a then-current *Doctor Who* film rumour, saying: "New *Doctor Who* will be a major news story, and you can expect to see it confirmed through reputable news sources (on the BBC, through publications like *SFX* and *Doctor Who Magazine*, and on creditable fan news sites like Gallifrey One)."

"Officially, we didn't have a relationship, and that was fine," explains Shaun Lyon. "The BBC has always been very proprietary with *Doctor Who* and that's always been the case, from the 1990s through today. They left me alone and vice versa.

"In reality though, the BBC digital services in those days were filled with wonderful people. Folks like James Goss and Rob Francis, and Moray Laing and Paul Condon and Jim Sangster and Jac Rayner at the BBC, and Karen Parks and Laura Palmer at BBC Worldwide Americas – lovely people who have been friends and acquaintances of mine ever since. We had a great relationship and many participated in fandom at the time too."

From the BBC side, Rob Francis agrees with Lyon's assessment.

"I think there was a lot of mutual respect between us and Outpost Gallifrey, as we recognised that they were a significant force in fandom, who had earned that through a huge amount of hard work. I know I used to be a bit sensitive about being the first with news scoops, and it was sometimes annoying when they and others beat us to it! As I got older and wiser though, I realised that the most important thing was to be authoritative and a trusted source of information. Who got the story about a new CD release up half an hour earlier seems very petty now. Shaun Lyon was also extremely accommodating when it came to involving us in his conventions, so things always ran very smoothly when we visited LA to interview his guests."

One thing both the official site and Outpost Gallifrey had in common by the early 2000s was that they both ran message boards where fans could discuss, debate and speculate about all aspects of *Doctor Who* – past, present and future. This was different to where online *Doctor Who* discussion, such as it then was, had mostly taken place in the 1990s, as Shannon Patrick Sullivan explains.

"At the time, there were basically two types of online forums. Some individual Internet providers, like CompuServe, offered bespoke message boards that were themed around various interests. But Usenet was different because it could be accessed by anybody with an internet connection and a little bit of know-how. Usenet was divided into literally thousands of text-based message boards called newsgroups, each devoted to a specific subject.

"The rec.arts.drwho newsgroup was created in the mid-1980s and had been around long enough to generate a following. By the time I got online in 1994, there were already a few dozen regular posters and any number of more casual participants. What really drove interest in rec.arts, though, was the presence of Jean-Marc and Randy Lofficier, the authors of the original *Doctor Who Programme Guide*. The Lofficiers had a semi-official relationship with Philip Segal, executive producer of the *Doctor Who* TV Movie, and had begun posting updates with his blessing. I think that really legitimised rec.arts in the eyes of a lot of fans."

Shaun Lyon agrees and explains how this then gradually began to change.

"The Usenet newsgroups, specifically rec.arts.drwho, were well known. CompuServe and AOL had *Doctor Who* communities, but there wasn't a lot of external interaction. Once you were in one community you pretty much stayed there. With the web still in its infancy, cross-linking between sites was generally the only way for people to find you. This was when AltaVista was the main search engine.

"I think there were a few things that really started to bring online *Doctor Who* fandom together in the late 1990s. The main one was a wonderful website called Nitro Nine, run by Siobahn Morgan. Siobahn's website was basically a listing of other *Doctor Who* websites and locations, and it was really the first major index of online fandom. Other websites cropped up like Shannon Patrick Sullivan's news page, Benjamin Elliott's wonderful regular post called *This Week in Doctor Who*, and a plethora of different sites that suited people's needs. My site was one of many, still mostly locally-focused until the end of the century.

"There was really a hunger for a different sort of online community than the Usenet newsgroups, and people had really begun turning away from the dial-in services like AOL. I started the Outpost Gallifrey Forum in 2001, roughly around the same time that the BBC started its own *Doctor Who* forum to go along with its official website. I genuinely don't remember which one came first. I think the BBC did one first, and we began ours as a fan alternative.

"I started the Outpost Gallifrey Forum as another experiment, using proprietary forum software called Ikonboard that was buggy and frustrating; I think if more than one person clicked on the post button at the same time as another, the database couldn't handle it. So about six weeks in, I moved us entirely to a hosted forum service called ezBoard where we remained for, I think, two or three years until we outgrew that. Eventually, around the time the show came back, we were on our own server using vBulletin board software, paying a lot of money for the server bandwidth.

"The people who were with me for the entire history of Outpost Gallifrey's forums from 2001 to 2009 were Steve Hill, who in 2009 opened our successor forum, the still-operating and still wonderful Gallifrey Base; and our dearly departed friend Jennifer Adams Kelley, who opened Gallifrey Base with Steve and whom we lost to cancer in 2019. Steve and Jennifer are two of the main reasons we did what we did so well, and I think their legacies speak for themselves.

"My forum was only one community among many. There were so many other places to chat online by then – Roobarb's, the *Doctor Who* Restoration Team Forum, Ian Levine's forum, *Doctor Who* Online's forum, and quite a few sites calling themselves Outpost whatever. That miffed me a little at the time, but I look back at it all with great fondness these days."

The message boards on the official BBC *Doctor Who* site lasted until April 2004, closing the year before the new series arrived on screen. Speaking on Twitter 16 years later, James Goss admitted that the closure had come at the direct instruction of Russell T Davies himself.

THE VELVET WEB

"The main reason Russell ordered us to shut down the BBC's Godawful forums was his fear that after [the debut episode] *Rose* new viewers would post on them to say they'd enjoyed it and would immediately be told how wrong they were and to go away," Goss explained, adding in subsequent tweets: "Running that site, it was heartbreaking that most of my budget went on paying for a forum where people spent most of their time saying how much they hated the show... We could have animated six missing episodes a year for what those hate-pits cost us."

"The message boards were often a challenge," agrees Rob Francis. "A challenge that certainly hasn't gone away since they evolved into our current social media world. What *Doctor Who* means to a fourteen-year-old will understandably be somewhat different to how a 50-year-old perceives it. With age, unconscious bias can sometimes creep in. So there was a lot of tact involved in trying to manage some of those conversations, before we ultimately thought it best to step away from running forums."

The Outpost Gallifrey forum certainly benefitted from the closure of the BBC message boards, and for the first few years of the new series became the focal point for online fan discussion of *Doctor Who*. However, Lyon eventually became disheartened by some of the same issues which the BBC team had faced – and in 2009 he took the decision to close Outpost Gallifrey.

"I got a lot of flak for shutting down the forum entirely," he admits. "But by then I'd been made aware of a truth that was very difficult to swallow; the words 'Outpost Gallifrey' were held in extremely low regard by the people making the show. At least two of the series' writers decided not to continue working on the show specifically due to the things said about them on my forum. I decided to shut down entirely, with Steve Hill starting Gallifrey Base to replace it as a fresh start. We gave everyone about two months to save whatever text they wanted from the old forum, and then it was gone. To this day, I still stand by that decision. Nothing lasts forever, not even the internet. Sometimes, not having access to the terrible things people say in the moment – unburdened by having to show their face or use their name – is a very good thing."

THE LONG GAME

At the turn of the century, though, such concerns were still a long way off. The main online 'casualty' of the time didn't disappear because of anything to do with its *Doctor Who* content. In 2000, BBC Worldwide's commercial beeb.com site was refocused to become almost entirely based around online shopping. The *Tomorrow's World Plus* site, with its *Doctor Who* webzine, had already gone by the end of October 1999. The site as a whole did not last for long after its switch to become a shopping portal, shutting down for good in 2002.

Beeb.com did, however, manage to leave one significant milestone in the history of *Doctor Who*. In 1999 the service hosted the official website for the Comic Relief appeal, and in spite of all the technical limitations of the period provided a live video stream of the whole BBC One telethon on Friday March 12. This, of course, included the evening's comedy *Doctor Who* serial, *The Curse of Fatal Death*. By the following Monday, the Comic Relief site had also made available on-demand individual streaming videos for all four of *The Curse of Fatal Death*'s episodes.

This was the very first time that episodes of *Doctor Who* had been broadcast online by an official BBC service, and – being the early days of such things – they were available internationally without restriction. This gave fans around the world, provided they had the technology to access it, the ability to react together in a collective *Doctor Who* viewing experience that would not have been possible before. They may have been short comedy episodes made available only in very low technical quality by today's standards, but in 1999 it was a glimpse of the future.

Within just a few years, the *Doctor Who* site at bbc.co.uk had taken up that baton and run with it, providing their own newly-made *Doctor Who* stories direct to the web. This would end up setting in motion a chain of events within the BBC which eventually helped to smooth the path for the return of *Doctor Who* to television itself.

7

"A JACUZZI OF SPARE PUBLIC CASH"

IT WOULD BE WRONG TO SAY that the BBC operated some sort of reverse Midas touch when it came to television drama in the 1990s, with all of its efforts somehow turning to dust and disaster. There were many high-rating shows, acclaimed productions and programmes, such as *Our Friends in the North*, *This Life* and *Pride and Prejudice*, which rank among the most lauded and successful the Corporation has broadcast in its long and distinguished history. Equally, even the critical mauling given to the likes of *Rhodes* was no greater an embarrassment than, say, the failure of *Churchill's People* in the 1970s, a period regularly regarded as a golden age.

Nor was the BBC the only British broadcaster to suffer failures, or even to be struck with internal divisions in its drama output. The ITV network may have been well on the way to consolidating into a single organisation by the turn of the century – across England and Wales, at least – but it still carried much of the legacy of its original fragmented regional structure. As one ITV producer put it to researchers from the University of Westminster for a report published in 1999:

> "It's odd because we're very independent of each other in the companies – Yorkshire, Tyne Tees, Granada, LWT – and we all compete with each other for the

commissions. So there's no cohesive policy between the companies, we're all operating like little independent companies, all fighting for the same slice of the cake."

Nonetheless, such things always came under greater scrutiny at the BBC – perhaps inevitably, due to its status as the UK's publicly-funded national broadcaster. There has probably never been a time, ever since regular television programming began on the BBC in the 1930s, when the Corporation's drama output hasn't been being criticised by someone, somewhere. 'It's too elitist.' 'It's too populist.' 'It's too glossy.' 'It's too cheap-looking.' 'There's too much of it.' 'There isn't enough of it.' Because of "the unique way the BBC is funded" as its much-parodied 1990s licence fee trails used to say, there is always a great sense of ownership when the BBC is discussed – and justifiably so.

The BBC has to try, in its various media and across assorted genres, to appeal to as wide an audience as possible throughout its different programmes and services. This, indeed, was sometimes an argument used by *Doctor Who* fans during the time the show was off-air to complain about its absence from the schedules: "I pay my licence fee, so why isn't the BBC making the programme I love most above all the others?"

So it's always difficult. But it would be fair to say that both BBC One and BBC Drama faced particularly testing times in the 1990s, especially in the second half of the decade. The chopping and changing of personnel at the top, brickbats from the critics and sliding audience figures meant that it was a challenging period for possibly television's most popular genre, on the BBC's most prominent service.

In Drama Series, Mal Young's background may have been mainly in soap opera, but after the debacle of *Eldorado* earlier in the decade there was no way that the BBC would contemplate another attempt at launching a new soap to try and entice the viewers. However, he was quite cleverly able to spearhead some programmes which did the next best thing.

Post-*Eldorado*, the BBC had already upped *EastEnders'* schedule from two episodes per week to three in 1994. Director-General John Birt had forbidden any further increase; but after Birt departed and Greg Dyke took over the BBC, the go-ahead was given and a fourth weekly episode of *EastEnders* duly arrived in the summer of 2001.

By the time Young had joined the BBC in 1997, their other most popular drama series, the Saturday night medical procedural *Casualty*, had already increased in length from the fifteen episodes of its first series in 1986 to running for half the year. Young, however, sought a further increase, and by the time he left the Corporation at the end of 2004, *Casualty* was running for nearly 50 weeks per series.

But it didn't stop there. In the late 1990s, Young co-created a spin-off series from *Casualty*, reasoning that instead of having a new, unconnected hospital drama on weeknights, BBC One could have a series that explored other areas of the hospital in the fictional city of Holby, away from the Accident and Emergency ward viewers saw on Saturdays. The result was *Holby City*, launched in January 1999, initially as a run of just nine episodes. From October 2001 it ran all the year round, becoming a weekly fixture of the BBC One schedule until its cancellation was announced in June 2021.

"They had a big box that they gave me," Young recalls. "A box of files and scripts and documents, and it was for a hospital show that they wanted to run on Tuesday nights against *The Bill*. I'd just finished relaunching *The Bill*, so I knew what had made it good again, but I also knew its weak points – like the Death Star, I had the plans!

"So I said yes, we should do an alternative hospital show, and they told me they had one which had been in development for ages. It was called 'Project Y', and they gave me this box and it was full of all this stuff. Pictures and sketches of what the hospital would look like, and this and that. But none of it was about the scripts – it was all back-to-front. They were doing this thing of, 'How do we design another *Casualty*?' rather than just saying, 'What's a great idea?'

"So I said that we had a hospital show, it's called *Casualty*, but what happens when you open the doors and they send the patient upstairs? Wouldn't it be fascinating to see what happens upstairs? It was like a light bulb going on in their heads – it was so simple. So we spun it off into what became *Holby City* and it became its own show. It became a very emotional, slower-burn show for Tuesday nights. We launched nine episodes, went to sixteen, went to 32, and then went to all-year-round, really fast. We got a great cast and it tapped into something."

Holby City was also the last major drama series ever to be launched on British television with the 'video look' of live programming. It would have been inconceivable by 1999 for almost any other drama series to have been launched like this, but *Holby City* was deliberately made in the style of its sister show, *Casualty*. This had maintained the video look since its launch in 1986, when it had still been common for a range of dramas.

By the late 1990s, this was no longer the case, and outside of *Casualty* and *Holby City* and most soap operas, the video look was now gone from British television drama. It's hard to say exactly why the look fell so swiftly out of favour, when it had been used in British primetime dramas on both the BBC and ITV for decades. Perhaps it was the influence of American imports; perhaps simply changing tastes, but there can be no denying that in the 1990s it came to be seen as giving a 'cheap' appearance to non-soap drama.

This had been commented on by *The Guardian* as far back as 1989, when journalist Bob Woffinden wrote in an article on the state of BBC television drama that:

> "A decade ago, the received wisdom was that the advent of videotape would cut costs substantially. In the event, few creatively engaged in TV drama are happy to work with it. At the beginning of the eighties, David Hare and others passionately argued that video was unsuitable for drama; and their view has prevailed. Writers, directors and producers prefer film; and, so they tell us, audiences expect it."

"A JACUZZI OF SPARE PUBLIC CASH"

By the late 1990s film was now the dominant production method for British television drama, as it had been in the US for decades. This change is one of the reasons why seasons of British dramas, outside of *Casualty* and the soaps, tended to be so much shorter than their US counterparts. British broadcasters rarely had the time, money or resources to make long series of all-film shows, with runs of between six and ten being the norm in most cases. The comparatively quick turnaround of the multi-camera studio dramas of old was now a thing of the past.

Jane Tranter had begun her career in television drama in the mid-1980s when multi-camera production had still been common. She then saw such production methods die off rapidly as her career progressed into the 1990s. She says:

"I think it's just that once things shot entirely on film and location began to show themselves, once you started using video in a different way and it brought down the cost of it, we were never going to look back, really. It just grew and grew from there."

There were attempts to achieve a similar effect without the expense of shooting on film, by using video that had been treated with a film 'look', but early on they were not terribly successful. When *Casualty* tried an early form of so-called 'filmising' at the start its 1994-95 series – in an effort to "enhance the emotional power of the programme," as producer Corinne Hollingworth put it – the effect was quickly dropped after viewer complaints. Possibly stung by this bad experience, *Casualty* and *Holby City* stuck with the 'live' video look until 2007.

"We actually did do some tests to make it look filmic," says Mal Young, recalling *Holby City*'s launch in 1999. "We put a filmic sheen on it, and it just felt wrong. We tested it with people, and they freaked. The clean video of our soaps has taught the audience to expect something different from them. It feels like it was shot this afternoon, it feels more instant and of the moment – and it felt out-of-sync with *Casualty*, if it looked too filmic. But we pushed the lighting more. We did a lot more locations. We made it look pretty good. But they resisted it looking like film, which is a very British thing, isn't it?"

THE LONG GAME

By the early 2000s, much better video-processing techniques were available, which is why by the time *Doctor Who* returned it could be shot on video and given a film 'look' afterwards without any particular complaints about the quality of the picture. It eventually began shooting with a built-in film look when the show moved into high definition in 2009. Indeed, HD cameras brought film's decade or two of dominance in British television drama to an end. If you could now shoot on a high-resolution video format that looked like film, there was no need for film itself. But there would be no return for the old studio multi-camera system, as these productions were still made in the manner of single-camera film shoots.

Whatever the picture quality of *Holby City*, when it began in 1999 it was undoubtedly Mal Young's first great success at the BBC with a new show, providing BBC One with a regular weeknight hit it badly needed. *The Guardian* commented in September 2000 that:

> "Series such as *Holby* are what the BBC really needs, the fresh but reliable mid-week regular drama that ITV is best at. Young, perched in a hospital chair on the *Holby* set, underscores its significance. This is the first successful new BBC One one-hour drama format and it has risen above the very public failures of *Harbour Lights* and *Sunburn* – slapped down by Dyke in Edinburgh for relying on ex-soap stars. The man who once vowed he would use former soap stars above all others is repentant. 'We're all guilty of grabbing a face, but it's a short-term gimmick. Viewers see right through it. It's the scripts that count. On the other hand, the soaps are so prevalent it's hard to find someone who hasn't been in one,' says Young equably."

Harbour Lights and *Sunburn* – the latter of which was about the life and work of a group of holiday reps – were two other dramas launched at the start of 1999 to try and capture some of that ITV territory, neither of them to very great success. The problems with *Harbour Lights* had continued after Patrick Spence's attempts to get Russell T Davies to come on board and save it, to such an extent that one of the episodes made for the first series was never even broadcast by the BBC.

Harbour Lights does, however, represent a fascinating snapshot of the midpoint in an era of BBC television drama. The higher production values of full single-camera shooting on film were now the norm, for the sort of series that, even just a decade earlier at the end of the 1980s, would probably have been made with multi-camera interiors. But it's also a series that was used as a stick with which to beat the BBC for its casting of a former soap star as the name to hang it on.

Part of the problem with *Harbour Lights*, *Sunburn*, and perhaps *Badger* can be thrown in too – a drama about a police officer who investigates animal crime, which like the other two lasted for a couple of series in 1999 and 2000 – was that they were neither one thing nor the other. They didn't offer the relatively cosy nostalgia and populism of the likes of *Heartbeat*, but nor were they the hard-hitting yet still engaging contemporary drama delivered by ITV's other 1990s mega-hits, *Prime Suspect* and *Cracker*.

You don't have to be gritty to be good, of course, but the issue with *Harbour Lights* and *Sunburn* was that they didn't seem to be much of anything at all, to anybody. The BBC had been criticised for stodgy, unpopular literary or historical drama serials such as *Rhodes* and *Nostromo* a couple of years earlier, and was now equally criticised for lighter, frothier productions. What they were rarely able to do at this point was to hit that vital balance between quality and popularity which ITV had mastered. As future *Doctor Who* showrunner Chris Chibnall put it to interviewer David Darlington for *Doctor Who Magazine* in 2007: "There had been series like *Badger* and *Harbour Lights*, which had been slightly humourless, and didn't have a real sense of joy at their own existence..."

The BBC could occasionally manage ITV's knack of making popular, critically well-received dramas that still captured the attention of the audience and gained good ratings – *Silent Witness* being probably the most notable example of this to emerge from the Corporation during the 1990s. But *Silent Witness* had originally been commissioned by Nick Elliott during his brief stint at Television Centre as Head of Drama Series and had even been cancelled, until it was saved by Young and his Head of Development Patrick Spence when they took over. "I thought that was a show that was in need of a bit of love," says Spence. "We tore up the format and started again and relaunched it."

There were other popular drama successes on BBC One in the 1990s, such as the Sunday night hits *Hamish Macbeth* and *Ballykissangel* – but these were independent productions which had come from BBC Scotland and BBC Northern Ireland respectively, making their commissioning perhaps less complex than that in the system which had so frustrated Elliott. Speaking to *The Guardian* for an article about the state of BBC drama in December 1996, Channel 4's drama boss Peter Ansorge claimed that the successes coming from outside the BBC's central Drama department in London were no coincidence. "Only the regions with their set quota for the network now have real autonomy," was his verdict.

"The indies were doing great because the in-house had sort of lost their way," remembers Mal Young of the time when he took over. "So I said I was going to run our department like an indie. I was very competitive. We aggressively chased after writers and for ideas that we liked. Patrick was a big part of that. I felt we were competing with the indies, because that was the only way to make our department feel like it had an energy and a purpose. Otherwise, you could just drift on in development for ten years, and what's the point in that? You never make a show."

It perhaps demonstrates something that one of the few other returning drama hits that BBC One had managed in the late 1990s was the Saturday night mystery series *Jonathan Creek* – which didn't come from Drama at all. It was made by the Entertainment Department, as writer David Renwick was used to working with them and didn't want it to be done through Drama.

So there were certainly misfires at this pretty low time for BBC Drama, but looking back – particularly from the perspective of a

Doctor Who fan – it's interesting just to see how many names that would eventually come to be connected to the revival of the series were involved with a programme like *Harbour Lights*. Indeed, there was one name already heavily associated with *Doctor Who*. *Harbour Lights* was based on an original idea by Dave Martin, co-writer of many 1970s stories and co-creator of K9.

The very first behind-the-scenes name you see on *Harbour Lights* is that of Mal Young as Executive Producer, right after the leading actors in the opening credits. The director of the first episode is Keith Boak, who would later of course helm the first production block of the revived *Doctor Who*. Coming immediately after Patrick Spence in the end credits is the show's script editor – one Julie Gardner. Gardner also script-edited the first series of *Sunburn* before, with Young's encouragement, being promoted to become the show's producer for its second and final run.

If Mal Young was still in the process of sorting out Drama Series, then how about across at Drama Serials? There, too, changes were taking place, and another of the names that would be vital to *Doctor Who*'s return was making her way up the ladder.

In February 1998, Michael Wearing resigned from his role as Head of Serials in the drama department, with *Variety* reporting that he was quitting:

> "...in disgust, claiming that 'rampant commercialism' has made it 'creatively impossible' for him to remain... He has long been a vociferous critic of the current BBC regime headed by director-general John Birt, which Wearing – along with many of his past and current colleagues – regards as stifling creativity with management dogma."

There's no doubt that this was a blow – Wearing was a giant of BBC television drama, having forged his reputation as the producer of hugely successful serials such as *Boys from the Blackstuff* and *Edge of Darkness* in the 1980s. As Head of Serials since 1989, his department had put out some of the BBC's most successful productions of the past decade, including the *House of Cards* trilogy, the 1995 version of *Pride and Prejudice*, Tony Marchant's *Holding On* and the 1996 adaptation of Peter Flannery's play *Our Friends in the North*. The latter was an expensive, epic serial which Wearing had stood firmly behind and attempted to get into production since seeing the theatre version on stage in 1982. The television version ended up helping to accelerate the careers of stars Christopher Eccleston and Daniel Craig and became one of the defining BBC dramas of the period.

In her book *Uncertain Vision: Birt, Dyke and the Reinvention of the BBC*, academic Georgina Born writes of the serials department under Wearing that:

> "Freer of the dead hand of market research than Series, Serials' double achievement was to serve up both classy standard adaptations for the heritage market (*Middlemarch*, *Pride and Prejudice*) and, in varied ways, to renew the genre by exceeding routine horizons. Serials was blessed with the leadership of the recalcitrant Michael Wearing... Under his protection its producers had the strength to seek out and exploit opportunities for innovation. Inevitably, if risks were taken, some failures were made."

Wearing was a link to a disappearing age, his frustrations with the changing commissioning landscape for drama perhaps summed up as *Variety* continued: "The last straw came when new BBC One controller Peter Salmon rejected his plans to adapt a novel by crime writer Janet Neel after negative feedback from US-style focus groups." In *Uncertain Vision*, Born said of Wearing and his struggles to get *Our Friends in the North* commissioned by then-BBC Two controller Michael Jackson that: "Jackson... seemed to say that he feels alienated – he didn't use that word – from a kind of Seventies, Eighties social realist political drama. He sees that as the past, as having always characterised BBC Drama. Wearing must embody that for him."

But now Wearing was gone, and the BBC chose to replace him with two people – a Head of Serials each for BBC One and BBC Two. Jane Tranter was given the BBC One job in April 1998, less than a year after from her return to the BBC from Carlton.

Unlike many, Tranter did not find the BBC system to be overly tangled when it came to the process of getting a programme commissioned, telling *The Guardian* in 2000:

> "You have got to understand the structures, but you have to look outside, to the audiences, concentrate on making programmes. I never changed my modus operandi. So [in serials] we put our heads down and made the programmes. Coming from ITV, the BBC was simple. I wrote out commissioning forms for development funds [for new dramas]. To have them green-lit I went across the road to [BBC One Controller] Peter Salmon, who'd joined at the same time. He gave backing for Peter Kosminsky [*Warriors*] and William Ivory [*The Sins*]."

Warriors was perhaps Tranter's signature commission while working in serials. Starring Ioan Gruffudd, Damian Lewis and Matthew Macfadyen, it was set among a group of UN peacekeepers during the 1990s war in Yugoslavia; according to its author Peter Kosminsky, it was the most expensive contemporary drama the BBC had ever made. It went on to win the BAFTA Award for Best Drama Serial and, by the time of its broadcast on BBC One in November 1999, Tranter had already been promoted. That month, she was given Wearing's old role as overall Head of Drama Serials, working across both BBC One and BBC Two.

"There is this real myth about the BBC that it's incredibly complicated to get things made," Tranter told *The Observer* at the time of *Warriors*' broadcast. "But if you have a good idea and you take it to one of the channel controllers it will get made."

Not all BBC One programmes of the era were as successful, however, and in many areas, the channel was seen to be struggling.

THE LONG GAME

In 1999, it was revealed that BBC One's average share of viewers had fallen below 30 percent for the first time in its history, prompting talk in the press of a 'ratings crisis' at the broadcaster.

This was at least partly down to the increasing fragmentation of audiences with the rise of multi-channel television. Analogue satellite and cable systems had become increasingly common in British households since the end of the 1980s, and digital broadcasting had been launched in the UK in 1998, with the BBC providing its rolling news channel and BBC Choice as new extra services on these platforms. But there was also some feeling that BBC One simply lacked the money to adequately compete with its main commercial rival.

At the Edinburgh International Television Festival in August 1999, Peter Salmon made the case for BBC One needing to be better-funded, with something of an open plea for more money to be given to the channel. *The Times* reported:

> "BBC One is appealing for a £100 million 'fighting fund' to produce more sitcoms and dramas and to stop audiences deserting to the commercial channels. Peter Salmon, Controller of BBC One, is asking for a bigger slice of the licence fee fund to put him on an equal footing with ITV. BBC One's annual budget is less than £500 million, while ITV gets £600 million, and Mr Salmon wants an extra £100 million to make up the shortfall."

Salmon would get his money – or rather, his channel would. But he would not be at BBC One to spend it. The extra funds would be given to a new channel controller, by a new man at the top; Someone who had never worked for the BBC before, but who saw BBC One as the shop window through which the Corporation's success or failure was ultimately judged by the majority of the licence fee payers.

In January 1999, John Birt had announced that he was to step down as the Director-General of the BBC the following year.

"A JACUZZI OF SPARE PUBLIC CASH"

Birt had joined the BBC as Deputy Director-General, as well as Head of News and Current Affairs, in 1987. In 1992 he was appointed to the top job, becoming the Corporation's twelfth Director-General at the start of the following year. His time in charge saw huge changes being made to the BBC, with the aim of making it fit for purpose in the modern world.

Birt implemented a system called 'Producer Choice,' which introduced an internal market and also gave a wider scope for BBC producers to buy services from outside contractors rather than having to use the Corporation's own in-house units for things such as costumes, scenery, special effects or even editing and studios. Many of these departments eventually closed; even though they could now in theory also sell their expertise outside of the BBC, in practice they were generally run uneconomically and could not compete on a commercial basis.

Birt was criticised by many – with the lauded television playwright Dennis Potter famously labelling him as a "croak-voiced Dalek" – and he was never widely popular with staff. His use of complex management jargon was mockingly labelled as 'Birtspeak', and he drew criticism a few weeks into his term as Director-General when it emerged he had been doing the job of running the entire BBC on a freelance basis rather than having joined the staff – something he subsequently did, and claimed in his autobiography to have already been in the process of doing.

In fairness to Birt, he can also take credit for some positive changes within the BBC. He helped to ensure that it was well-prepared for the arrival of digital television; he was key to the establishment of the BBC's online presence, and he negotiated a generous licence fee settlement with the Labour government in the late 1990s – of which his successor was able to reap the benefit.

"The BBC needed to be sorted out because you didn't know what you were spending," is Jo Wright's assessment of Producer Choice, which arrived while she was working as a BBC producer in the mid-1990s. "I remember years back when I was working in Factual, we had no idea what our budget was; nobody really worked to a budget. So somebody needed to put their foot down.

"People were spending money editing for months and months, and you couldn't go outside [to employ people]. I did a show called *Move Over Darling*, where we had an editor and we asked how long they thought it would take. They said 'two', and we thought two weeks might be alright. But they meant two months!

"The in-house editors could work for months without anybody stopping them. So we said we wanted to get an editor from outside who could move quicker, and they really went mad. But my boss at the time was Janet Street-Porter, and she just told them to eff off! I think she was the first person to get editors from outside, because ours were too slow. It wasn't their fault, they were good editors, but they were just used to taking forever to do everything.

"So I think there was definitely a good intent by John Birt. He just had no charisma and no way of pulling people with him. He didn't really care."

Birt's BBC Television, with its split between BBC Broadcast and BBC Production, was also stereotyped as being overly bureaucratic, with excess layers of management and administration that made it difficult to tell who precisely was in charge of what, or what the exact process was for getting a programme commissioned. One unnamed executive complained to *The Times* in November 1997:

> "It's Kafkaesque for production heads, because there are now seven bosses they have to doff their caps to. And under them are reams of consultants on both sides, plus a whole board structure on both sides. Senior executives are required to go for away days, strategy days and board meetings with each. It's the biggest disease of the BBC. Too many senior people are made to spend their time in endless repetitive meetings, chaired by bosses who overlap in their job responsibilities. So they have their eye off the ball."

When it was announced in 1999 that Birt would be leaving, *Doctor Who* fans – on the lookout for who could be good for the future of the series – might perhaps have favoured Alan Yentob as his successor. Since 1997, Yentob had returned to the broadcasting side of things as the BBC's Director of Television, following his brief stint as Director of Programmes for BBC Production. Touted as a contender, he was widely believed to be a strong candidate. A profile in *The Independent* wrote of him that:

> "If he gets the top job, many will see it as a possible return to a golden age. Certainly, he is a champion of the programme maker and an instinctive and mercurial scheduler. He paid a social visit to the Royal Opera at Covent Garden, liked the production enormously and cleared the schedules for it the following Saturday. He was so taken with his young son's delight in the animation *The Wrong Trousers* that he put it on BBC One on Christmas Day."

The same profile also pointed out that Yentob was, "Notoriously disorganised (he once left a meeting with a producer to take a phone call and never returned, having totally forgotten about the meeting)." Perhaps it was this factor that led to Yentob being overlooked; he never did get the very top job at the BBC. In June 1999, it was announced that the Director-General role had gone to an outsider – Greg Dyke, the chairman and chief executive of Pearson Television, who officially took over in January 2000.

Dyke was a controversial appointment. His support for the governing Labour Party, to which he had donated money, was criticised in some quarters as infringing on the BBC's political neutrality. Yet he was also praised by others, particularly within the BBC, for being a complete contrast to Birt. A straight-talking populist who had famously turned around the fortunes of ITV breakfast broadcaster TV-am in the early 1980s, before running LWT and making millions after its takeover by Granada, he arrived at the BBC pledging to reduce some of the layers of management, and plough funds back into programme-making.

Or, as he later put it, to "cut the crap" at the organisation.

In June 2000, the BBC's Board of Governors criticised the performance of BBC One in their annual report – for the second year in a row. The board's chairman, Sir Christopher Bland, said that, "BBC television programmes as a whole did not reach a high enough level of quality and ambition and the average quality of programmes across the year on BBC One needs to be improved."

Summarising the governors' report, *The Guardian* wrote:

> "Sitcoms have been poor, and BBC One is too reliant on light, popular factual shows – an implication that the likes of *Changing Rooms* and *Airport* have had their day. There was much praise for other parts of the corporation – notably radio – but the criticisms about BBC One represent a serious blow for the channel controller, Peter Salmon, who is under increasing pressure. At a press conference today, BBC Director-General Greg Dyke notably failed to endorse his position."

By early September, it was widely speculated that Salmon's days were numbered. Reporting on the 2000 Edinburgh International Television Festival, *The Guardian* pieced things together:

> "The evidence was all there. First, in his MacTaggart lecture, Director-General Greg Dyke laid into BBC One, saying it simply had to do better. Then, the following day, he attacked the use of soap stars in poor TV dramas (think *Harbour Lights* and *Sunburn*) and called time on tired old docusoaps. Next, it was his trusted lieutenant Mark Thompson, and not Salmon, who fielded questions about how BBC One would take shape after the *Nine O'Clock News* is moved to 10.00pm. Finally, Salmon pulled out of a seminar on TV drama, at which he was to be a panellist... It is not a question of if, but when – and it is certain that he'll be off to another top BBC job before the month is out."

"A JACUZZI OF SPARE PUBLIC CASH"

There was already one name being tipped to take control of the channel, so it was little surprise when the confirmation of Salmon's departure from the role followed on September 13. That day, the BBC announced that Salmon was to become the corporation's Director of Sport – technically a promotion within the BBC's new structure under Dyke, but widely interpreted as his having been "shunted sideways," as *The Times* put it.

In Salmon's place would come the person the media analysts had been talking about for weeks as his probable successor. This was the BBC's Joint Director of Factual and Learning, Lorraine Heggessey; becoming the first woman to be Controller of BBC One in the channel's history.

Born in 1956, Heggessey grew up in the London suburbs and studied English Language and Literature at Durham University. After having been rejected for a BBC traineeship in 1978, she had volunteered at a hospital radio station and then began working as a local newspaper journalist. She then reapplied to the BBC in 1979, this time being accepted.

In the early 1980s, she worked as a producer on BBC One's *Panorama*, a flagship current affairs series and one of the BBC's longest-running programmes. She then left the BBC to work for Thames Television on their prestigious current affairs series *This Week*, effectively ITV's equivalent of *Panorama*. She followed this by moving to the small independent company Clark Productions and becoming the assistant editor of *Hard News* for Channel 4, later working on their acclaimed documentary series *Dispatches*.

Heggessey returned to the BBC in the 1990s, and in 1994 she became the editor of BBC One's main regular science series *QED*. She also racked up a populist hit when she launched the hugely successful BBC One series *Animal Hospital*, one of the channel's great early evening successes of that decade.

In 1997, she became Head of Children's Production at the BBC's in-house programme-making wing, BBC Production. Under the new split structure introduced by John Birt, Heggessey joined the new Head of Children's Commissioning at BBC Broadcast, Roy Thompson, to replace the retiring Anna Home. This appointment represented a change of heart for Heggessey; she had already agreed to leave the BBC again to join the independent production company MBC, when she was tempted to reverse her decision and stay at the Corporation to take the Children's job.

It was as Head of Children's Production that Heggessey had perhaps her highest-profile moment before taking charge of BBC One - although hardly in ideal circumstances. In 1998, a tabloid newspaper revealed that Richard Bacon, a presenter on the long-running children's magazine programme *Blue Peter*, had taken cocaine. Heggessey decided that Bacon would leave the show and, in an unprecedented move, recorded a direct-to-camera piece introducing the edition of *Blue Peter* that followed Bacon's sacking. In this widely-reported - and sometimes parodied - broadcast, she explained to the audience that she felt Bacon had to leave because he had let the viewers down.

In 1999 Heggessey became the Director of Programmes for all of BBC Production, also serving as the in-house programme-making unit's Deputy Chief Executive. But when Dyke took up the reins as Director-General, one of his moves to try and reduce the complexity of the BBC's structure was to do away with much of John Birt's split between BBC Production and BBC Broadcast. So in 2000 Heggessey's job disappeared, and she was instead made Joint Director of Factual and Learning. However, this was also to be only a brief appointment - and by August some of the media had already named her as a favourite of Dyke's, and Salmon's likely successor at BBC One.

What does Lorraine Heggessey recall being the main problems facing BBC One when she was officially announced as the new Controller in the autumn of 2000?

"Because of various things - but partly because the BBC's always got a limited pot of money, and partly because there was all this focus on building websites and the BBC's digital capability - BBC One had suffered through lack of resources and couldn't compete with ITV, in terms of the amount of drama or entertainment it did. Those tended to be the more expensive genres, and so BBC One became overly reliant on factual.

"A JACUZZI OF SPARE PUBLIC CASH"

All of the factual programmes were good in their own right, but when you had a stack of three docusoaps after each other, inevitably they slightly lost their lustre.

"John Birt was very strategic, and I think positioned the BBC incredibly well for the digital future, and became very focused on that – on the internet and starting new channels. To some extent, the BBC took its eye off the ball of its bread-and-butter, its core services, and under-invested in BBC One.

"Greg Dyke came in. His background was ITV and he immediately saw how valuable BBC One was. In fact, when research was done, it showed that the way the public felt about BBC One affected the way they felt about the whole BBC – more than any other single factor. So if you didn't get BBC One right the public perception of the job the BBC was doing was adversely affected."

In early September, just ahead of Heggessey's appointment, but when she was heavily rumoured to be replacing Salmon, *The Times* wrote:

> "Some of her colleagues are concerned that she lacks experience in popular drama, where BBC One is usually outgunned by ITV, and which will take on added importance in the schedule when the main news is moved to 10.00pm. But the new commissioning system introduced by Dyke, giving an enhanced role to specialist editors, should help to plug that gap."

The commissioner who would take on that role and work closely in tandem with Heggessey to revive the fortunes of BBC One's drama output was another appointment made that autumn. As with Heggessey, the job went to a woman who had been widely tipped in the press beforehand. But it was some time before this was confirmed, as the details were hammered out and she ensured that she had the control she wanted.

Colin Adams had retired from the BBC at the end of 1999 and had been replaced as the Controller of Drama Production by his deputy Susan Spindler. Like Adams, Spindler had no real background in drama before joining the department as a senior executive in 1997; she had spent much of her career in science programming. However, her appointment was to be a brief one – she was in the job for less than a year.

On October 12 2000, the BBC announced that Jane Tranter had been promoted from her job as Head of Drama Serials to become the BBC's overall Controller of Drama Commissioning. This saw her overseeing not just the commissions from the in-house Drama department, but also those from independent companies. Indies had previously been looked after by Tessa Ross of the defunct Independent Commissioning Group, which had been disbanded under Dyke's reforms.

This meant that Tranter was now ultimately in charge of all of the BBC's television drama output – from the in-house departments making series, serials and singles, along with drama coming from the nations and regions and from independent production companies. She was in control of it all.

As *The Guardian* titled its profile of her shortly after she was appointed to the role, "If I say it will happen, it will happen." There was some suggestion in the media that the BBC had initially tried – not for the first time – to tempt Nick Elliott back from his post in charge of drama at ITV to take on this new role. However, *The Guardian* asserted that: "Such is her standing that Director-General Greg Dyke preferred her modern take to the more traditional tastes of ITV's drama controller, Nick Elliott."

"I really, *really* had to think about whether or not I wanted the job and took a great deal of persuasion," Tranter admits today. "Mark Thompson [then the BBC's Director of Television] always said that it took longer to write the press release for that job than anything, because I didn't really want to give anything up. I really liked the job I was doing, and I was trying to work out how I was ever going to be able to do the commissioning job. Was I going to be able to *do* anything? When I look back on it now it's just all such rubbish. It took a long time to work that out because I just really needed some persuasion to do it.

"In the end, I think I did the job, really, for the same reason I've taken any new job in my life. I wanted the oxygen of being able to make some of the decisions for myself – not all of them, but *some* of them. I like the oxygen that provides to your creativity. Of course, as soon as you actually start doing the job, it doesn't really matter who's got what tick or who holds what power; people are ultimately going to respond to what it is you say, if you are reasonable about it and if you're doing it for the right reasons. So it was a very, very good run, after four months of undoubted dithering."

"It was very good," Heggessey says of their relationship. "I think we mutually respected each other. Jane's the most fantastic drama practitioner, a really good eye for quality. I would say she was good at every aspect of it – casting, making sure the scripts were good enough."

Dyke's new system meant that the channel controllers and the various genre commissioners needed to 'double tick' any project to get it going. What this meant for drama on BBC One is that Heggessey and Tranter both needed to approve a project for it to be made – but fortunately, they worked well together.

"We had commissioners for each genre, and the channel controllers were equal partners with the genre commissioners," remembers Heggessey. "So we both had to agree or disagree on whether something should be commissioned. The channel controller had the overall strategic vision for the channel, and obviously decided where money was allocated, and the genre commissioners were trying to source the best programming possible for each of the channels, and worked across all of them."

"It's funny thinking back about the whole 'twin tick' thing, which meant so much at the time," says Jane Tranter. "I don't think there was anything that we didn't do that I had wanted to."

Tranter quickly found a rapport with Heggessey: "She was just really good. It was great having a woman as a boss – I think that's the first time I'd ever had that. I say 'boss', but we were on an equal level. She was a powerful and a more experienced broadcaster, and we had very similar tastes in a lot of things. I think Lorraine was much more overtly populist than I was in some ways, despite my ITV-ness. I was always looking for the salt in the mixture, believing that the particular qualities of public broadcasting needed a bit of that. I think Lorraine thought that was absolutely right, but we should just get an audience in there first, because public service broadcasting is no service to anyone if no one's watching it. So we just had some fun."

Tranter has fond memories of that time: "It was scary, and it was hard work, but we just absolutely *went* for it," she says. "I think it's no coincidence that the drama we made was more firmly female-skewing; it was much more modern, it always had something to say. Some of it had an awful lot to say about female empowerment and relationships and all sorts of things. It was a very good run for making drama that put strong women front-and-centre, both in terms of contemporary and classic pieces."

Over the next few years, Heggessey and Tranter commissioned a slew of popular, long-running series for BBC One. For *Doctor Who* this close working relationship, as well as the overall culture which Greg Dyke helped to create within the BBC, would be vital to its eventual return.

One of the things that came with Dyke's arrival was money. He had been able to allocate BBC One the extra funds that Peter Salmon had pleaded for the previous year to help take on ITV. The government had by now granted the BBC the above-inflation licence fee settlement negotiated by John Birt before his departure. Indeed, the BBC would be perceived by some to be so well-off in the coming years that in April 2002, Channel 4's new chief executive Mark Thompson – who had been the BBC's Director of Television under Dyke, and would later succeed him in the top job – declared that the BBC Director-General was "basking in a jacuzzi of spare public cash."

In September 2000, when it had been announced that he was moving to the Director of Sport position, Peter Salmon was asked by BBC Radio 5 Live's Brian Alexander whether he was frustrated that he hadn't had the money which was now being made available to his successor as Controller of BBC One. Salmon claimed to be

"A JACUZZI OF SPARE PUBLIC CASH"

philosophical about it, saying:

> "You're a caretaker. You're doing the best you can in the period of time you look after a channel or a station. At the same time, you're fighting for its future. So no, I'm very happy that the foundations are laid and the next person coming in can design that wonderful building. So it's a very kind of positive moment to leave the channel, I think."

One reason why Dyke needed Heggessey and Tranter to quickly come up with popular new dramas using the new money he was making available was because of the changes he'd made to the BBC One schedule. For decades, the BBC had run their news programme at nine, with ITV having theirs at ten – the *Nine O'Clock News* and *News at Ten* respectively both becoming household names and anchors within their schedules.

However, in the spring of 1999, ITV had elected to take the risk of losing the well-known *News at Ten* name by pushing the bulletin to later in the evening. After he arrived at the BBC, Dyke decided to take this opportunity to move the BBC's own nightly news to 10.00pm in its place. It was originally announced that the move would take place in late 2001, but in October 2000 the change was suddenly sprung with just two weeks' notice. This was because ITV had been ordered by the industry regulator to restore its own news to 10.00pm for at least three nights per week, and Dyke did not want to lose the initiative.

The 9.00pm news had long been an issue for weeknight BBC One dramas. It had meant they either needed to be suitable to be aired earlier in the evening, or else they would start after the news at 9.30pm and have to go on until 10.20pm, in the days of episodes of the BBC's dramas typically being 50 minutes long.

Now, Heggessey and Tranter were charged with developing long-running, mainstream hour-long dramas to run in the new primetime 9.00pm slot opened up by the moving of the news. Over the coming years, they were able to deliver a parade of new and returning dramas that proved to be both high quality and popular with audiences, reversing the recent trend that had seen ITV dominate this area.

"It had been much talked about before then," Tranter says of the news move. "But he just went and did it. We got some more cash, which was always the really big thing, because when we were going out at nine we were doing a full hour's worth of drama and so we needed more money. They decided they were really going to back the drama and our rebuilding of that whole drama output. So it was a perfect storm of good stuff."

Casualty writer Barbara Machin had already taken to Mal Young and Patrick Spence her idea for a drama about a police 'cold case' unit, and Young and Peter Salmon had commissioned the resulting two-part pilot for *Waking the Dead*, which had aired in 2000. Heggessey was then able to commission a full series, and the programme ran until 2011. Young's department delivered another hit with GF Newman's courtroom drama *Judge John Deed*, a popular – if sometimes controversial – series, which ran from 2001 until 2007.

Successes from independent companies included the spy series *Spooks*, launched in 2002 which also ran until 2011, before later spawning a feature film spin-off. *Hustle*, a con-artist drama and a stablemate of *Spooks* at independent producers Kudos, arrived in 2004 and ran until 2012. *New Tricks*, from production company Wall to Wall, followed a group of retired detectives recruited by the police to also tackle cold cases. It debuted in 2003 and ran for twelve series, outlasting all of its fellow Heggessey-Tranter era drama commissions.

Well, unless you count a certain *re*-commission, of course.

Other dramas were also tried and, even if they weren't always successes, at least showed a desire to experiment. Mal Young's Drama Series department piloted an adaptation of the stories of EW Hornung's Edwardian 'amateur cracksman' Raffles, in a one-off called *Gentleman Thief*, starring Nigel Havers and Michael French and screened in June 2001. It didn't lead to a series but was another demonstration that the department was looking

"A JACUZZI OF SPARE PUBLIC CASH"

outside of cops, docs and soaps for its subjects.

"We were the biggest commissioner of development scripts in the country," says Patrick Spence. "I think in my two years there I commissioned about 120 pilot scripts. We got about fifteen shows greenlit during my time there, in the first eighteen months."

In a *Doctor Who Magazine* article published at the end of 2001, writer Jonathan Blum cited the *Gentleman Thief* pilot as an example of how the BBC might possibly experiment with dipping its toe into the water with *Doctor Who*, by perhaps commissioning a one-off that could lead to a series. Like *Doctor Who*, *Gentleman Thief* had attempted to revive a once-popular character with an illustrious history across various media.

However, the scriptwriter of *Gentleman Thief*, Matthew Graham, believes that the efforts of the Drama Series department to make shows outside of the tried-and-trusted staples were not necessarily always appreciated or encouraged higher up in the BBC.

"I don't think people really wanted Mal to be making high-concept television," asserts Graham. "What they had brought Mal in to do was to make long-running, mainstream, white bread TV drama. That's what they wanted him to do. So I think anything outside of that they were going to close down fairly quickly."

Patrick Spence offers a measured response to this suggestion.

"I would hope that my career since leaving the BBC – and then coming back, by the way – speaks to the kind of ambition that Matthew is alluding to," he says. "Of wanting to do stuff that had its own vision and voice. I'm not going to refer to soap as good or bad, but I think it's fair to say that there were some of us within that department who wanted to make shows that had ambition. I think it's fair to say that there was a pressure from above to deliver ratings on things with soap stars as the leads. That didn't always sit well with some of the work that we wanted to be doing. I didn't leave because I didn't like it there, I left because I moved to America. But I think there's some truth in that, yes."

There is no doubt, however, that hits such as *Holby City*, *Waking the Dead* and *Judge John Deed* – added with the successes being produced by the independent companies – helped to bring the

THE LONG GAME

Drama department under Jane Tranter and Lorraine Heggessey's BBC One a renewed sense of confidence in the early 21st Century.

And justifiably so. In 2001, BBC One overtook ITV's main channel in average audience share across the year for the very first time since competition between the two began in the 1950s.

It's possible, though, that *Doctor Who*'s recommission arrived only just in time to benefit from this successful and confident era. Greg Dyke resigned as BBC Director-General at the beginning of 2004, over the controversy involving the Corporation's news output in the wake of the publication of the Hutton Report; one of replacement Director-General Mark Thompson's early interactions with Tranter was to ask if they could stop the *Doctor Who* project.

Heggessey was gone the following year, leaving to run production company Talkback Thames. Within a few years, the BBC had a new licence fee agreement that locked their income in place, without any rise for inflation, resulting in a raft of cutbacks across the Corporation.

But all that was yet to come. In the early 2000s BBC One's drama offerings under Heggessey and Tranter, and the BBC as a whole under Dyke, were very definitely on the up. Soon after the news of *Doctor Who*'s return was first announced in the autumn of 2003, Russell T Davies commented to *Doctor Who Magazine* that:

> "As BBC Drama goes from strength to strength, it strikes me that they want something for everyone on screen. They want every type of drama! *Byron*, and *Cutting It*, and *Holby City*, and *Strange*, and *State of Play*... look at the range of material, it's brilliant. Science fiction had to feature on the list sooner or later, so why not use the best property of all?"

'The best property of all' was at this point still waiting in the wings. But actually, science fiction and fantasy hadn't been as absent from BBC One as it might have seemed in the years of *Doctor Who*'s hiatus... It was just that the channel's efforts hadn't always worn their genre trappings with pride.

8

NOT DOCTOR WHO

"IT'S A BBC ONE SHOW ON SATURDAY NIGHTS – it wouldn't be there if it was actually labelled science fiction."

A decade on from the last time *Doctor Who* had appeared on BBC One on Saturday evenings, and another decade before it would return there, this was the verdict of Colin Brake on the drama series *Bugs*, which he both script edited and wrote for during the 1990s. Brake was speaking to *TV Zone* magazine in the summer of 1996, when the *Doctor Who* TV Movie was already past tense and *Bugs* was about to start the second of its four series on BBC One.

It's hard not to feel a little sorry for Brake, a *Doctor Who* fan through-and-through who arrived both too late and too early to work on the show on television. When *Doctor Who* fans speculate about who might have taken over from Andrew Cartmel as script editor had the series continued past 1989, they often talk about the likes of Ben Aaronovitch or Marc Platt – but it's much likelier that it would have been Brake who got the job.

By 1989 he already had three years of experience as a script editor for BBC Drama, working on one of its most popular shows, *EastEnders*. He was known in the department to be a *Doctor Who* fan and was probably the only script editor working there who actively *wanted* the *Doctor Who* job. Brake had visited the set of *Ghost Light*, which turned out to be the final *Doctor Who* serial to be made at BBC Television Centre, and the last production of the classic series; there Cartmel had introduced him to Sylvester

McCoy as his possible successor. Then the BBC cancelled the show, and nobody was needed to replace Cartmel when he left to script edit *Casualty*.

Come the mid-1990s and Brake was working on *Bugs* which – outside of *Red Dwarf* – was the only long-lasting series broadcast by the BBC during *Doctor Who*'s absence that even vaguely qualified as science fiction.

Bugs was made independently for the Corporation by producer Brian Eastman's company Carnival Films. Had *Doctor Who* returned as a BBC series at this point then Brake's experience of writing 50-minute self-contained action-adventure episodes for a Saturday evening family audience would quite possibly have stood him in good stead as a writer for the show – especially given how rare such programmes were on British television at the time.

But of course, it didn't return then, and by the time *Doctor Who* did come back *Bugs* had long gone; Brake's chance having again slipped away.

Bugs, as Brake suggested to *TV Zone*, was never out-and-out branded as a science fiction series, and at the time of its launch in 1995 was more often touted as a thriller show in the mould of ITV's 1960s hit *The Avengers*; "Avengers for the 90s" was even how the *Radio Times* titled its feature marking the show's first episode. The comparison seemed particularly apt, since original *Avengers* stalwart Brian Clemens worked on *Bugs* as a consultant.

But *Bugs*' tales of a group of investigators who dealt with crimes involving futuristic technology, computers, cyberspace and the like definitely gave it the *feel* of a sci-fi show. The two-part opener to the second season, written by Brake, even involved a space mission that wouldn't have seemed out of place during *Doctor Who*'s early 1970s UNIT era.

There were also *Doctor Who* alumni involved – *Warriors' Gate* and *Terminus* author Stephen Gallagher wrote for the show, and *Destiny of the Daleks* director Ken Grieve was behind the camera for some episodes. There was a future *Doctor Who* director involved too, with *The Long Game*'s Brian Grant helming several episodes later in the run, and in 1996 the holders of the *Doctor Who* book rights,

NOT DOCTOR WHO

Virgin Publishing, put out five novelisations based on episodes of the first series.

"The hardware/bugging stuff was sold as being state-of-the-art, real-world but, of course, we knew we were making it all up, most of the time!" says Colin Brake. "One factor that was interesting was the tone. On *Bugs*, Brian Eastman was determined to have no serial element – so international broadcasters could show them in any order – with little or no sense of the domestic lives of the characters, which is how season one worked. By the second series, however, I managed to persuade him to allow us to have some serialisation and begin having some personal stories for the characters. By season four we had a show that was much more like *Doctor Who* is now, with stronger character arcs across the season. I wonder if the show would have lasted longer if it had more of that earlier?"

Was there a deliberate attempt from Brake and other writers to see how far they could push the sci-fi elements?

"We all knew what we were doing," he admits. "We just had to let Brian Eastman – and more importantly the BBC – think that it was all in the realms of the credible. My two-parter was a clear statement of intent, I guess. Although I was very annoyed that Brian insisted on us cheating some kind of anti-gravity, rather than have the expense of faking zero gravity!"

It says something about the way in which science fiction as a genre was regarded on British television during this era that it effectively had to be smuggled in. While science fiction might be acceptable on the more niche-orientated BBC Two, in the form of *Red Dwarf*, *Doctor Who* repeats or US imports such as *Star Trek*, for the most part, it now struggled to find a home on BBC One, or indeed on ITV. Brian Clemens told the *Radio Times* of *Bugs* at the time of its launch that:

> "There have been so many years of realism on British TV that we've got to keep one foot in the real world. Nowadays it's all medical programmes and cop programmes – all very well done, but you don't see

a cop jumping on a balloon the way Bond would have done. We don't even make movies like that any more – with helicopters and people falling off the Eiffel Tower. British movies are three people in a room, or in an Italian garden, examining their navels. *Bugs* is plugging that gap."

Colin Brake recalls that the lack of such sci-fi-tinged adventure shows also caused problems behind the scenes, as there was now a dearth of writers still working in British television who were able to adapt to the genre.

"There were no experienced writers of this kind of adventure show around, save for a few of Brian's generation who were mostly retired," he explains. "Apart from the four episodes written by Stephen and the one I wrote [for the first series], the final drafts of all the other five scripts were essentially written by me and [producer] Stuart Doughty between us."

During the run of *Bugs*, Carnival also produced another Saturday evening science fiction series for BBC One, although in this case it only lasted for a single series. *Crime Traveller* aired in the spring of 1997, written by Anthony Horowitz – now best known for the *Alex Rider* series of children's novels, and the ITV drama *Foyle's War* – who even by 1997 was an experienced TV hand, with years writing for series such as ITV's *Robin of Sherwood* and *Poirot*. *Crime Traveller* starred ex-*EastEnders* actor Michael French and *Red Dwarf*'s Chloë Annett as a pair of police detectives who use a time machine Annett's character secretly possesses, to aid their crime-solving efforts. However, despite *Crime Traveller*'s time-travel premise, those involved were again reluctant to explicitly label it as sci-fi.

"Carnival were convinced that sci-fi was the kiss of death," explains Colin Brake. "I consulted a bit on the development and was commissioned to write an episode before Anthony decided he wanted to write them all. For him, it was a chance to do a crime series in a different way – he really wasn't interested in the time travel *per se*. I worked hard to make the time travel make sense, to impose some rules, but no one was really interested."

Jo Wright was the BBC Head of Drama Series from 1996–1997, overseeing both *Bugs* and *Crime Traveller*. She agrees with Brake's suggestion that British fantasy shows at the time had an uneasy relationship with the genre.

"I was a big science fiction fan, so I would have loved *Crime Traveller* to work," says Wright. "Do you know what the real problem with a lot of them was? That people weren't taking them seriously enough when they were making them. If you compare it to Russell T Davies and how seriously he took the remake of *Doctor Who*, there wasn't really anybody with their finger on the pulse, making it believable in its own way. To me, the best science fiction is where somebody has invented a world that is so clever that you can't say, 'Well, that wouldn't happen!'

"But unfortunately, I felt that people thought science fiction was an easy thing to do, when it's the most difficult thing of all. *Bugs* was good, but it went a bit downhill. The only reason they brought *Bugs* back was because they got it cheaply from Brian, because he found some more money [overseas]. But I think that they would have done more science fiction if they'd felt that there was somebody serious trying to make it. That was the problem with it."

Crime Traveller does perhaps give a flavour of what *Doctor Who* might have looked like had it returned around this time – if, say, Mal Young had arrived at the BBC a couple of years earlier, and been in a position to commission a BBC-only series off the back of the TV Movie's success in the UK. *Crime Traveller* ran for eight 50-minute episodes, was made entirely on film, and its star Michael French might conceivably have been the sort of actor who could have been a contender to play the Doctor had a series been in the offing at this point.

French was much in demand for BBC dramas around the turn of the century, his run in *EastEnders* as David Wicks having led first onto *Crime Traveller* and then in 1999 one of the leading parts in *Holby City* when that series began. He was the sidekick to Nigel Havers' Raffles in the one-off *Gentleman Thief* pilot in 2001, and

THE LONG GAME

from 2002 starred in the BBC One Sunday night 1950s rural period drama *Born and Bred*, which was co-created by Chris Chibnall and initially overseen by modern *Doctor Who* producer Phil Collinson. Russell T Davies himself even suggested French as a possible series star to *Doctor Who Magazine* in 1999 – although prefaced this suggestion with "anyone, so long as they can act."

Crime Traveller never returned after its initial run, and was somewhat overshadowed by the programme which immediately replaced it on Saturday nights, *Jonathan Creek* – a quirky mystery series that blended surreal crime stories with stage magic, starring the comedian Alan Davies. Off the back of *Jonathan Creek*'s success, Davies himself became a name often linked with the role of the Doctor by the media in the following years.

It's fair to say that *Crime Traveller*'s demise after a single short series was the subject of a certain amount of schadenfreude from some *Doctor Who* fans. Some didn't rate it simply because they didn't think it was very good, but there was also a distinct element of dislike for it having the temerity to be a time travel show on BBC One on Saturday evenings which wasn't *Doctor Who*. This wasn't exactly helped by the way in which the series almost seemed to be deliberately provoking such a reaction at times – the title sequence and music had a whiff of *Who* about them, and the sixth episode even featured a cameo appearance from a police box, complete with a *Doctor Who* theme reference snuck into the accompanying music score.

It wasn't just that it felt like teasing, it was that this also felt like a charming little reference to a show now dead and gone, while *Crime Traveller* was of the now. *Doctor Who Magazine* even got in on the act by running an edition of its spoof *The Life and Times of Jackie Jenkins* column gently mocking the show. They later printed a photo of French as *Crime Traveller*'s Jeff Slade, with the caption "No second season Jeff? Perhaps you can change your jacket now" – although, in fairness, this was there to illustrate a reader's letter defending the programme.

Having thus tried and failed with time travel in 1997, BBC One briefly experimented with science fiction again the following

NOT DOCTOR WHO

year, this time with another staple of the genre – alien invasion.

Invasion: Earth was a six-part serial shown on BBC One on Friday nights in May and June 1998, produced by BBC Scotland in collaboration with the Sci-Fi Channel in the US. Beginning with a UFO being shot down over Scotland in the present day, it told the story of Earth becoming caught in the crossfire of a war between two alien races, with a storyline reaching back to the Second World War.

The serial was written by Jed Mercurio, then best known for his acclaimed BBC medical drama *Cardiac Arrest*, which he had written under a pseudonym while still a practising medical doctor himself. *Invasion: Earth* was widely heralded in the media as a British answer to *The X-Files*, the US paranormal series which had become a sci-fi phenomenon during the mid-to-late 1990s – even briefly earning a primetime Saturday night BBC One timeslot, an honour seldom bestowed on imported programmes by that time.

"*The X-Files*' success has made television realise that science fiction is once again fashionable," Mercurio told *The Sunday Times* in September 1996, when *Invasion: Earth* was still in pre-production. "It has also made a lot of TV companies say, 'We must have a British *X-Files*.'"

This viewpoint was shared by Carlton Television's Jonathan Powell – the man who, as Controller of BBC One in 1989, had cancelled *Doctor Who*. Powell told journalist Steve Clarke in the same article:

> "Nobody is going out and saying, 'Let's recreate *The X-Files*...' If you tried to do that, you're bound to end up with a turkey and, anyway, audiences would see straight through it. But the success of *The X-Files* has given commissioning editors the confidence to take another look at science fiction drama."

Powell did, however, then go on to concede that:

> "One of the problems with doing television science

fiction is that you are setting yourself up to be compared with high-budget Hollywood feature films... We just don't have the money for those kind of production values and the special effects audiences expect."

If *The X-Files* was the standard to which the makers of *Invasion: Earth* aspired, at the same time it was also being distanced from its own UK sci-fi heritage. Mercurio told *The Independent* newspaper:

"I used to watch *Blake's 7* and think, `Why does this spaceship have a blue line around it when the Starship Enterprise in *Star Trek* never does?' That used to annoy me. Nowadays you can't broadcast dodgy special effects and then put up a caption saying, 'Sorry, this is what the budget was'. You have to do it with high production values because the audience has been spoilt by the special effects on things like *The X-Files* and *Independence Day*."

Speaking to the official *Invasion: Earth* page on the BBC's short-lived beeb.com website, the writer was more forthright, declaring that "a certain Time Lord should be consigned to the dustbin."

Radio Times, in a similarly uncharitable mood, went to great lengths to praise *Invasion: Earth*'s lavish visuals, simultaneously using them as a stick with which to beat *Doctor Who*:

"[It] slaps a leather glove in the face of British TV's previous sci-fi efforts. But then, look at them: *Doctor Who*, whose monsters used up enough rubber to erase the mistakes of a nation's youth... A multi-million-pound BBC co-production with the US Sci-Fi Channel, boasting computer-generated images, full-scale models, 85 sets... Beats pepperpots on casters!"

This *Invasion: Earth* love-in continued in the *Radio Times* editor's weekly column, where Sue Robinson complained that *The X-Files* had become dull and boring, while enthusing that:

> "*Invasion: Earth*, which lands on BBC One this week, is a slick, sophisticated thriller that should have the nation pinned back in its armchairs (or hiding behind them) for the next six Friday nights. Light years away from British television's previous sci-fi efforts, there's not a wobbly set or tin-foil costume in sight."

In the end, for all of its production values, *Invasion: Earth* came and went without ever leaving much of an impression. Even on Mercurio's own CV, it rates as a mere aside, given his subsequent successes with award-winning series such as *Bodies* and *Line of Duty*. But it did demonstrate that if the will – and more importantly, the money – was there, then the BBC could produce science fiction that was up to modern standards.

The series even helped give rise to a short-lived *Doctor Who* revival rumour of its own. While *Invasion: Earth* was still in production in October 1997, Scotland's *Daily Record* newspaper printed an article claiming that the BBC and the Sci-Fi Channel were about to sign an agreement to produce a new series of 30-minute episodes of *Doctor Who*. The rumour quickly turned out to be completely unfounded, probably based on nothing more than the fact that the two were already working together on *Invasion: Earth*. But when it was reported in *Doctor Who Magazine* 259 in November 1997, they pointed out that:

> "By the following afternoon, a statement headed unequivocally 'No Truth to *Doctor Who* Rumours' had been issued by the Sci-Fi Channel's US headquarters. More positively, however, the statement quoted Barry Schulman, vice president of programming for the channel, who said of talking to BBC representatives about future co-production of *Doctor Who*: 'We'd consider the opportunity, but as of yet there have been no discussions.'"

Nothing ever did come of this rumour, and when the *Doctor Who* production team were seeking US co-production funding in 2004 the Sci-Fi Channel declined the chance to come on board. They did, however, later premiere the first four series of the revived show in the US as bought-in programming.

Science fiction may only have been an occasional sight on BBC One during this period, but that certainly wasn't the case for its sister channel BBC Two. Designed as it was to cater for less mainstream tastes and interests, science fiction had been a regular presence on the channel in the 1990s – there was even a fairly steady stream of *Doctor Who* repeats from 1992 to 1994. Indeed, in 1999 University of Westminster researchers Steven Barnett and Emily Seymour published a study into British television drama which found that in 1997–1998, 55 percent of all drama shown on BBC Two had a science fiction theme. However, the vast majority of this was accounted for by either American imports or repeats – or, in the cases of *Star Trek: The Next Generation* and *Battlestar Galactica*, both.

There was at least one original, British-made genre effort on BBC Two around this time, though. *Neverwhere*, a six-part serial written by Neil Gaiman and set in a subterranean London fantasy world, aired on the channel in the autumn of 1996. *Neverwhere* has developed something of a cult following since its broadcast, despite being dismissed by *The Sunday Times* as "the sad Ealing version of *The X-Files*" – a series it didn't, in fact, particularly resemble in any way. Nonetheless, budgetary constraints were evident; particularly in the fact that it was shot on video and broadcast with the 'live' look to the image. This decision, unusual by this time in British television history, left it looking very cheap indeed.

It wasn't just the BBC channels where science fiction didn't get much of a look-in, when it came to home-produced primetime series. During the 1990s until the early 2000s sci-fi was also rarely seen on the BBC's main competitor ITV; but like the Beeb, they occasionally dipped a toe in the water.

ITV's *The Vanishing Man*, a modern take on *The Invisible Man* formula, had a pilot in April 1997 followed by a six-part series over a year later, with plenty of talent involved. Like *Crime Traveller*, it was created by Anthony Horowitz. Tony Jordan, an *EastEnders* stalwart and later the co-creator of *Life on Mars*, wrote four of the six episodes. The star of the show was Neil Morrissey, a familiar face to many millions of viewers from the popular sitcom *Men Behaving Badly*. Digital effects were from The Mill, the company which would later perform the same role on the *Doctor Who* revival, while on-set practical effects were by BBC Visual Effects – despite it being an ITV show, albeit one made independently for the network by ABTV.

Visual Effects were one of several in-house BBC production departments now being encouraged to adjust to the commercial imperatives of the 1990s by selling their services to other programme makers. However, it didn't do them much good, and over the next few years many of these departments at the Corporation closed down as the BBC switched to buying or renting-in production services from outside contractors. The Visual Effects Department's work on *The Vanishing Man* does, however, demonstrate just how much more complicated the world of television production had perhaps become even in the few years since *Doctor Who*'s original run had come to an end.

"It's not very often that money goes into British-originated sci-fi these days," *The Guardian*'s preview of *The Vanishing Man*'s pilot episode noted, "So this is a bit of an event: A two-hour special (which may or may not become a series)." The paper was not particularly complimentary about the script, but the preview did conclude that: "Given its rarity value, though, it deserves a second chance. Just." Although *The Vanishing Man* pilot did get that second chance, in terms of leading to a series in 1998, despite the very capable names involved, it then vanished without leaving much of a trace.

Another ITV effort arriving on screen in 1997 was a four-part serial called *The Uninvited*, a *Quatermass*-tinged tale of infiltrating aliens replicating the population of a vanished village. Written by Peter Bowker, it was based on an original idea by co-star Leslie Grantham, best known for his starring role in *EastEnders*.

THE LONG GAME

The Uninvited is perhaps most notable to *Doctor Who* fans for the fact that the tie-in novelisation featured a cheeky cameo by a character clearly intended to be Brigadier Lethbridge-Stewart, courtesy of the book's author, *New Adventures* regular and future TV *Doctor Who* scriptwriter Paul Cornell.

There was one footnote to *The Uninvited*'s story. In 2004, the Sci-Fi Channel in the United States bought the rights to remake it. This US version never actually emerged, but they appear to have been on a UK spending spree, also purchasing the rights to remake another ITV science fiction serial from the late 1990s – 1999's *The Last Train*.

Written by Matthew Graham and perhaps owing a creative debt to Terry Nation's 1970s series *Survivors*, *The Last Train* was a post-apocalyptic six-parter, heavily promoted by ITV, concerning the passengers of a carriage who are cryogenically frozen and emerge 52 years later into a vastly-altered Britain.

Graham recalls the broadcaster had reservations about running with a story that was explicitly high-concept. ITV's Controller of Drama Nick Elliott, when speaking to *The Sunday Times* for their piece on British television science fiction in September 1996, made the point that: "Science fiction is an area where we have to tread carefully because we don't want cult shows. We want shows that the main audience will watch."

"Nick Elliott was one of the great commissioners because he just believed in going for bums on seats," says Graham. "He looked for good ideas but he never micro-managed a programme. He would just say, 'Okay, if this is what you want to do, that's interesting.'

"*The Last Train* he never got. Literally, I pitched it to him and he said he didn't know about that. But his deputy, Jenny Reeks – who I also really, really liked – said she thought it sounded fun, she'd loved *Survivors*, and told Nick they should do a *Survivors* show! So he agreed to give it a go, and that was kind of how it was in those days. It was a wonderful time. There wasn't so much deep analysis – people just took a punt."

Why then, given that comparative freedom, does Graham think

that commissioners in the 1990s and early 2000s so rarely took that punt on sci-fi or fantasy?

"I think anything fantastical – science fiction, fantasy of any description – was out of whack with the vast majority of thinking amongst commissioners and broadcasters in general... producers at the indies, as well. If you look at the big shows back then, things like *Inspector Morse*, *A Touch of Frost*, *Silent Witness*, a lot of them were basically procedural shows.

"This is not to decry these shows. They were extremely good and made to the very highest standards of British television, but they were predominantly shows made by middle-aged men for middle-aged men and women to watch. And they were about the melancholia of people of a certain age, and it was just a certain type of television.

Graham feels that sci-fi's place in British television's heritage had been largely dismissed by the late 1990s. "It's funny, because we do have a great tradition in this country of doing science fiction," he asserts. "We did *Quatermass* and *Doctor Who* and *Blake's 7* and *The Tomorrow People* and *Sapphire & Steel* and *Children of the Stones*. It's not like there hadn't been a history of doing these shows, and doing them extremely well. So it is kind of strange."

Home-grown science fiction and fantasy may have been rare on the BBC or ITV in the late 1990s and early 2000s, but on the UK's fourth main national television channel it was almost nonexistent. Channel 4 had begun broadcasting in 1982 – except in Wales where the Welsh-language S4C was launched in its place at the same time. Throughout much of its existence, Channel 4 provided a home for various fantasy imports from the US, but it has only very occasionally commissioned such programmes itself.

In the autumn of 1998, however, Channel 4 broadcast the well-received vampire thriller *Ultraviolet*, starring Jack Davenport, Susannah Harker and Idris Elba. The six-part serial was both written and directed by Joe Ahearne, who would later go on to direct much of the first series of the *Doctor Who* revival. At this point, both Ahearne and the production company behind *Ultraviolet*, World Productions, were coming off the back of the success of the critically-acclaimed BBC Two drama *This Life*, which ran for two series in 1996 and 1997. With Ahearne's career riding high, moving from the wide acclaim of *This Life* to a potentially niche genre series might not seem like an obvious choice. But as he explains, *Ultraviolet*'s roots stretched further back.

"I came to World with a vampire show having been obsessed with horror and science fiction and Marvel comics from childhood," says Ahearne. "When Sophie Balhetchet joined World she read the treatment and the spec script I'd written and we met and hit it off. If it – and me – hadn't been to her taste I think that would have been the end of it. I had no broadcast credits apart from a short film so it was impossible to sell me as a writer, let alone a director on a big-budget, technically complex show like *Ultraviolet*. She got me a writing gig on *This Life* which developed into two scripts and then I directed another block of three. It wasn't a genre show in any way, but I loved it and it provided some confidence to World and Channel 4 that I could take on something bigger. *Ultraviolet* was always my end goal before I saw *This Life*. I was desperate to do something in the genre I love and it was pretty much impossible to break in on anything – let alone anything high risk – until I met Sophie."

Ahearne's fellow *This Life* writer Matthew Graham agrees that it was the success of that series, rather than any particular interest in fantasy from the commissioners, which enabled them to get such projects made and broadcast.

"The way I got *The Last Train* off the ground really was that *This Life* had sort of exploded, and all the writers – including Joe Ahearne, Richard Zajdlic, Amelia Bullmore, myself – suddenly got approached by broadcasters who said they'd love to do something with us, because we did the coolest show on television."

Ahearne's recollection is similar. "I think me and my vampire idea were the biggest obstacle to any sale, but World Productions were riding high. To Channel 4, *Ultraviolet* had to be presented as a tale of turn-of-the-Millennium angst rather than what I was interested in, which was doing modern Hammer Horror," he says. "That hasn't really changed, by the way. A show always has to fight for its reason to exist: 'It's a good story' isn't good enough. The pressure to make a case is more intense the more outside the norm it is. It's self-evident to many why there should be a drama about Iraq, say, or Hillsborough – less so with vampires."

"The main channels were embarrassed by science fiction," remembers *Bugs* script editor Colin Brake. "It was silly and childish and juvenile. It looked cheap, and no one ever won awards or big audiences with it. Of course, at the movies it was a very different story! I worked in the BBC drama department from about 1985 to 1994 and throughout that time sci-fi and fantasy was always looked down on. No one wanted to be involved; no one wanted to produce *Doctor Who*. Peter Cregeen asked me once, in a staff review meeting, who should be the next producer of *Doctor Who*. I often wonder what might have happened if I'd said 'Me!'"

Joe Ahearne agrees that this sci-fi stigma was evident when dealing with certain executives.

"I pitched a show in the early Noughties which was not science fiction, but had a fantasy premise," he remembers. "And was told by one head of commissioning that they could see and appreciate the themes and ideas being expressed but couldn't I just express those things within the format of naturalistic drama like everyone else? Which about sums up most of my commissioning experience around that time – not just from broadcasters but production companies too. A lot of people who make decisions about what gets made simply like what they like as we all do. They deep down don't really 'get' science fiction or horror in the same way they do, say, social realism. I think they find the genre a real barrier to their enjoyment and can only allow it in if there's an alibi like 'psychological' horror – not all commissioners at that time, but I would say most.

Ahearne also brushes aside the familiar arguments about the prohibitive budget demands of making science fiction, which by this time had become a mantra among television high-ups.

"It's true that the US imports then had production values we couldn't begin to compete with, but I don't think that's the real reason. There was and continues to be a fetishisation of character and social concerns to the detriment of anything else that might contribute to a show, and just a plain old embarrassment factor. They were generally more at home with projects that have an obvious social import or relevance."

Even *Ultraviolet*, in spite of its success, fell victim to the whims of the commissioners, not being brought back for a second run in spite of the positive reaction to the first.

"I have no complaints about the promotion and scheduling," Ahearne says. "We had a very decent press campaign and trails, and good media pick-up. The figures were very good but it was a new regime at Channel 4 by the time it aired, and very much out of step tonally with everything else they were doing. Incredible it got made at all, really."

What of the views of the commissioners and executives themselves, though? Several of those who would be responsible for bringing about *Doctor Who*'s return were already in senior positions in television by the late 1990s. What do some of them feel was the attitude towards the genre among the upper levels of the broadcasters at this point?

"I think it was completely out of vogue with commissioners," says Jane Tranter, who became the BBC's Controller of Drama Commissioning in 2000. "I never thought that it would be out of vogue with an audience if you did it right. British culture throughout the 20th Century had been ripe with brilliant sci-fi and fantasy pieces – in the Sixties and the Seventies there were loads of them. It's just in television drama the wheel turns, and after the Sixties and Seventies, when maybe there was quite a lot, in the Eighties came the rise and rise of police drama.

"I always think you can mark out the decades of television drama by what the police drama is; it tends to give you a sense of where the cultural zeitgeist is. So in the early Sixties, it was *Dixon of Dock Green*, leading into *Z-Cars*; the Seventies led into *The Sweeney* and *The Professionals*; and then the Eighties led into the more thoughtful and respective mode of *Inspector Morse*, and in the Nineties, obviously into that whole precinct, procedural, very dark stuff. It felt much less 'genre' and much more a way of very

NOT DOCTOR WHO

directly reflecting who we were."

Tranter believes that a parallel line can be drawn through the science fiction shows across the decades: "I think that the sci-fi became more miserabilist in feel – it was more bleak... which sci-fi can be, but it doesn't *have* to. It had become one of those things which audiences thought they didn't like. But they were still reading it and were still going to the movies to see it, but they weren't seeing it on television. So it was just clear to me that there was something that wasn't working.

"It wasn't that there was no one there for it, but it just wasn't working in the intimacy of a sitting room. You neither had the scale of the movies, but nor did you have that open, imaginative box of a book. So we just had to work out what we were doing and why. But I always knew it was something I would do. I just knew that if I did sci-fi I had to get it right because, up to that point, it had been a spectacular failure, really."

Mal Young had arrived at the BBC as Head of Drama Series at the end of 1997, and before the *Doctor Who* revival there was little to link his name to any enthusiasm for science fiction.

"People were trying. But it never got any traction, did it?" he suggests. "It didn't go to multiple series or become these huge hits. They were great ideas, and they were always by a group of writers who were really into that genre – Ashley Pharoah, Matthew Graham and those guys – and Jed Mercurio was fishing in those waters. But it always felt a bit self-conscious because they were *so* British. The Americans, they just throw themselves into it and go, 'Yeah, it's an alien! Believe it!' There's a confidence. Whereas we kind of go, 'Oh, sorry! Sorry, he's an alien.'

"There was a nervousness about doing anything that we now call 'genre'. Sci-fi – you didn't talk about it, you smuggled it in. You would always have to sell it on being about the world: 'It's about politics, it's about emotions.' But if you went in like you do in America and sell it on the concept, you're dead.

"But we also grew up loving sci-fi, and I had my own obsessions coming from the States – all those imports. So we had that in us. That same generation of writers and producers all wanted to find

THE LONG GAME

a way of mixing it all up and saying we could do sci-fi. But how did we sell it to a British broadcaster?"

After *Bugs*' run on BBC One came to an end in 1999, little more science fiction was seen on the channel over the next few years, aside from showings of feature films. However, there were other programmes that, while not science fiction as such, were certainly fantasy-based, and are interesting to now reflect upon, knowing what was soon to come with *Doctor Who*.

In March 2000 BBC One launched a revival of a long-cancelled cult drama, in Saturday night primetime, with high production values and a wealth of modern CGI effects. This was *Randall & Hopkirk (Deceased)*, starring comedians Bob Mortimer and Vic Reeves as a private detective and his ghostly partner. The original had been made by ITC Entertainment for ITV in 1969 and 1970, with this new version 30 years later made by Working Title Television for the BBC, and masterminded by comic writer and actor Charlie Higson.

The new *Randall & Hopkirk* began with an audience of ten million, but the strong figures tailed off across the run. After a series of six episodes in 2000, and another of seven episodes in the autumn of 2001, the show ended. In retrospect, though, this revival looks like an interesting trial run for *Doctor Who*'s return, and there are many names in the credits that *Who* fans would recognise: Murray Gold provided the incidental music, Mark Gatiss and Gareth Roberts both contributed scripts, Rachel Talalay directed two episodes of the first series, and Tom Baker had a regular role as a ghostly mentor for Reeves' character. It's even perhaps tempting to wonder whether *Randall & Hopkirk* ended up filling a slot that might, in other circumstances, have gone to a Russell T Davies-penned *Doctor Who*, had Mal Young and Peter Salmon's desire to commission such a series come off.

In March 2002 BBC One broadcast a one-off pilot for a supernatural thriller series called *Strange*. This starred Samantha Janus alongside Richard Coyle – then best known as Jeff in Steven Moffat's BBC Two sitcom *Coupling* – as the eponymous John Strange, an ex-priest who hunts demons. Written by Andrew

Marshall, who was behind the acclaimed sitcom *2point4 Children*, the pilot was sufficiently well-received for a series of six one-hour episodes to follow, although not until over a year later, on Saturday nights, starting in late May 2003.

"The previous controller, Peter Salmon, and Jane Tranter had been very, very supportive in the set-up," says Andrew Marshall. "But Peter moved on before production, as people often do, and then the usual manoeuvres began, when they suddenly change their minds; cancelling trails and publicity, relegation to a summer slot – not the best thing for a spooky story. This was very upsetting as I had literally put my life on hold for six months to be at every day of filming and was pretty exhausted. So that was a great disappointment for me."

Does Marshall agree that there was resistance from British television executives at the time to anything that ventured into the science fiction or fantasy genres?

"Yes, at that time there was no other fantasy series on TV at *all*, and I decided rather bravely – and as it turns out, stupidly – to make an attempt to bring fantasy back. The show, in order to not frighten the horses, was framed as a kind of spooky whodunnit, and I developed it over quite a long time unpaid, until BBC One finally accepted it. There were quite a number of problems making it; nobody was left in the Corporation who had worked on anything like this for a while, and we only had a budget extrapolated from *Jonathan Creek*, which made FX and the like very hard to achieve, though I think we did a fairly good job in the circumstances."

The pilot and three of the following six episodes of *Strange* were directed by Joe Ahearne, who agrees with Marshall about the challenges posed by trying to make a show requiring special effects on a budget not really built for them.

"Like all good filmmakers, Andrew had big ambitions and that's what I loved about his stories," Ahearne says. "They were unashamedly visual and there was something for a director to do other than just point the camera at whoever's speaking. We did our best, but set pieces are the hardest thing to pull off on almost any TV budget, especially back then with CGI on TV in its infancy."

"It was a brutal schedule," Marshall recalls. "I remember remarking at one point 'If they don't like this, I don't know what I'll do,' and when – apparently – they didn't like it, I consequently didn't know what to do. I was unable to write anything for some considerable time, and my parents and parents-in-law were dying simultaneously, so it was a very dark part of my life. I'm not sure I shall ever get over it, actually."

Strange never returned after the sixth and final episode of the series was broadcast in July 2003 – a story that guest-starred Tom Baker. As was often the case for dramas broadcast over the summer months, the viewing figures had not been high, and changeable timeslots for the episodes – as well as the long gap between the pilot and the series – can't have helped either.

"Interestingly, looking at it now, it's the kind of thing that might well have a good home on Netflix if I'd been making it at this moment," Andrew Marshall reflects. "I think, in the end, BBC One at that moment was probably just the wrong place for it."

Following his work directing *Strange*, Joe Ahearne moved on to write and direct the two-part docudrama *Space Odyssey: Voyage to the Planets*. This was an Impossible Pictures production about a fictional space mission, broadcast in 2004 on BBC One in the UK and on the Discovery Channel in the USA. It seems likely that Ahearne's experience on this as well as both *Strange* and *Ultraviolet* – making him one of the few British-based television directors who had worked on a significant amount of drama involving special effects – was one of the factors that led to him being recruited to helm several episodes of the initial run of the *Doctor Who* revival.

"I would imagine so," he agrees. "*Doctor Who* was as full-on a show as I've ever done – CGI, prosthetics, stunts, pyrotechnics. There weren't many genre shows that big in recent years. I think they wanted someone who could get through the schedule as well as making it look good. I can't remember if my agent chased it or they approached him, but I was insanely keen to get on it as a director, *Doctor Who* being one of my formative experiences."

Just as *Strange* was coming to an end in the summer of 2003,

NOT DOCTOR WHO

another contemporary supernatural series destined for BBC One was just starting production. This was BBC Scotland's *Sea of Souls*, written by David Kane, which told stories of the exploits of a parapsychology unit at the fictional Clyde University in Glasgow. Like *Strange* it was a six-parter, but rather than consisting of standalone episodes it was made up of three two-part stories, aping BBC One's successful 'Crime Doubles' format.

Broadcast in early 2004, *Sea of Souls* would fare better than *Strange* and ended up running for four series of varying lengths and formats until 2007. In this respect, it perhaps benefitted the beginning of a return to fashion for fantasy and science fiction productions on British television, of which the *Doctor Who* revival ended up being the flagship. Making a fantasy-based show with special effects also provided useful experience for its producer Phil Collinson, who left after the first series to become the producer of *Doctor Who*, taking up that role from January 2004.

Like *Strange*, *Sea of Souls* was broadcast on BBC One under the aegis of channel controller Lorraine Heggessey, perhaps indicating that there was something of a sea-change taking place under her stewardship of the channel. But even she was cautious about science fiction and fantasy in general.

"I think it's always a tricky genre," she says. "It may be easier to get wrong than to get right. Something like *The X-Files* obviously bust through. It's not necessarily a mainstream genre, but I would put *Doctor Who* in a different category to normal sci-fi or new sci-fi because it had this amazing heritage. It was part of British cultural heritage, and was done in a peculiarly British way."

There's little doubt that *Doctor Who* dominates the discourse when it comes to science fiction and fantasy television in the UK. If the series were to come to an end again today and not return for decades, the size and passion of its fanbase and the impact it has made on British popular culture means that it would still continue – as it did in the years it was previously off-air – to be the yardstick against which all other such home-grown sci-fi shows are measured. New programmes in the genre will be compared to or contrasted with it, and will be positioned in relation to it – if

THE LONG GAME

not by their makers then certainly by the fans.

When Steve Clarke was writing about the then-forthcoming *Crime Traveller*, *The Vanishing Man* and *Invasion: Earth* for *The Sunday Times* in the autumn of 1996, he referred to them as: "A batch of new series that echo the fantastic world inhabited by Mulder and Scully, one of which may give British television a long overdue sci-fi hit to equal the international reputation of *Doctor Who*."

All these years later, such a feat has still never really been achieved by a British science fiction show. The best way of matching the success of *Doctor Who* in the genre since then has been with reviving *Doctor Who* itself.

At the end of his superb book of essays *Doctor Who: From A to Z*, published in 1998, writer Gary Gillatt concluded that the space in the BBC's schedules which *Doctor Who* had been created to fill back in 1963 once more appeared to be present.

"Now that gap exists again," Gillatt wrote. "There is only one programme that can possibly be called upon to fill it."

In the early 2000s, Lorraine Heggessey and Jane Tranter also seemed to have concluded that they had a *Doctor Who*-shaped hole in the Saturday evening schedules. It was to be a little while yet before they were able to get *Doctor Who* itself to plug that gap – but, more than almost anybody knew at the time, the will was there.

Events were in motion. However, it was to be another BBC One programme entirely which was to provide the catalyst – a half-hour comedy-drama series called *Linda Green*.

9

RUNNING IN WEDGES

NEITHER LORRAINE HEGGESSEY nor Jane Tranter can recall exactly when it was that the notion of bringing back *Doctor Who* first occurred to them, after taking up their respective new positions as Controller of BBC One and Controller of Drama Commissioning in the autumn of 2000. However, both agree that it was something of a gradual process – an idea which only slowly started to seem viable.

"We had to reinvent Saturday night," Heggessey remembers. "I had to get a big entertainment show, that was a priority. Out of that came *Strictly [Come Dancing]*, but then I realised that you needed light and shade within a Saturday night, and certainly my childhood viewing had always had drama as part of Saturday. I remember shows like *Bonanza* and of course *Doctor Who*. I knew it was an iconic title. It was going to be so hard to launch something that nobody had ever heard of, so I thought we should bring it back. I mentioned it to Jane Tranter and she liked the idea. In fact, she was the one who got Russell T Davies lined up to write it."

"When I became a drama commissioner, I began to get the creeping beat of *Doctor Who* as an idea," says Tranter. "Obviously when I came back to the BBC in 1997, the Paul McGann single film attempt was sort of still there. I'd been aware of its demise [in 1989], which I thought was absolutely the right thing to do. I mean, no show, however brilliant, doesn't benefit from a rest – unless it's a soap and the whole point is it's designed to be there forever. I often think, as a commissioner, your job is as much to know when to stop as it is to know what to start. So I understand that it was necessary to have stopped *Doctor Who*."

Tranter always envisaged any *Doctor Who* revival as a series rather than one-off films, a view very much reinforced by her memories of the TV Movie.

"I wasn't sure, when the Paul McGann film was announced," she admits. "Obviously, I'm a massive *Doctor Who* fan and always was, but even I wasn't sure that was right – as a single film. Because it put too much emphasis on it, and that encourages pretension, which in my view is the one thing *Doctor Who* can never ever be. It's just not enough – you wouldn't be able to tell a big enough story.

"When I went back into the BBC, it didn't really occur to me at all. I developed a lot of fantasy in those early years, which I wasn't able to persuade the BBC to do. But it really didn't occur to me until I was made Controller of Drama Commissioning, and I got stuck in and I began to see what it was possible to achieve. Between about 2001 and 2003, I could see what we were doing, and I could see the way clearly and I thought, 'Okay, it's time.' That's when I said, 'It's time to do *Doctor Who*.'"

Over in the BBC One office, *Doctor Who* fans had a secret ally in the camp. This was in the form of Helen O'Rahilly, Lorraine Heggessey's principal deputy at the channel. O'Rahilly took up the position in November 2002, having previously been in charge of the BBC's interactive television efforts, and before that Director of Television at the Irish public broadcaster RTÉ.

"I was called a 'Channel Executive' – *the* Channel Executive. Basically, it's a deputy editorial role to the controller's role, which was Lorraine Heggessey," O'Rahilly explains. "It was helping out with editorial decisions; accompanying Lorraine to commissioning meetings, contributing to the commissioning process. Every time the independents came in, or the in-house groups came in, you'd be part of the team along with the scheduler, who would obviously be looking at the slots that were available, the budgets that were available, and so forth.

"I basically had to be, on a daily basis, aware of breaking news stories that might affect channel content; I had to be across all our press every morning; I would view tapes, with regard to editorial content and possible issues, and would brief her on things. I mean, it was a billion-pound channel – she was a pretty busy woman, you know! So anything that could be delegated to me was. It was an important, full-on role – I loved it. I had a good relationship with Lorraine and that's where the whole *Doctor Who* thing came in.

"I was a mad *Doctor Who* fan, and I'd actually met Jon Pertwee when I was a young researcher up at the BBC in Birmingham, Pebble Mill, and it was the highlight of my life! Usually, when you're a television researcher you meet all sorts of people – you're never bowled over, you know? But to meet Jon Pertwee was just... my God! It was sort of the pinnacle of my career! He was so charming and lovely, and he was my era – him and the early Tom Baker years.

"I was a huge fan, absolutely massive fan, and you could get the BBC for free then in Ireland. Because of the overlap of the link between Wales, we got it without paying the licence fee. So I grew up being a non licence-fee viewer of *Doctor Who*, and every Saturday night my poor dad would move from the sitting room and I watched every episode.

"I went into media in the factual area. I was never a part of Drama or anything like that, and I got on with being good in that department. But when you go to a multi-content place like BBC One, you're dealing with entertainment, you're dealing with news, you're dealing with drama. So here we were – within a few weeks I was fully engrossed in all of our output."

It wasn't long before *Doctor Who* cropped up during discussions:

"We would have these future planning meetings, just the small BBC One team, about six of us. And *Doctor Who* would come up, rare enough. There'd be a little bit of long-finger talk; if only we could, if, maybe... It was never anything being pushed on. Of course, at the first mention of *Doctor Who*, I got incredibly excited, just to myself – my God, the idea of bringing back *Doctor Who*! This was amazing! Wouldn't it be great?

"Lorraine was a fantastic controller, she really was. She was open to suggestions, and she was very fair about letting other people have their say. As a child, she wasn't into *Doctor Who*, particularly, but a few other people on the team were. But I was the mad, passionate fan, and you can be a real bore if you're a fan. So you have be careful.

"But I thought this was an opportunity here. Because Lorraine would always listen to ideas. I'd drop it into the future planning meetings – little gentle hints, not all the time. It was not a cul-de-sac, but it was one thing, always way, way down the list. We were concentrating on comedy series, and of course, we knew *Doctor Who* would be a huge CPH – cost-per-hour – because of the CGI involved, et cetera."

However, even before O'Rahilly's arrival, Heggessey was also being occasionally reminded of just how keen on *Doctor Who* a certain person in the industry outside of the BBC was, too. Russell T Davies may have claimed to Gay.com in November 2000 that he wouldn't have known Heggessey to look at her, but that didn't in the event stop him from making it known to the new Controller of BBC One that he was keen to get his hands on one of her channel's most famous past shows.

Davies' conduit for this gentle, from-a-distance lobbying was his friend Nicola Shindler, the woman behind Red Production Company. Since Red's initial success with Davies' *Queer as Folk* for Channel 4 in 1999, the company had quickly continued on an upward trajectory. In 2000 Red's first major series for BBC One had been broadcast, the Sunday night drama *Clocking Off*. Set around the lives of a group of workers at a textile factory in Manchester, it had been created by Paul Abbott, a friend and contemporary of Davies' from their Granada Television days. Abbott was rapidly becoming one of the most acclaimed and sought-after writers in British television drama.

Clocking Off had been renewed for a second run, and in the summer of 2000 Red had also been commissioned to make another Paul Abbott series for BBC One. This was *Linda Green*, also set in Manchester, and focusing on the life of the title character, a 30-something single woman played by Liza Tarbuck.

Linda Green was an unusual series as, despite being a non-soap drama, its episodes were only half an hour each, making it pretty much unique in British television at the time.

Red's increasing workload for BBC One meant that Nicola Shindler would periodically find herself in meetings with that channel's controller – and she agreed to be Davies' messenger to Lorraine Heggessey, mentioning to her that he was very keen to write a *Doctor Who* revival for the channel. Davies told *Doctor Who Magazine* in 2005:

> "Every time Nicola went in there, she said, 'By the way, Russell is still asking about *Doctor Who*!' Apparently, at one point, Lorraine went, 'Oh that bloody show! Everyone nags me about it!' I went to Nicola, 'Oh thanks, that's not going to get me very far,' but I had to keep nagging and drip-feeding my name in there – not just my name, but the idea of the programme."

This isn't, however, something which Heggessey herself recalls.

"I certainly often had meetings with Nicola Shindler – she's the most amazing producer, and she was doing *Clocking Off* and various other things," she agrees. "But no, I don't remember a lot of people asking me about *Doctor Who* – apart from after it became known that I wanted to get it off the ground and I was being stopped from getting it off the ground. So it was probably in that period that she asked me. I would imagine it was when I was frustrated because of the fact that I couldn't do the thing I wanted to do, because BBC Worldwide were stopping it."

The tackling of the issues posed by BBC Worldwide's desire to make a film version of *Doctor Who* did not happen, however, until after Davies himself finally had an opportunity to directly make his ambitions known to those at the top of BBC Television – although not initially to Lorraine Heggessey.

Probably sometime in early 2001, Davies had a meeting at the BBC with a woman called Pippa Harris, who was one of the executives working under Jane Tranter in the Drama department.

Davies recalled in *Doctor Who Magazine* 463 in 2013 that he had a meeting with Harris about *Doctor Who* in either 2000 or 2001. Given that in November 2000 he thought the *Doctor Who* idea was dead, and that he specifically remembered the meeting taking place not long after the debut of the American version of *Queer as Folk* – which took place in December 2000 – it seems very likely that it was early 2001 when they met. His reputation at the time was still riding high after the success of *Queer as Folk*, which had come to an end with a two-part special in February 2000, so it is little surprise that the BBC might then have been interested in snapping him up for a future project.

Davies, of course, was keen that this project be *Doctor Who*. He enthusiastically outlined to Harris how the recent BBC One natural history series *Walking with Dinosaurs* had shown what could now be achieved effects-wise on television budgets, and also related to her an idea he had about a story involving a version of the then-popular BBC game show the *Weakest Link*, hosted by Anne Robinson. He explained to *Doctor Who Magazine* in 2013:

> "I'd just been to New York for the launch of *Queer as Folk* USA. Anne Robinson was plastered all over the city for the American version of the *Weakest Link*. I suspect they weren't that interested, and used *Doctor Who* as a pretext to talk to me about other projects, but I had plenty of work from ITV and Channel 4. For me, it was *Doctor Who* or nothing."

This was not, however, entirely true. In 2001 Davies did his first writing for the BBC since the broadcast of *Century Falls* eight years earlier, and it wasn't for *Doctor Who*. But it *was* a piece of writing that would end up, indirectly, being very important for *Doctor Who*'s future.

Linda Green had been a Peter Salmon commission for BBC One, but it turned out to be a series enthusiastically embraced by his successor at the channel. In April 2001, *Broadcast* magazine reported that Heggessey thought so highly of the work done on the show so far that she had commissioned an extra four episodes, to bring the run up from six to ten ahead of its scheduled premiere in the autumn.

This meant that four more scripts were needed at short notice. Although Davies' career was now moving past the point of simply contributing episodes to other people's programmes, as it was for his friends at Red, he agreed to write one of the extra instalments. Nicola Shindler later explained why to Davies' biographers, Mark Aldridge and Andy Murray.

> "Paul couldn't write all of them, and Russell's friendly with Paul, and friendly with me. He loved the idea, and loved what he'd seen, so he said, 'Yeah, I'll do one.' For someone like Russell, when he's got an idea in his head, a half-hour show can take days to write. He didn't mind writing for somebody else's show at all, because he had the time, basically, and he's not a snob."

Davies wrote the fifth episode of the first series of *Linda Green*, called *Rest in Peace*. His involvement with the programme meant that he ended up attending a press launch event the BBC held at The Lowry theatre and exhibition centre in Manchester, in mid-October 2001, a couple of weeks before *Linda Green* made its debut on BBC One.

It was at this event that the path to new *Doctor Who* really began, when Nicola Shindler introduced Davies to the BBC's Controller of Drama Commissioning, Jane Tranter, for the first time. The way they tell the story, it almost sounds like a pair of nervous teenagers finally being brought together on the dance floor by a mutual friend at a school disco.

Davies told his side of events in the DVD documentary *Doctor Forever: The Unquiet Dead* in 2013.

> "When you write an episode of someone else's series, you're kind of in a lesser status as a writer. And so I was really pissed off that I was meeting Jane Tranter

in a really lesser status, just when I wanted to talk about *Doctor Who*... So I almost didn't bother, and there was this big launch party, and Nicola Shindler went 'Go over and talk to her, go and talk to Jane Tranter, go and say that you want to do *Doctor Who*.'"

Shindler wasn't only prodding Davies towards Tranter; she was also directing Tranter towards Davies as well.

"That was true, Nicola saying that," says Tranter. "So obviously, I had, like everybody, been a massive fan of Russell T Davies. I just thought he was one of the best and cleverest and funniest writers around, and he did an episode of *Linda Green*, which was brilliant. Everything Russell does is just brilliant.

"I was just completely in awe, but had never worked with him. Nicola said to me, 'In case you really are genuinely looking for someone to write *Doctor Who*, you know Russell is a major fan?' Which I hadn't known at all. I was quite heavily pregnant with my twins, I'm wearing a pair of wedges, but I literally sprinted from one side of the room to the other to say, 'Is it true?'

"I'm very instinctive like that, but there were really no big conversations. As soon as I knew that, I thought that's how it was meant to be. It never occurred to me for one second to doubt that Russell was the right person to do it, because of his ability; he's so witty, he's so clear in his writing – his ability to access the nature of the human condition. He was clearly a major fan and he wasn't afraid of it. He could throw it all up in the air and pull out things he'd like to include and what he wouldn't. But to be honest, we really didn't talk that much about it. I said, 'Look, I really want you to do it.'"

Davies makes it sound slightly less dramatic, and also disagrees over who actually ended up breaking the ice and approaching who. He recalled in the 2013 documentary:

"I literally thought I bored her and annoyed her. I went up to Jane Tranter and said 'Hello, nice to meet you properly, and don't you think we should do *Doctor Who*, we should do it properly, and make it marvellous, and blah blah blah blah blah.' And she sort of went, 'Oh yes, that's a nice idea,' like they do... And I remember thinking... I was really sort of kicking myself. And do you know what? I wouldn't have done it again after that meeting. Because I sort of walked away from that thinking, this is getting embarrassing now. It was literally that *Linda Green* press launch in the Lowry Hotel that forged the entire creation of *Doctor Who*."

Davies may not have necessarily felt that Tranter was genuine with her enthusiasm for bringing *Doctor Who* back, but he was mistaken. Indeed, in the *Doctor Forever* documentary, she says that even before this point she had already broached the subject of *Doctor Who* with Lorraine Heggessey, and floated the possibility of it returning. However, she did admit that without Nicola Shindler's matchmaking at the *Linda Green* press launch – and despite Davies' previous dealings with the BBC regarding *Doctor Who* – she might not have realised Davies was so keen to revive the show: "I don't know, if I'm really honest, that I would ever have necessarily put two and two together and found Russell for *Doctor Who* myself," she explained in the *Doctor Forever* programme.

Lorraine Heggessey had also been present at the *Linda Green* launch, although was apparently not privy to Davies and Tranter's brief discussion about *Doctor Who*. After they had returned to London, Tranter put the idea of asking Davies to take charge of a *Doctor Who* revival to Heggessey. When the return of the show was finally officially announced in September 2003, Heggessey told the *Daily Telegraph* that she had been "waiting for two years" to be able to revive the programme – pinpointing the timing of those attempts to get it underway almost exactly to the time of the *Linda Green* launch.

At least part of the delay may have been down to the fact Jane Tranter didn't have much of an opportunity to make any headway with the *Doctor Who* idea that autumn. Not long after this first encounter with Davies she temporarily left the BBC for a period of maternity leave, giving birth to twins in December 2001.

But Tranter was by no means the only person in BBC Drama who was keen on working with Davies. In the autumn of 2001 Davies' latest collaboration with Red hit television screens. *Bob & Rose* was a six-part serial for ITV, starred Alan Davies and Lesley Sharp. It told the story of a gay man who falls in love with a woman, based on something which had actually happened to a friend of Davies'.

Bob & Rose was much admired by one of Jane Tranter's main lieutenants in the BBC's Drama department, Laura Mackie. Mackie was the Head of Drama Serials – and so in charge of the branch of the Drama department that had originally made *Doctor Who*, and had been its home for most of its existence.

By Davies' reckoning, it was early in 2002 when he went to meet with Mackie at the BBC, as her enthusiasm for *Bob & Rose* meant that she was keen to bring him on board. According to Davies' recollections to *Doctor Who Magazine* in 2005, she told him that "'I love *Bob & Rose*, and I'd like to work with you.' I said 'Well, I'd only like to do *Doctor Who*.'"

It seems that Mackie had been keen for him to collaborate with the novelist China Miéville on a science-fiction version of *A Tale of Two Cities*, but Davies stuck to his guns on the *Doctor Who* front. According to the story, as Davies related it in *Doctor Who Magazine* 359 and in *The Unquiet Dead* documentary in 2013, he was then later called in for a follow-up meeting, specifically to discuss his ideas for *Doctor Who*.

This is where the narrative becomes slightly blurred, as when Davies talks about this second meeting, he relates the same stories about pitching ideas based around *Walking with Dinosaurs* and the *Weakest Link* that he would later ascribe to his meeting with Pippa Harris a year earlier. Obviously, Davies would have attended a great many meetings with a great many television executives, and it's no surprise that some of the details may have become conflated, with memories of one such meeting bleeding into those of another.

So it's unclear whether Davies pitched the same *Walking with*

Dinosaurs and *Weakest Link* ideas to Mackie as he had to Harris or whether, over the intervening years, he simply confused the two discussions.

Whatever the case, it all had the same outcome as before. There was no more progress with *Doctor Who* on this occasion than there had been in 2001, or when he had met with Patrick Spence just before *Queer as Folk* was screened. Once again, it all seemed to be down to the mysterious and ill-defined area of 'rights issues'.

"I was very excited, but they said, 'We've got to inquire about the rights,' and still nothing happened," Davies told *Doctor Who Magazine* 359.

It seemed as if Davies had once more missed his chance with *Doctor Who*. He busied himself with work on *The Second Coming*, a drama about the Son of God returning to Earth in modern-day Manchester. Developed with Nicola Shindler's Red Production Company, this script had been initially commissioned and then subsequently cancelled by Channel 4, and then turned down by the BBC, before being picked up by ITV.

This project, filmed in 2002 and screened in two episodes in early 2003, brought Davies together with one of the most prominent British television actors of his generation, someone well-known for his association with serious dramatic roles. His name was Christopher Eccleston, and his and Davies' collaboration on *The Second Coming* would not be their last on a major television drama production – although, of course, not even the two of them had any idea of that yet.

10

WHAT DO WE WANT?

"Ask any two fans what their 'fantasy *Doctor Who*' is, and you're almost certain to start an argument. If someone said 'Bring back *Bergerac*!' or even 'Bring back *Blake's 7*!' you'd instantly have a pretty good idea what they meant. With *Doctor Who* it's different – it could be ten-minute animations before *Newsround* or 15-rated TV movies with a huge budget."

WHEN *DOCTOR WHO* NOVELIST Lance Parkin made the above remark in the summer of 1999, he was speaking in a feature piece about the show's possible future printed by *Doctor Who Magazine*; a publication which was by then approaching its 20th birthday later that year. Originally run by Marvel UK before being bought by Panini in 1995, the magazine continued to be available on British newsstands throughout the periods when *Doctor Who* itself was off the air.

"Even now that it's on TV, my partner boggles that they can fill a magazine about it every month," says Gary Gillatt, the editor of *Doctor Who Magazine* from 1995 to 2000. "I don't recall any panic at Panini about sales, though of course the figure was always slowly dribbling down. Odd thing is, I'll bet the magazine's current sales aren't so very different, even now that *Doctor Who* is supposedly a global brand."

Clayton Hickman became *Doctor Who Magazine*'s assistant editor shortly after Gillatt's departure, and then editor himself at the end of 2001. "It was still selling fine," agrees Hickman. "I mean, not brilliantly, but we didn't have much of a budget for it anyway, and everyone was so fond of *Doctor Who Magazine* that they'd do stuff for very little. It hadn't occurred to me that it might have been a very strange career move. When I came to London, I'd go to the monthly meet-ups in the Fitzroy Tavern pub, the first Thursday of every month I think it was. So I'd always see all the people I'd heard of – people I knew, people I'd just befriended. It felt like a little community.

"*Doctor Who Magazine* was like the newsletter of that community. So I'd put things in thinking it would make such-and-such a person laugh, or it would appeal to my friend Peter! It sounds ridiculous for a commercial magazine, but it seemed to work. I think the readers felt like they were part of a little club."

Much like *Doctor Who* within BBC Worldwide, *Doctor Who Magazine* had evolved to become a steady, albeit modest enterprise, essentially self-contained within the rest of Panini's business.

"The high-ups at Panini didn't understand a blithering thing about *Doctor Who*, but were happy to just let it go on because it brought in money for them," says Hickman. "I'm not saying that they were horrible, nasty, rich businessmen types – they weren't, they were creative. But they were part of comics really, and *Doctor Who Magazine* was a complete aberration in the Panini line-up.

"They were happy to support it because it had a very loyal readership – a lot of whom would subscribe, which isn't typical with magazines – it's usually an impulse purchase at the newsagent's or the station or something. But with *Doctor Who Magazine* they could almost guarantee a certain number of copies each month. It meant that they left us alone because they pretty much threw their hands up and said, 'We don't understand a thing about this, you get on with it'."

The magazine's annual reader survey always continued through the years when the show was out of production, polling fans for their views on the year's official novel releases, Big Finish audios, comic strips and the like. There's always *something* going on in the world of *Doctor Who* to ask the fans about, and always something

WHAT DO WE WANT?

about which fans like to speculate.

In 2000, the magazine decided to add something extra to the annual survey. Perhaps as a reaction to the various film rumours going around at the time and the news of the abandoned approach to Russell T Davies for a new television version, they asked their readers the following three questions:

"Who would you cast as the Doctor in a multi-million-dollar Hollywood *Doctor Who* film?" "Who would you cast as the Doctor in a new BBC TV series of *Doctor Who*?" And finally... "Who would you choose to shape and produce a new TV series of *Doctor Who*?"

The survey form was published in *Doctor Who Magazine* 287 in January 2000, and the results of the polling for these categories were printed as part of a special feature in issue 293 at the end of June. Perhaps unsurprisingly, the winner in both the film and TV fantasy Doctor categories was the man who then currently held the role – Paul McGann.

Although the 1996 TV Movie had divided opinion in fandom, McGann himself had been almost universally praised for his performance. Many were keen for him to get another crack at the part. At the time the poll was conducted, McGann had yet to return to the role for the *Doctor Who* audio licence holders Big Finish, making his TV Movie outing a true one-shot; in May that year, McGann was finally persuaded to record new stories for the company, which were released from early 2001.

The runner-up in the film Doctor category was Hugh Grant, star of *Four Weddings and a Funeral* and *Notting Hill*; at the time probably the most bankable British name at the worldwide box office. He had actually played the Doctor the previous year – for 1999's Comic Relief spoof *The Curse of Fatal Death*. To accompany the poll results, Steven Moffat, the charity skit's writer, provided a short prose story 'starring' Hugh Grant as the Doctor, to accompany his position as the top non-McGann candidate in the movie Doctor category.

Coming second to McGann in the TV Doctor poll was Ian Richardson – best known as the star of the BBC adaptations of

THE LONG GAME

Michael Dobbs' *House of Cards* trilogy; he had also played the eponymous magician in the BBC One Sunday teatime children's fantasy serial *The Magician's House* the year before. Richardson was by this time 66 years old, showing perhaps that in terms of the small screen, fans were keen for a more mature take on the Doctor. Richardson was also cast in a short prose scene to accompany the poll, this one written by prolific *Doctor Who* novelist and up-and-coming TV scriptwriter Paul Cornell.

Cornell's vignette was interesting when viewed as a little taste of what a future *Doctor Who* series might be like. The impression is given that companion Alice has yet to travel with the Doctor in the TARDIS - despite them having experienced several adventures together. This perhaps reflected a prevailing view at the time that to make any new version of *Doctor Who* affordable for the BBC - as well as palatable to the general BBC One viewership - it might have to be much more Earthbound than previous iterations.

Of all the actors who would go on to star in the modern series, Peter Capaldi might have been expected to garner a few votes in 2000 - but he didn't feature in the poll's top ten TV contenders, nor even in the general round-up of others also mentioned. Future Master John Simm did merit a few votes, although he also failed to make the top ten. Behind Richardson were the main *Curse of Fatal Death* Doctor Rowan Atkinson, perennial Doctor speculation target Alan Davies, and another *Fatal Death* Doctor - and future voice of an animated version - Richard E. Grant.

Then there were the responses to the third question - who the magazine's readers would like to see masterminding any television return for the Doctor?

Steven Moffat and Mark Gatiss both featured in the top ten here, having each been responsible for generally well-received *Doctor Who* comedy pieces broadcast by the BBC during 1999 - Moffat's *The Curse of Fatal Death*, and Gatiss' *Doctor Who Night* sketches for BBC Two in November that year. 'The BBC' generally, audio producers Big Finish Productions, and previous *Who* hands Philip Hinchcliffe, Terrance Dicks and Philip Segal also garnered votes. There were, however, some fans who clearly felt that there should be a completely clean slate, and that anybody with a previous connection to the series or who was even a fan of it should be ruled out – with the magazine recording nominations for "Any Bugger To Whom It's Not An Ambition" and their close relative "Anyone Who Has Had Nothing To Do With It Before."

"I think the sentiment behind that wish still exists today," says Gary Gillatt, who was editor when the poll was put out. "*Doctor Who* is forever fated, I feel – however imaginative the revival or relaunch or new producer – to decay, or maybe merely relax, to a lower energy state. That lower energy state is men in Time Lord collars shouting at each other about the imminent collapse of the tachyon barrier, or some such.

"Even Russell and Steven, for all their skill, couldn't escape it. Chris Chibnall tried for a year, then ended up right back there. All the spin-offs end up there as well. At the moment they're piling up faster than ever. Some fans love it, but others fear it. That whole alienating, *Arc of Infinity* squabbling rubbery-ness. So when they say they want someone 'new' to take charge, they mean someone to keep *Doctor Who* away from that for as long as possible. To take it somewhere new for that delicious, precious five minutes before Gallifrey's tachyon barrier fails again."

Two percent of the respondents voted for Matthew Robinson to take charge of any new version. As a young director in the 1980s, Robinson had helmed the *Doctor Who* serials *Resurrection of the Daleks* and *Attack of the Cybermen*. He'd since gone on to produce the long-running children's drama *Byker Grove*, and most recently run the BBC's flagship soap opera *EastEnders* – which, given its high profile, probably accounted for his appearance in the poll.

However, Robinson had left the *EastEnders* job in January 2000 to become the Head of Drama at BBC Wales – making it seem very unlikely that he might now have anything to do with the future of *Doctor Who*. BBC Wales did, however, had its sights set on a bigger share of network exposure across the UK.

When Robinson was appointed to the BBC Wales job, *Broadcast* magazine reported that: "One of Robinson's key tasks, according to a BBC source, will be to secure a network commission for a returning drama series."

Meanwhile, top of *Doctor Who Magazine*'s fantasy producer poll were two joint winners, each of them receiving 16 percent of the votes. One of them was Verity Lambert – the original producer of *Doctor Who* in 1963, who since then had become one of the foremost producers in the history of British television drama, with a string of successful, popular productions on her CV. At the time of the poll, she was still very much an active producer, as she remained for the rest of her life, at this point producing the BBC's successful Saturday night mystery series *Jonathan Creek*. Clearly many fans felt that Lambert, the woman who had brought *Doctor Who* to the screen in the first place, was the best person to be trusted with breathing new life into it.

Sitting alongside Lambert at the top of the poll was someone whose professional connection to *Doctor Who* at this point extended no further than a single novel in Virgin's *New Adventures* range – Russell T Davies. But Davies' success with *Queer as Folk* had propelled him to the forefront of well-known current television writers, and the fact that he was also a known fan meant that he was someone who a significant chunk of a fandom appeared to trust not to make a mess of the series.

Doctor Who Magazine pointed out in their commentary on the poll result that it was fitting for Lambert and Davies to have jointly come top; several respondents had evidently suggested that the pair of them should work together on any new series.

Davies also probably did well because his views on how a new series of *Doctor Who* could be tackled, and what form it might take, were by now familiar to *Doctor Who Magazine* readers. A year before these poll results had been published, in June 1999 the magazine had printed what has probably become one of their best-known and most analysed features. *We're Gonna Be Bigger Than Star Wars!* was an article published in issue 279, looking at how a new series of *Doctor Who* could possibly be made to appeal to "the *Phantom Menace* generation," tying in with the new *Star Wars* movie released in cinemas that summer.

For the feature, Gary Gillatt gathered the thoughts of a variety of *Doctor Who* fans – nearly all of them *Doctor Who* novelists – who also had careers writing for television. In his introduction to the piece, Gillatt pointed out that it seemed likely that one of these people might well end up running a new series of *Doctor Who* at some point in the future. Among those to whom Gillatt spoke was Davies – who by now had already had his first meeting with the BBC about bringing *Doctor Who* back, although this was not yet public knowledge at the time. The feature is therefore a fascinating insight into what Davies' thinking was at this juncture, and perhaps a glimpse of what might have happened had Peter Salmon been able to commission his series of *Doctor Who* for BBC One in 1999.

"With lots of things I do, the title comes first," explains Gillatt. "Or the look of a page – the 'promise' really, or perhaps just a gimmick – then I'll chisel out something to help make it all stand up. You'll see a lot of it in *Doctor Who Magazine* in my time. The giveaway is if I'm the writer. I hate writing, will do anything to avoid it, and would only do it if I couldn't communicate the idea adequately to someone else.

"So it really started with the idea of *Doctor Who* Lego. I wanted to see what it would look like. They'd just released *Star Wars* Lego for the first time, and I'd met two guys at a convention who knew how to CG me some – it was all very cutting edge! The article was the justification for the graphic, basically trying to answer the question; how do we get from here to there? I thought it would be fun to rustle up some expert insight. Anything that followed is just down to good journalistic instinct, I guess."

Taking Gillatt's starting point of the 'promise', did he really believe that long-rested *Doctor Who* could scale those heights? "It all felt very plausible to me, not some mad flight of fancy," he says. "Then it was kind of how it all happened, wasn't it? We even got the Lego. Not quite bigger than *Star Wars*, though. But size isn't everything. Certainly broader than *Star Wars*!"

As well as Russell T Davies, also contributing their thoughts to Gillatt's piece were Steven Moffat, Mark Gatiss, Paul Cornell, Gareth Roberts and Lance Parkin. All of them except for Parkin would go on to write for *Doctor Who* when it eventually returned, adding to the article's prescience.

At the time of the feature's publication in the summer of 1999, Moffat had already been writing for television for a decade, having seen great success with his ITV children's drama *Press Gang* from 1989 to 1993, and written two series each of his BBC sitcoms *Joking Apart* and *Chalk*. He was about to embark on his most successful sitcom, *Coupling*, which would begin its four-series run on BBC Two the following year.

Mark Gatiss was at the beginning of *The League of Gentlemen*'s success on television, with their first series having been broadcast on BBC Two at the start of the year. Cornell was probably the most acclaimed of all of the panel as a *Doctor Who* novelist, and in the past few years had been writing for television, with two series of his own ITV children's drama *Wavelength* and a contribution to *Coronation Street* among other work. Roberts had also worked on *Coronation Street*, as well as ITV's other main soap opera *Emmerdale* and Channel 4's soap *Brookside*, while Parkin had been another contributor to *Emmerdale*.

The piece ended with a rather comically prophetic statement from Russell T Davies: "God help anyone in charge of bringing it back – what a responsibility!" Before this, however, he'd pointed out a potential pitfall with *Doctor Who Magazine*'s group of runners and riders: "One of the problems with fan writers making their way in the industry... [is] it reaches the point where the return of *Doctor Who* could be, for them, a backward step."

Given the results of the magazine's poll in 2000, Paul Cornell's comments in the piece about who should be in charge of any new series were noteworthy: "The only person who could take it on without worrying is someone like Verity Lambert, with a vast bullet-proof reputation. That would get the business interested again." By the time his chance finally came, Davies himself had accrued exactly that kind of reputation, to the extent where his name alone was enough to get the business to sit up and pay attention.

What is interesting is how much of Davies' thinking for the

series was already in place and recognisable as what would eventually turn up on the screen. "I think you should set all that high flown end-of-the-world stuff in a very real world of pubs and mortgages and people... emotional content has got to be stronger, more interesting, more open, to grab a wider audience."

When it came to the potential format of the show, Davies was somewhat more cautious in 1999 than he would be when he came to make the programme for real: "Self-contained stories, maybe – only maybe – trying a two-parter towards the end of the first series," he told the magazine.

It's the format that sparked the most debate amongst the fan panel. Lance Parkin came close to hitting upon the eventual modern format for the series when he suggested, "The Saturday post-Lottery slot seems like a natural place these days, where *Crime Traveller* and *Jonathan Creek* went. That would seem to dictate 50-minute filmed episodes, aimed at the 'older family.'" Davies, however, disagreed that the series could ever end up on Saturdays again at all: "I don't think you'd put a 50-minute film series on during Saturday teatime. That slot has been consigned to history now. It would have to be weekday evenings at 8.00pm."

Quite aside from episode numbers and lengths, the types of stories a new series could tell would be dictated by budget. Davies pointed out that, "If it was, say, a series of thirteen 50-minute episodes, that means thirteen batches of new sets. Nightmare!"

If the format of a returning *Doctor Who* was an issue for debate, then the content of a new version was in another league altogether. With such a long, rich history and an opinionated fandom, making sense of all that past continuity was one issue upon which the majority of those asked seemed to agree.

Parkin: "The Police Box and the theme music [should be retained] – everything else is up for grabs". Gatiss: "Throw it all up in the air, I say. Nothing is sacred. Start from scratch and keep the show vivid and alive." Roberts: "No need for any Time Lord mythos or complex continuity – who cares?" Paul Cornell felt that unless a better deal was struck for their use, then the Daleks almost certainly wouldn't be back. Given that their appearance in

THE LONG GAME

the first series of the revival did involve a last-minute deal, after initially hitting contract stalemate, Cornell clearly wasn't totally wrong about that – however inconceivable bringing the show back without the Daleks might now seem in retrospect.

In a sense, this desire for a fresh start was all understandable and admirable, wanting to capture new audiences for a new series rather than simply appealing to the existing fanbase. But it also reads a little like fans being overly defensive; perfectly prepared to throw out all past continuity and start again from the beginning, rather than risking ridicule. In the event, there was nothing quite so drastic come 2005 – this was still very recognisably the very same Doctor with the very same history, just with one pretty major development since we last met him.

"To be realistic," Paul Cornell said in 1999, "I'd chuck away half the background – the moment the Doctor started talking about Gallifrey or the Time Lords, I'd just cut it. Excess baggage." Davies did cut it, of course, but not by erasing the Doctor's history and backstory. Instead, he added to it with the epic new mythos of the Time War and the destruction of the Doctor's home planet. It turned out that the perfect solution to continuity was not to ignore it, but to create a little more of it.

Steven Moffat had some firm thoughts about just what *type* of actor should play the part – thoughts that are interesting with the knowledge that a decade later he was responsible for casting the youngest Doctor to date. "I don't think young, dashing Doctors are right at all," he said to *Doctor Who Magazine* in 1999. "The Doctor should always be a bit more Picard and a bit less Kirk. He should be 40-plus and weird-looking – the kind of wacky grandfather that kids know on sight to be secretly one of them."

So at this stage, the likeliest prospects for a *Doctor Who* revival according to those closest to being in the know seemed to be fairly well set. It would probably be a 50-minute slot on a weeknight at 8.00pm, with continuity-light Earthbound stories and perhaps even be a reboot of the entire series.

But could it make any impact at all? Would it last?

In December 2001, *Doctor Who Magazine* 312 published another feature looking at the future of the show across various media. This piece was called *50 Essential Questions*, and covered assorted points about the future direction of *Doctor Who* in books, on audio and on television. The section devoted to questions about the potential future of the series on television was written by *Doctor Who* novelist Jonathan Blum.

Blum consulted widely with fans and experts for his piece, and assured readers that ratings of five million would probably be good enough to get a new series recommissioned for a second run. Matt Jones, a *New Adventures* novelist who had script edited *Queer as Folk*, explained to Blum, "Get 35 percent [of the audience] and the champagne flows!" Such an audience must have seemed unlikely to the magazine's readers at the time, however; its own resident historian Andrew Pixley was quick to warn that, "the UK public perceive [*Doctor Who*] as an old property, and are unlikely to tune in repeatedly unless it is something very special."

One thing is very clear from both of these articles. Although *Doctor Who*'s eager gaggle of fans now included emerging television professionals who loved the series, and all would be prepared to work on it should it come back, they all to a greater or lesser degree had doubts about whether such a revival would work.

This didn't, however, stop several of them – as well as others working in the industry – actively making efforts to try and revive the series. Indeed, going into the early years of the 21st Century, it seemed as if there were quite a few different people and groups actively courting the BBC to try and be the ones given the task of bringing the Doctor back to the screen.

Whether or not the BBC itself was particularly keen to let any of them actually take charge of a television revival of *Doctor Who* was, of course, another matter entirely.

11

THE BIDDERS

"WHAT'S A BID? Who bids? I've never 'bid' in my life."

That's what Russell T Davies told the official BBC *Doctor Who* website in December 2003, when interviewed by them in the early days of pre-production for the show's revival. But even if Davies claimed to find the whole idea of bidding a bit of a nonsense, it can't be denied that only a couple of years before this, *Doctor Who* seemed to have enough interested parties to stage a small auction.

What fandom generally meant by the term 'bids' was anybody who had approached the BBC, either publicly or privately, with a proposal to bring back *Doctor Who* in some way, shape or form. Of course, some of these propositions might be more serious than others – you could technically count any fan writing to the BBC saying they should be placed in charge of a new multi-million pound series of *Doctor Who* as a 'bid'.

Nonetheless, whenever *Doctor Who* has been out of production, there has been no shortage of people working within the television industry who were interested in bringing it back. The various efforts and proposals of the early 1990s are well-chronicled – and while it was Philip Segal who always held the BBC's attention, there were also assorted others who tried their luck from time to time; or at least stated their intentions to do so. Former *Doctor Who* writers Terry Nation and Gerry Davis had a pitch in mind, and even Verity Lambert's production company, Cinema Verity, briefly became involved in considering a proposal.

This didn't all stop after the 1996 TV Movie, either. In August 1997, an American producer called Karen McCoy claimed to be developing a proposal for an animated series of *Doctor Who*, although it quickly became apparent that McCoy's claims could perhaps most charitably be described as a little over-enthusiastic.

Certainly, it seems that she was never in any serious contact with anybody in authority at the BBC regarding developing such a proposal, and in any case it appears unlikely that another project – especially another American co-production – would have been able to get off the ground so soon after the TV Movie.

A couple of years after this, at the 1999 Edinburgh Festival, a radio comedy writer and producer named Dan Freedman met the seventh Doctor actor Sylvester McCoy. They were introduced by their mutual friend Sophie Aldred, who had played McCoy's companion, Ace, in the final years of the classic series. Freedman knew very little about *Doctor Who* and later claimed, in an interview for *Doctor Who Magazine* in 2002, that at this point he hadn't even been aware that the series was no longer running.

During the course of his friendly drink with McCoy and Aldred, they had discussed *Doctor Who*, and why it hadn't been successfully brought back by the BBC. Despite not being a *Doctor Who* fan, and by his own admission having scant knowledge of the show, Freedman was inspired by this discussion and decided that *Doctor Who* could be returned to life as a radio series.

Audio *Doctor Who* was very much in vogue at this point, as that summer Big Finish Productions had launched their licensed range of professional *Doctor Who* audio dramas for retail. However, Freedman had in mind a series which would actually be broadcast by the BBC; the first time *Doctor Who* would have appeared on the radio since two serials starring Jon Pertwee were made earlier in the 1990s.

Freedman had experience working on programmes for BBC Radio 4, the national radio station which broadcast most of the Corporation's comedy, drama and documentary output for the medium. Although his background was in comedy programming, he was able to persuade the Controller of BBC Radio 4, James Boyle, to pay for a pilot for a new radio series of *Doctor Who*.

The pilot was formally commissioned on January 18 2000,

and news about it broke in *Doctor Who Magazine* Issue 288, published the following month. By this point, Freedman had recruited a collaborator - fellow BBC radio comedy writer Nev Fountain. Unlike Freedman, Fountain was an avid fan and had been intrigued by the *Doctor Who* logo Freedman had placed on the door of the office he was working from at Broadcasting House, the BBC's radio headquarters in central London. After introducing himself to Freedman and learning about the *Doctor Who* radio project, Fountain had volunteered his services to check anything about the show's continuity or mythos that Freedman might be unsure about. He ended up being brought aboard in a more formal capacity, becoming the project's script editor.

"The BBC Comedy department, headed by John Pidgeon, had commissioned the pilot," Fountain explains. "I know it sounds like an odd thing to do, but John Pidgeon was quite an eccentric head of department and Dan was quite an eccentric man, so he'd sold John Pidgeon on the idea of doing *Doctor Who* on the radio."

The script for the pilot, as well as the subsequent series, was credited to one 'Colin Meek' - which turned out to be a pseudonym for Dan Freedman himself. This was never revealed publicly during production; not even to Nev Fountain, although those overseeing the project at Radio 4 had been aware that Freedman and Meek were one and the same.

"I was dealing with two very eccentric people here," says Fountain. "Dan Freedman is quite eccentric and John Pidgeon was quite eccentric. When it all came out - because Dan didn't tell me at the time - he said that John Pidgeon told him to keep the identity of the writer secret, which I didn't understand. The other reason he gave was that it was working out so well - with me making comments directed at Colin Meek and Dan forwarding them to New Zealand, where he said Colin Meek lived - that it was a nice working arrangement which he didn't want to ruin.

"He said that if I knew that he was writing it I would pull my punches, which I was quite offended by, because I would never pull my punches on any script. It would have made things a lot easier to deal directly with Dan as a writer. But I think Dan was quite secretive because he just was quite sensitive about his writing, and didn't want to have a direct discussion with me about his work. So I'd give criticisms to Colin Meek, I'd make notes to Colin Meek, and Dan would forward them to Colin Meek, and then Colin would turn up with rewrites."

Freedman himself has now dropped the 'd' from his surname and goes by the name of Dan Freeman. When approached for this book he declined an invitation to be interviewed, explaining that he felt he had already "said everything there is to say about it."

By the early summer of 2000, the project officially had the title of *Death Comes to Time*, and various casting news began to emerge. Sylvester McCoy and Sophie Aldred had already been announced as reprising their roles as the Seventh Doctor and Ace, and an impressive list of names was gradually assembled to join them. These included actor and writer Stephen Fry, comedian and actor John Sessions, and *Blake's 7* star Jacqueline Pearce.

"I think Dan was very persuasive," says Fountain of the ability to attract such a high-profile cast. "Of course, Radio 4 is a great name to work on, and at the time *Doctor Who* was a bit of a myth. It was like Brigadoon – it floated up from nowhere and there was excitement, and then it would disappear again. So I think Stephen and John and all those people were very excited to be working on any *Doctor Who* project. At the time, Big Finish was very much in its infancy – it was very much a fan organisation. So the idea that the BBC was actually smiling on doing a *Doctor Who* project probably meant a lot to other people."

Recording for the pilot began with a session at Broadcasting House on July 7 and was completed over two further days at the Soundhouse Studios in Acton, on October 2 and 3. There was then a wait of some months until the editing of the episode was completed in December, and Radio 4 then made up their minds about what to do with it.

In January 2001, Dan Freedman posted on the message board of the official *Doctor Who* website to deliver the news that the hoped-for series had not been picked up by BBC Radio 4. James Boyle had by this point moved on as the station's controller, and his successor Helen Boaden was evidently not minded to pay for the story begun in the *Death Comes to Time* pilot to be concluded.

"I never had any illusions that this would get taken up by the BBC," says Nev Fountain. "I didn't think it would for a second. The fact that it was being made was the thing that was exciting to me, and just getting involved in it, because at that time Helen Boaden had taken over. They'd done their demographics and polls and things, and they were much of a mind that Radio 4 was a woman's channel. A woman's channel back then was consumer programmes, dramas with ladies sitting there discussing their menopause, genteel comedies and kitchen sink dramas. It was very much of that bent. They did not think that genres like horror or science fiction or Westerns were anything to do with women. So I thought *Doctor Who* didn't have hope in hell of getting on Radio 4. There was a fond hope in the back of my head, but I was 90 percent certain it wasn't going to happen."

There, even just a couple of years earlier, it might all have ended. But by this time, the BBC was no longer operating only as a television and radio broadcaster. Over the past few years, it had been increasingly active in a third medium, one that had exploded in popularity and accessibility over the course of the 1990s – the internet.

By the early 2000s, the BBC's official *Doctor Who* site in their online Cult section offered a growing range of content related to the series. The site had been supportive of *Death Comes to Time* from the start, giving the project its own dedicated page for the latest updates and running interviews. By 2001, internet bandwidth had reached a point where the site could take things a step further – not just covering the series, but offering users of the website actual new *Doctor Who* adventures to enjoy.

On June 10 2001 the website published a news story announcing that they would be making the *Death Comes to Time* pilot available, in what was heralded as the BBC's first-ever example of putting out an online-only drama. Although the technology of the time meant that the half-hour episode would need to be split up into five smaller chunks for users to stream to their computers, it was presented in a then-innovative fashion. Artist Lee Sullivan was commissioned to produce some accompanying artwork, which was then partially animated to provide a sort of visual slideshow of the characters and scenes for an 'enhanced' version of the story.

"Dan was going to put it somewhere, I knew that," Fountain recalls. "I can't remember whether or not I knew he was going to go to BBC Cult if it didn't get commissioned properly. But it just seemed to be an inevitable next step. I honestly can't remember if that was a prospect at the time, but it felt quite optimistic just doing it."

At the time, Martin Trickey was one of the BBC's online team responsible for overseeing the work of the *Doctor Who* site.

"This was down to James Goss, and generally our experimenting with new technology," he explains. "I think the whole point of some of this happening was asking how technology could allow you to do the thing you wanted to do.

"So Dan had made this thing, and James had got it. The BBC's then-current streaming video platform was RealPlayer, so we had to deal with RealPlayer. They had just allowed you – in quite a simple way – to be able to put images into it, so you could play streaming audio with accompanying still images. It was a *Jackanory*, rostrum camera kind of vibe.

"Audio by itself didn't really work – online was a visual medium. James had looked at this and said we could take the audio from *Death Comes to Time*, and put some images over it, but it would work at low bandwidth; everyone was mostly on dial-up at that point.

"I said that sounded great, and everyone was on board, saying this was the sort of thing we should be doing. So that was the first one, and I think the response was pretty positive."

The *Death Comes to Time* pilot was released on the BBC *Doctor Who* website on July 13 2001, and was a staggering success for the time – 100,000 users created 1.6 million page impressions while accessing the episode. It was also generally well-received critically, with praise from the likes of *Doctor Who* novelist Paul Cornell and the science fiction magazine *SFX*. Despite the fact that it starred an existing Doctor and companion from the end of *Doctor Who*'s original run, Freedman's take on the series was at least seen as offering something a little different.

"Oh it was bloody huge!" says Nev Fountain. "I mean, the hits when it went out were just *ridiculous*. It was like becoming rock stars overnight. The appetite for *Doctor Who* was incredible. Money was absolutely sloshing around the BBC at the time. All these little departments sprung up – BBC Cult and BBC Online. There was money everywhere to make these little departments, and they all had budgets. BBC Cult spent a lot of it on *Doctor Who*, making a great website and putting original material out there. It was a glorious time, the early 2000s, for being inside the BBC."

In August, it was confirmed that the success of the *Death Comes to Time* pilot webcast had resulted in a commission for a full serial to be made, completing the story – this time produced specifically for BBC Online. However, this wasn't to be the thirteen-part series that Freedman had envisaged in his original pitch to BBC Radio 4. Instead, it would be another four half-hour episodes, each split into three segments of approximately ten minutes each, with one new section made available each week on the official *Doctor Who* website. The recording for the rest of *Death Comes to Time* was concluded in December 2001, and the first part of the second episode made its debut online on February 14 2002.

"That was Dan who did that, and we weren't so involved with it," says Martin Trickey. "In all of these things, my role tended to be running around everywhere, trying to find the rest of the money to put it all together – a little bit from our budget, some from here, some from there. The commercial unit was the bridge between public service and Worldwide, and you'd talk to them to see if you could find some investment to do things. It was relatively low-cost to do the audio, so you'd find the money to put it together, then work on it in a collaborative fashion."

By this point, however, it was clear that Freedman didn't simply have a web series of *Doctor Who* on his mind. He had his sights set much higher – he now wanted to be the one to bring *Doctor Who* back to television as well.

Rumours of this began to spread in the autumn of 2001.

THE LONG GAME

In early October, *SFX* magazine reported that an unnamed producer was putting together a proposal for a new *Doctor Who* TV series, with an aim to debut in time for the programme's 40th anniversary in 2003. Soon after the *SFX* story appeared, the fan website Outpost Gallifrey confirmed on their news page that Freedman was the man behind this new series pitch.

Nev Fountain told *Doctor Who Magazine* Issue 314, published in early February 2002, that he had been asked by Freedman to be the script editor of the new *Doctor Who* TV series if it managed to get off the ground. However, these days he gives the impression of not having been particularly involved in the television proposal.

"The idea of Dan being given a television series was the same as BBC Radio taking up *Doctor Who*," he explains. "I thought the chance was miniscule in both instances. But I'm not the kind of person to just flounce out if there's a cat in hell's chance of something happening. I always thought they would give it to someone else, but just in case, I wanted to stay in the picture.

"Dan was always making deals and trying to get things up and running. He'd occasionally tell me something and I'd smile and nod. I didn't want to spend a lot more of my time than was needed. I didn't get a lot of money for working on *Death Comes to Time*, and I certainly didn't want to run around and do a lot of stuff for the television proposal. Not that I was invited to, particularly. If things happened then he might turn up on my door again, and I'd get to write an episode or something like that. But he put the proposal together himself. I thought it was pretty weak – but it was his thing. He'd put *Death Comes to Time* together; it wasn't for me to sit on his back and say he was doing it wrong, because he got that far."

But Fountain wasn't the only person with whom Freedman was discussing his proposal. While working on the idea, he travelled to the United States to spend a few days with some of those responsible for making the hit American series *Buffy the Vampire Slayer*, which had been one of the most successful fantasy series of recent years. David Fury, who was one of writers and producers on *Buffy* and its spin-off *Angel*, recalls Freedman's visit.

"Dan had visited the *Buffy the Vampire Slayer* writers' room for a few days while he was trying to develop his proposal, and asked a few of us if we'd be interested in consulting," Fury explains. News of this emerged in the summer of 2002 – after Freedman's *Doctor Who* television bid had already come to nothing – when it was reported by the UK sci-fi magazine *Dreamwatch*. Fury admits that this was probably due to him.

"I made the mistake of mentioning the possibility at a *Buffy* fan convention, naively unaware how news of any potential *Doctor Who* revival would catch fire," he says. "I did not make the same mistake again. Regardless, nothing ever came of it."

That didn't stop one of the UK national newspapers, the *Daily Express*, picking up on the *Dreamwatch* report in an article published on July 2 2002. Under the headline "Return of *Dr Who*," the piece claimed that...

> "[The BBC has] hired leading American TV scriptwriter David Fury... to be an adviser on the Doctor's comeback. Fury said: 'They want to do what we do on *Buffy* – produce 22 episodes a year and sell them internationally. I'm helping to take *Doctor Who* into a new universe."

"I can only guess that I was trying to explain what Dan was looking for at *Buffy the Vampire Slayer*," says Fury of the quote, if it even did come from him. "But 'taking *Doctor Who* into a new universe' was certainly someone else's contribution. I did *not* work as a consultant on any *Doctor Who* project."

The article in the *Express* had been accompanied by a large photograph of the actor Anthony Head, well-known in the UK for starring in a series of coffee adverts for Gold Blend but also one of the regular cast of *Buffy*; he had also made a brief appearance in *Death Comes to Time*. Head was suggested by the *Express* as a candidate to play the Doctor, but is also perhaps another reason for the talk at the time of links between the BBC and the *Buffy* production team. There had been tentative discussions in 2001 about the BBC being involved in a UK-based *Buffy* spin-off called

THE LONG GAME

Ripper, focusing on the British character Rupert Giles whom Head played. In the event, these discussions and rumours dragged on for some years without ever eventually amounting to anything – something they had in common with various *Doctor Who* ideas during this time.

In Britain, *Buffy* had developed a strong following among younger viewers and general fantasy television enthusiasts. It had been first broadcast on Sky One and was later shown by the BBC, in one of the 6.00pm weeknight slots on BBC Two that had very much become established as the home of 'cult' programming since the early 1990s.

In *Doctor Who Magazine*'s *Death Comes to Time* feature, published in February 2002, Freedman seemed to make it clear that this was where he envisaged his new *Doctor Who* idea being scheduled, sidestepping the more exposed, competitive arena of a primetime BBC One slot:

> "There's a place you can go with all these cult sci-fi programmes on telly – *Farscape*, *The X-Files*... We could make a really good one with this format. Do I wish that Pertwee was still around? I don't care! I only give a toss about producing a great show. Mainstream for BBC Two is a cult audience, but it's a big cult audience. The sort of thing that kids will beg to stay up for, you know, a bit risqué. I'd like to stay with it. I'd like to get a series up and running on television. And produce it for a bit. I'd love to go to LA and show them what we can do – have *Doctor Who* as a focal point for a new wave."

Freedman also told the magazine that he had a candidate in mind to play the Doctor, although he didn't reveal to them who the actor concerned might be. "We have cast him – theoretically – but I can't say who," he teased. With the benefit of time and distance, Nev Fountain is a bit more forthcoming.

"The TV proposal was very traditional," he says. "Not very

imaginative. I think the companion was very much in the *Buffy* mould; someone who was a good fighter. The Doctor was going to be Stephen Fry. But I can't remember anything more of that – it was quite a thin document, as I remember."

In 2002, Freedman told *Doctor Who Magazine* about the more general aims of his series proposal. His conviction was that any new series had to represent a fresh start:

> "I'm aware that the fans have kept it alive, you know, but in order to produce it... The moment I get it, I think people will stop whining... When it comes to a TV project... Any fan involvement will kill it instantly. And nobody will touch with a barge pole anything that has any continuity baggage. A bloke in a time machine shaped like a police box that's bigger on the inside than the outside travelling through time and space. And that's *Doctor Who!* No regeneration scene, no continuity references, no nothing. You've got to get to know the character and his companions again. I would like to have the Daleks back, and maybe the Cybermen. I mean, everybody in Britain knows what a Dalek is, so that's an exception, but when you see the Cybermen, it'll be explained afresh what they are. It'll be like starting from scratch."

These days, Nev Fountain doesn't recall being aware of any involvement from the *Buffy* team with Freedman's proposal, asking "Who's David Fury?" when I put the question to him. In late March 2002, though, with *Death Comes to Time* well into its run on the BBC website, Fountain posted an update on his own official site, stating that: "The proposed series outline, which has been put together with the assistance of the team behind *Buffy The Vampire Slayer*, has been submitted, and we should know the results before *Death Comes to Time* has finished."

In the end, the verdict came shortly after *Death Comes to Time* had completed its run, and the news was delivered by Freedman himself. The serial had concluded on the BBC website on May 3, and it would be fair to say that reactions were mixed. Some fans had taken exception to certain elements of the story, and also to the characterisation of the Doctor – as well as his apparent death at the end of the final episode.

Freedman had, during the course of the making and webcasting of *Death Comes to Time*, been continuing to interact with fans on the official *Doctor Who* site's message board. On May 17, the site's news page reported on a post that Freedman had made to the forum, announcing his decision to pull out of the running to try and make a new *Doctor Who* TV series:

> "The TV thing is really over now, for me anyway. I've kind of decided to drop out, given the strength of feeling amongst the majority of fans... I'm sure someone will do it eventually, so don't give up hope! But don't overestimate my importance here, I'm just not going to do any more *Doctor Who*, that doesn't mean other people can't, and they might have more success... It's not as if it was on TV and I pulled out. It still wasn't on and it still isn't, so nothing drastic has happened."

This wasn't *quite* the end – in October 2002, Freedman told the *Doctor Who* website that he was working on developing a series based around the Minister of Chance, a Time Lord character who had been played by Stephen Fry in *Death Comes to Time*. He claimed to be working with David Fury on this idea, and that it was "intended as a sort of *Doctor Who: The Next Generation*." Whether he meant this in a literal or more of a thematic sense isn't clear – Nev Fountain, however, believes that Freedman may still have had the Doctor in mind for this:

"I think if we were going to continue on the radio, down the line the Doctor would return. The Doctor would die, the Minister of Chance would have a couple of adventures as the Doctor, and the actual real Doctor would return. That was the last thing he said to me. But his plans were always constantly shifting. I think he'd come up with an idea in his head and someone like me would say he couldn't do it, and then he would adjust himself accordingly."

No Minister of Chance television programme ever materialised – although a decade later Freedman did launch an audio series based around the character, albeit without any involvement from Stephen Fry or David Fury.

Whatever the reception *Death Comes to Time* had received from fandom, there was no doubting that it had been a success in terms of bringing attention and traffic to the *Doctor Who* website. BBC Online were therefore quick to carry on without Freedman to produce another webcast, this time starring Colin Baker's sixth Doctor and made in collaboration with the audio licence holders Big Finish. This project, a Cybermen adventure called *Real Time*, was announced in February 2002, just as the full *Death Comes to Time* serial began, and made its debut on the website in August that year.

So Dan Freedman wasn't the only one the BBC could make online *Doctor Who* with, and nor was he the only person trying to persuade the Corporation to make the series on television at this point – in spite of what the man himself claimed. Speaking in *Doctor Who Magazine* 314 in February, Freedman had insisted that:

> "There aren't any parties and they aren't bidding for anything. I haven't seen them. Which ones are they? Unless you've seen them, they're fictional! I mean, I know there are documents that say, 'Why don't we bring back *Doctor Who*?' but that's not really a proposal, is it? You can't just write on a piece of paper 'I want to bring back *Doctor Who*'!"

By this time, though, there had been at least one approach to the BBC that went a little further than simply "I want to bring back *Doctor Who*." It had been put together, at least partly, as a reaction to concerns about what Freedman might do with the programme were he to be given the responsibility of bringing it back to television screens.

Since speaking as part of *Doctor Who Magazine*'s panel of experts on how *Doctor Who* might be revived in the summer of 1999, Mark Gatiss had continued to enjoy great success with his fellow writers and performers in *The League of Gentlemen*. In 2000 they had won the BAFTA Award for Best Comedy Programme, and this success had helped to convince Gatiss that he at least had a voice that might be listened to in the BBC, as a recognised and acclaimed industry professional.

Gareth Roberts had also continued to enjoy success since 1999, becoming – as he phrased it to *Doctor Who Magazine* several years later – "the king of all *Emmerdale* for about a year," referring to his work on ITV's popular soap opera. He and Gatiss had both also contributed to the 2001 run of the BBC's *Randall & Hopkirk (Deceased)* revival, giving them first-hand experience of writing a Saturday night fantasy drama series on BBC One. That same year, the pair of them decided to take the plunge and assembled a proposal for a *Doctor Who* revival to submit to the BBC. *Doctor Who Magazine*'s then assistant editor Clayton Hickman also joined them in putting together the pitch.

"Myself, Mark and Gareth had been friends for quite a long time by then," explains Hickman. "I think Gareth and Mark had known each other from years back, but when I came into *Doctor Who* fandom we all became very pally. I think we'd all just been talking about it, and Mark was obviously becoming a sort of mover and shaker in TV.

"We were all round Mark's just talking about why nobody ever brought back *Doctor Who*, or trying to think of something that was a bit like *Doctor Who* that we could pitch to the BBC. Then I think Mark said that every time someone tried to think of something which is like *Doctor Who*, it's always much worse and less good than *Doctor Who*. So why didn't we just pitch for *Doctor Who*?

"I remember us all sitting there and realising that *yes*, we could actually do that. Because Gareth had been working a lot in television on the big soaps, I think he'd been working on *Randall & Hopkirk (Deceased)*, and he had some clout as well. So we just thought 'Yeah!'

THE BIDDERS

"I was involved because I was their pal, and I was on *Doctor Who Magazine*, and also I could write – I think they both knew I could write. So we put together this pitch. I remember working on it at the magazine offices, on downtime, when we'd just finished an issue and had a couple of days spare."

When interviewed for *Doctor Who Magazine* Issue 335 – published in September 2003, only very shortly before the revival of *Doctor Who* was finally announced – Mark Gatiss admitted that he had been "a little concerned about the content" of Dan Freedman's plans for *Doctor Who*, and this was what had spurred him on to team up with Roberts and Hickman to put an alternative proposal together. Knowing that he did at least have some television experience – something Freedman notably lacked – Gatiss couldn't bear the idea that some time down the line a revival of *Doctor Who* might emerge that he felt was approached in the wrong way.

Clayton Hickman is rather more frank about their worries about Dan Freedman and his proposal:

"He just seemed like a nightmare. The whole production was just *dreadful*. It was exactly the wrong thing to do. It was convoluted, continuity-heavy, mystical *guff*. I remember me and [*Doctor Who Magazine* journalist] Ben Cook going along to one of the recording days because we had to cover it. I think Dan had even contacted us himself to make sure we went along. I remember us sitting in the pub afterwards, me and Ben, just staring at each other going 'Christ on a bike! This is... Oh my God!'

"We were just willing it to fail, and it felt like it was *bound* to anyway, because it was just some terrible, impenetrable, audio thing with awful Flash animation. But I think Freedman had started talking about his plans to bring it back to TV, and we could tell no one was going to like it. But there was always that fear in the back of your mind that maybe the BBC might buy into him, he might go to a meeting and give a really good presentation saying this is the modern, new way of *Doctor Who*, and there might be someone at the BBC stupid enough to believe that."

However, what's striking from reading what Mark Gatiss says about his pitch in *Doctor Who Magazine* 335 is just how similar some

THE LONG GAME

of his thoughts were to those expressed by Freedman - in some areas at least. While Gatiss explicitly wanted to make the series "a mass-market programme again", as opposed to Freedman's BBC Two cult slot vision, like Freedman he believed that to appeal to a modern-day television audience and make any revival a success, it needed to make a much greater break with the past than was eventually seen in the 2005 series.

This is perhaps best illustrated by Gatiss' thoughts about Daleks, the only past element other than the Doctor and TARDIS that he planned to include in his revival:

> "They are up there with the Doctor as a national institution. But equally, all you have to know about the Daleks is that they are the most evil creatures in the universe. That's it. You don't have to mention anything else. As it transpired, in the idea we had for that story, there was also a lovely kind of game you could play, where the Daleks arrive in force at the end of Episode One, and the companion says, 'What are they, Doctor?' and he says 'I dunno.' Wouldn't that be lovely?
>
> "Now that, obviously, is appealing for people who do know, but there's so much pleasure to be had from the idea of just starting again. If anybody wants to say 'Well, he must be before Hartnell,' or 'He must be after McGann,' let them. But there's no reason on Earth why the programme should address those things. None at all. Because, in TV terms, what happened last week is ancient history. 40 years ago... is before electricity, practically!"

"We knew that the BBC wasn't that fussed," says Hickman of the possibility of the Corporation going for any new proposal. "But they *might* be interested if Mark and possibly Gareth's name were attached to it. But we were trying to do it in a way of not scaring them off. So it was all quite on-the-cheap - a certain number of episodes, saying it won't be that expensive, it'll be on location.

It was still a pretty good proposal, but it wasn't bold or exciting or all-guns-blazing like Russell's was."

So why does he think they were doing that?

"We all suffer from fan shame. It's ingrained into us, in that other people thought it was silly, and you'd cringe into yourself, even though you love it. Maybe people don't have that now, but there was always a slight embarrassment around *Doctor Who*.

"That is taken on even when you're talking to the people who own *Doctor Who*, and who actually might like to be making money from *Doctor Who*. You still feel like they're just going to look at you like you're crazy. We were trying to make this a non-threatening thing, because when they'd tried to bring it back previously they'd put all this money into it and it had done fine in Britain, but it hadn't done anything in America, and it all felt like a bit of a waste of time."

Hickman also points out that this was an era before the 'reboot' mentality had become a fast-track ritual for reinvigorating stagnant characters and formats.

"Things get rebooted now at the drop of a hat in a year or two, but in those days five years didn't feel like a very long time," he says. "So were they really going to want to try again? It was a coaxing and persuading sort of thing. The thing I'm most proud of in our pitch is that we specifically said that this must be a family entertainment series, not a cult show for sci-fi nerds. It must be something that the parents can enjoy, the kids can enjoy, and it must be on primetime BBC One.

"I'm glad we did that, because that was what Russell proved a few years later – that it was exactly the right thing to do. Rather than reducing your idea to appeal to a very small demographic. I think we thought of it as trying to do Season Seventeen, not Season Eighteen. Which I think is a fair comparison."

Hickman also feels there were other lessons to be learned from what had happened in the past – especially with the attempt at reviving the show in 1996.

"We knew that we had to reintroduce the character – that was another thing we took away from the TV Movie. Much as I quite

THE LONG GAME

like the TV Movie, it's a confusing load of old nonsense unless you know what *Doctor Who* is. It doesn't introduce the character in any way. So we had a strange man, he's got a strange box which is kept in an antique shop, and everyone in the village thinks he's a bit weird. He doesn't quite remember who he is or how to work his TARDIS. We find out with these two people. It was going back to the very beginning and just saying he can't work the TARDIS, he doesn't quite remember who he is, and we find out everything via the companions, like we did in the beginning.

"It's what Russell did, really. Again, it's the way to start *Doctor Who*. You just don't rely on knowledge. We didn't want to mention Time Lords and Gallifrey, and nor did Russell – which is great, we were thinking along those same lines. But then eventually, as with all these things, they creep in.

"The thing we always talked about was a cliffhanger in *Arc of Infinity* – Peter Davison going, 'Omega controls the Matrix!' Which is ludicrous! They hadn't mentioned really what the Matrix was, the Matrix hadn't appeared in the show for five or six years. You have to be thinking what the mum at home who's doing the ironing is thinking while this on the telly and the kids are watching. Make *her* laugh, you know? Make her interested. That's what Russell did. That's what we would have probably tried to do, but in a slightly different way, because I think we were nervous about it."

If Hickman, Gatiss and Roberts felt that the content of any new series should look to the future, then the same isn't necessarily true of the form. Gatiss spoke in his Dalek scenario about them turning up at the end of 'Episode One' of that particular story. When he'd earlier talked to Jonathan Blum for *Doctor Who Magazine* 312 in late 2001, he was even firmer in his conviction that if *Doctor Who* were to return then it should be in its old serial format.

> "I find it incredible that no one has noticed that the half-hour serial format is more popular than ever! They're called soaps, and they almost always end in a cliffhanger of sorts. *Doctor Who* couldn't be looked at as a rolling soap format, obviously, but in terms of a serial

spreading over six months of the year in half-hour episodes, it's still entirely viable. I really don't think that 50-minute episodes or TV movies suit it."

Speaking about the proposal to Russell T Davies' biographers in 2008, Gareth Roberts agreed that they had been keen to keep the format of the programme tied to that of its original 26-year run. "I think we were far too wedded to some of the aspects of the original series – posh Doctor, 25-minute episodes, etc. I think we saw those things as untouchable."

In 2016, Gatiss, Roberts and Hickman spoke more extensively about their 2001 proposal for the first time, in a special feature written by Graham Kibble-White for the 500th issue of *Doctor Who Magazine*. Sharing snippets from the original pitch document, Kibble-White was able to reveal that the proposal had been for seven three-part stories across a series of 21 half-hour episodes. The Derek Jacobi-modelled Doctor would meet young companions Dan and Holly in a rural English village, and would be unable to properly steer the TARDIS as it took them on journeys across time and space.

When speaking in 2016, Gatiss and Roberts felt that their idea of making half-hour episodes had perhaps been a mistake. Clayton Hickman, however, maintains that this was a good idea.

"We didn't want to go to that self-contained, 50-minute American model," says Hickman. "Because as kids we really loved the cliffhangers, and we really loved that over three episodes you felt like you got to know a place, and the guest cast. I do genuinely feel that it's a problem with the current show, in that they're trying to do mini-movies in 50 minutes. You don't really get to know anyone, you don't feel like you're in the place for any length of time. I still think three half-hour episodes would be great. I think people would really go for that.

"It would mean that the show could be on for longer each year, because rather than ten or thirteen hour-long episodes, you've got 20 or 26 half-hour episodes, so it's on for half the year. It's always there as part of the schedule. That's been one of the problems with

Doctor Who now; it's on and off so quickly, and takes all these massive gaps between. It doesn't feel like a regular show – it feels like a thing that occasionally pops up on some night of the week.

"It worked fine in Russell's time. Even though I think it would have worked even better had those stories been cut in half, because then you would have had 26 weeks a year of *Doctor Who*, and that would have been great. But there's just a thing about the 50-minute episodes. You can get away with more if you've got an Episode One – Episode One can be set-up, and character and world-building, and then you get all the exciting pay-off in Episode Two. When you've got 50 minutes and everything has to be in one thing, something has to be sacrificed. It's not my favourite way of storytelling, I have to say."

Gatiss, Roberts and Hickman gave their proposal for reviving *Doctor Who* to a man who couldn't have commissioned it himself, but who was Mark Gatiss' most senior working contact at the time within the BBC. This was Jon Plowman, the Controller of Comedy Entertainment, who was the executive producer of *The League of Gentlemen*. In *Doctor Who Magazine* 335 in 2003, Gatiss said that Plowman had passed the proposal to Jane Tranter – and possibly Lorraine Heggessey as well – but he and his collaborators had never been given a verdict on it. "It is incredibly hard to get a straight answer," he told the magazine. "But at least it's there, should it be needed. I think it's a very well-argued proposal."

There was also a concern in the back of Gatiss' mind, however, that the BBC might not go for their *Doctor Who* pitch; either because they wouldn't, due to not being interested, or because they *couldn't*, due to the unspecified, overhanging rights issues – which Gatiss in 2003 believed related to Universal Television's remaining options from the 1996 TV Movie. So he, Roberts and Hickman also came up with another idea for a new science fiction series to offer as an alternative to bringing back *Doctor Who*.

It later emerged that this was called *The Ministry of Time* and that work on it continued even after *Doctor Who* was back on television. Graham Kibble-White's feature in *Doctor Who Magazine* 500 revealed that a 30-minute recorded read-through for this took

THE BIDDERS

place at BBC Television Centre in 2005, but a lack of budget for any possible series saw the project eventually fade away without making it into production. It is another interesting parallel with Dan Freedman's efforts, however, that he attempted to make *The Minister of Chance* after failing to get *Doctor Who* off the ground, while Gatiss and company came up with *The Ministry of Time*.

One issue that both the Freedman and Gatiss-led proposals may have faced is that, although they had access to and connections with certain executives within the BBC, they didn't have any relationship with those right at the top of the drama commissioning process. In *Doctor Who Magazine*'s *The Way Back* feature in 2013, Russell T Davies remarked that one of the reasons for the show's eventual return was that after meeting Jane Tranter at the *Linda Green* launch in October 2001, he was then directly dealing with the person at the top when discussing *Doctor Who*. He pointed out that Tranter might well not even have been aware of his previous meetings about *Doctor Who* with those working under her in the Drama department, but now there was a line of communication with the person in charge of all drama commissioning.

The Freedman and Gatiss-Roberts-Hickman efforts may have been the best-known of the proposals to revive *Doctor Who* in the early 2000s, but they were by no means the only ones. In his piece about the future of the series in *Doctor Who Magazine* 312 in December 2001, Jonathan Blum wrote that there were, "four (count them!) proposals for a new series of *Doctor Who* which are currently doing the rounds at the BBC." Only one of these was specifically identified in the piece – Dan Freedman's. Asked about this claim today, Blum can only recall Freedman and Russell T Davies as being among those to which he was referring. It seems likely that Gatiss and company's work formed the third, but the fourth is a mystery – although there are some clues as to what it may have been.

Additionally, there was at least one further proposal – or more accurately, a discussion – which seems to have come about *after* Blum had written this article. In 2006, new series *Doctor Who* writer and *Life on Mars* co-creator Matthew Graham recalled that he had at some point a few years earlier "batted a few ideas around" for a potential *Doctor Who* revival. Speaking to *Doctor Who Magazine* 370 in May 2006, Graham explained that his meeting about *Doctor Who* had been with BBC drama executive John Yorke.

Yorke had taken over from Matthew Robinson as the executive producer of *EastEnders* in 2000, overseeing its increase from three to four episodes per week the following year. After a successful period in charge of the soap, he had been promoted in May 2002.

In the same shake-up which had seen Jane Tranter put in overall charge of drama in October 2000, Mal Young had also been given an effective promotion, with his position becoming Controller of Continuing Drama Series – 'controller' being a senior rank designation within the BBC, rather than simply a semantic change.

"They didn't want to lose what I was doing, or devalue that," Mal Young explains. "So they gave us both 'controller' titles so that we were equal. I was ring-fenced, so she was Controller of Commissioning, then I was Controller of Drama Series. All the existing shows I had, and any new development of drama series would all come through me, in-house. So I was still encouraged to treat my department like its own indie within the BBC."

John Yorke's 2002 promotion had seen him given Young's old title of Head of Drama Series, working as Young's deputy and overseeing the likes of *Casualty* and *Holby City*, and the other regular drama series output. He didn't stay long in this post, however. By February 2003 it was announced that Yorke was leaving the BBC to become Head of Drama at Channel 4.

Matthew Graham is very clear that his *Doctor Who* discussion was with Yorke. Therefore, it almost certainly must have taken place at some point between Yorke's promotion from *EastEnders* in May 2002 and the announcement of his departure from the BBC the following February.

Graham was at this point making the transition from being a writer on other people's shows to being a 'showrunner' in his own right. He had created and written the science fiction serial *The Last Train* for ITV in 1999, but had recently been writing episodes for BBC One dramas such as *EastEnders* and *Spooks*. In 2001 he had written the Raffles pilot *Gentleman Thief* for the BBC's Drama Series department under Mal Young, and he had co-created ITV's Second World War drama *P.O.W.*, which would be broadcast in the autumn of 2003.

"There were three things I was interested in at the BBC," Graham remembers of that time. "John said I should come and do something. We started developing a show called *Ghost Squad*, which was not supernatural; it was actually a 1940s London version of *The Untouchables*. It was about a group of police officers, detectives, against organised crime that was rising up in the void left by the Blitz and all the men going off to war. It was based on a factual book, and it was really good. But it was so bloody expensive, it had car chases – 1940s car chases during the Blitz! There was no way anyone was going to make it!

"But we loved developing it together, and then John asked me what else I wanted to do. I told him I'd love to do *Doctor Who*! I wasn't an uber fan of *Doctor Who*. I grew up with it, like everyone, but I wasn't in the Steven Moffat or Russell T Davies or Mark Gatiss camp of being absolutely obsessed with it and knowing every episode. I thought *Doctor Who* would be great fun to bring back. I was more excited about bringing *Blake's 7* back, actually – because, like a lot of people, my imagination hit a brick wall with *Doctor Who*. I couldn't see beyond the Kandyman and Sylvester McCoy – it didn't feel very cool.

"Whereas *Blake's 7*, in my head, still felt very cool. We talked about *Quatermass* as well. At the time, the rights for these things were all snagged up – it wasn't that they didn't want to do it, they *couldn't* do it. The rights were owned by different people. So it all became very frustrating."

Unlike with Freedman and the Gatiss-Hickman-Roberts trio, Graham's proposal for *Doctor Who* was just an informal discussion rather than a written document. He certainly never formulated any specific proposals for how he might relaunch the series.

"I can't remember the exact details of what I talked to John Yorke about," he admits. "But I can tell you that what amazed and impressed me so much about what Russell did was something I know I wouldn't have done– he kept the TARDIS as a blue police box. He kept the Daleks *basically* the same, apart from the levitation bit. He *basically* kept the Cybermen the same. I think I read an interview with him, or even had dinner with him – I had several dinners with him around that time – and he said something like: 'People have always fixated over *Doctor Who*, but they've always agonised over what to change. That's not the challenge – the challenge is knowing what to keep the same.' I thought that was brilliant. I think that's the essence of his genius. I think was very, very clever."

By comparison, Graham is honest about how his instincts for reviving the show would have likely missed the mark.

"What I can pretty safely say is my *Doctor Who* would not have been as good as his," he admits. "I don't think it would have hit that absolute sweet spot between nostalgia and reinvention. But also, he trusted it. It would be like me and *Star Wars*. I understand *Star Wars* the way he understands *Doctor Who*, and I feel I know exactly what you leave in with *Star Wars* and what you *can* change. I might be wrong, but that's how I feel, and Russell knew that about *Doctor Who* in his DNA. He knew *exactly* what you could change in *Doctor Who*, and *exactly* what you should leave alone."

Graham was also aware that he was not the only person at the time who had expressed an interest in perhaps bringing the Doctor back.

"I knew it was very common," he says. "I was told it was very common that people would come in and pitch a version of *Doctor Who* to the BBC."

Graham's discussions with John Yorke probably weren't one of the four proposals cited by Jonathan Blum in his *Doctor Who Magazine* piece in December 2001, given that this was written and published while Yorke was still running *EastEnders* and not yet involved with commissioning or launching other programmes. So if Freedman, Davies and the Gatiss-led proposal were three of the possibilities which Blum had in mind, what might have been the fourth?

A potential answer is provided by *Doctor Who* writer Robert Shearman, who wrote *Dalek* for the first series of the revived show. Shearman wasn't trying to get his own *Doctor Who* effort off the ground in the early 2000s – but he *was* a regular poster on the Outpost Gallifrey *Doctor Who* discussion forums. Shortly after the series came back in 2005, he wrote a post there outlining just how fortunate the fans were that Davies had been the one entrusted with being in charge of the revival:

> "A few years ago, I was aware of loose plans being formed at the BBC to revive *Doctor Who*. The people in question would have seen it as a complete reinvention of the series. To the extent, in fact, that they decided it would be much more fun and less distracting for the viewer if he wasn't an alien at all, but he was a human who had built this TARDIS thing in his back garden. None of us can appreciate how lucky we are that we have an executive producer who wants this to follow on from the original series, let alone the books and the audios. We can't appreciate it because we didn't see all the possible alternatives – all the potential revivals which would have been wholly distinct from the original show we love."

"I'd heard about the Cushing-style rumour but can't remember any details like who was attached to it," is Blum's response when asked about this. Nev Fountain also recalls being aware of this idea, and his recollection is that it came from some of those behind the Sunday evening BBC One drama series *Born and Bred*, set around a rural doctor's surgery in the 1950s. This makes sense, in terms of Shearman knowing those involved, as he worked on that programme, writing an episode for its second series, broadcast in the spring of 2003.

Born and Bred had various *Doctor Who* connections, past and yet-to-come. The first series was produced by soon-to-be *Doctor Who* producer Phil Collinson, and the second by 1980s *Doctor Who* director Chris Clough. Prominent 1990s *Doctor Who* novelist Paul Cornell also wrote for the second series, although has gone on record saying that he did not enjoy the experience, and his script was heavily rewritten. The show's co-creator and lead writer was Chris Chibnall, who later became the third showrunner of the modern *Doctor Who*.

Whether or not Chibnall was involved in a *Doctor Who* idea at this point, however – or even if Fountain's recollection is correct, and it was some or all of the *Born and Bred* team who might have been considering it – is unclear. One of the other main forces behind *Born and Bred* was executive producer Susan Hogg, who when approached for this book was quite certain that she, at least, had no involvement in any such discussions.

Whatever the case, it's clear that there was no shortage of people around in the early 2000s who were keen to write or produce a new series of *Doctor Who* if the BBC wanted to make one. But would the BBC ever have gone for one of these other options had Russell T Davies proved unwilling or unable to be involved? Or was it the prestige of having a writer of Davies' stature on board that made the whole thing possible?

"Once I knew Russell wanted to do it, that was that," insists Jane Tranter. "But before I knew Russell was doing it, I was thinking about other people, for sure."

Lorraine Heggessey recalls that while she was clear on wanting the show, she was happy to be guided by the drama specialists on who actually made it.

"I wanted *Doctor Who*. Jane was the one who said to me Russell T Davies really wants to do it. To me, there wasn't ever any debate about whether it was or wasn't going to be Russell. He came into the frame very, very early on when we were talking about it."

Mal Young believes that the show probably would have returned eventually, even without Davies' involvement, but perhaps not in quite the same way.

"I think it probably wouldn't have been one person [running it]," he says. "It probably would have been more along the lines of how we were doing our other dramas – where you would bring in four, five, six writers. You would create the team at the beginning and have a storyline conference with them all, then they'd go away and write their own episodes and have a producer overseeing that. It was probably going to be that. Russell was probably the only one who gave us the confidence to let him show-run it."

Whoever might end up being placed in charge of it, however, there was one question that needed to be answered before any possible television revival of *Doctor Who* could get underway. It was a question which seemed fairly extraordinary, given that *Doctor Who* had been created in-house by BBC staff members on BBC time, at the behest of BBC management. Particularly so, given that it was an issue that had never been in doubt during the original show's long run. But nonetheless, it was a question that caused some confusion, both among fans of the show, and within the BBC itself, during the late 1990s and early 2000s.

Did the BBC still actually have the rights to make *Doctor Who*?

12

DO I HAVE THE RIGHTS?

ON THE AFTERNOON OF Tuesday September 17 2002, Lorraine Heggessey appeared as a guest on the Simon Mayo programme on BBC Radio 5 Live – the broadcaster's national news and sport station. Ostensibly, she was there to promote BBC One's 'current affairs event' *Cracking Crime Day*, a schedule full of programmes looking at crime across the UK, taking place on the channel the following day.

However, she indicated that she was happy to discuss any other topics related to BBC One, and Mayo encouraged his listeners to get in touch with their questions about the channel and its output. Beginning just after the two o'clock news and sport, Heggessey had been supposed to be on-air until the headlines at half-past; but so many questions were submitted that she stayed on for a few more minutes after this.

Calls, text messages and e-mails put to Heggessey during the interview included questions about BBC One's comedy output, dramas being built around former soap stars, the issue of casting being ethnically diverse enough, the possibility of the BBC bidding for Champions League football coverage, the number of political programmes, and whether the channel's religious programming had been marginalised.

And then, at the end of the session, Mayo had one final question.

"Before you came on the programme, you could probably guess what one subject area was," he told her. He sounded almost apologetic about it as he explained that "the *Doctor Who* brigade" had been in touch, which prompted a laugh from Heggessey. Mayo continued: "As you knew they would be, and they probably turn up everywhere you go. They just want to know... is there any chance, ever, of under your tutelage *Doctor Who* making it back onto BBC One?"

Heggessey's reply was simple, straightforward, and surprisingly positive. "Yes."

Any *Doctor Who* fans listening – many of whom had grown cynical over the years about attitudes towards the series within the BBC hierarchy – must have pricked up their ears. Of course, Heggessey was not going to announce a new series off-the-cuff at the end of a radio interview, and there was immediately something of a qualification:

> "I think *Doctor Who* was a fantastic series... we should be looking at how we could reinvent it. The thing is, part of its attraction was the slightly cardboard, wobbly nature of the sets, and the fact that the Daleks didn't look realistic, and now we're used to fantastic special effects. So I'm not quite sure how we could do it, but I have been actively talking to some people about reinventing and writing some new *Doctor Who*s. At this moment it's in incredibly early stages, and there are all sorts of rights issues that have to be overcome, but there is hope, all you people out there."

When Mayo then suggested that *Doctor Who* would have to go out on Saturday evenings, Heggessey replied that she never gave away scheduling, but that Saturdays would seem quite a good place for it. However, it was clear that Mayo didn't regard the idea of bringing *Doctor Who* back as a serious one – possibly a reflection of how the series was perceived among many in the media industry at the time. He went on to list a Saturday evening line-up that could follow a potential revival of *Doctor Who* in the schedule: "Then *The Generation Game*, then *The Black and White Minstrels*, then *Match of the Day*, *Parkinson*! Those were the days – or not!"

Heggessey resisted pointing out that the most recent version of *The Generation Game* had only come to an end earlier that year, and that *Parkinson* and *Match of the Day* were both still ongoing BBC One shows – albeit with *Match of the Day* at this point limited to FA Cup weekends as the BBC were in a period without Premier League highlights rights, which ITV held from 2001 to 2004. Of the programmes Mayo listed, only *The Black and White Minstrel Show* was completely unthinkable in a modern-day BBC One schedule. This was for fairly obvious reasons, but it perhaps says something that he instinctively equated the idea of bringing back *Doctor Who* with the plainly ludicrous notion of reviving the minstrels.

Indeed, this was not the first time that such a comparison was put to Heggessey. Two years earlier, on that same radio station, she had appeared as a guest on presenter Nicky Campbell's mid-morning show. This was on October 18 2000, a month after she had been announced as BBC One's new Controller. Campbell had opened the interview with a sarcastic reverie for Saturday night: "Oh it was great! *Doctor Who, The Black and White Minstrel Show...* It's not just nostalgia, it's what we want – it's all going to come full circle!"

Heggessey laughed politely, and the interview had continued.

But even if Campbell and Mayo had been gently mocking, then it was clear from the tone of her answer in 2002 that Lorraine Heggessey herself was actually genuinely interested in the idea of bringing back *Doctor Who*. Her comments about low production values being part of the show's appeal may have indicated a misunderstanding of why people enjoyed *Doctor Who*, but her open admission that she had been looking into it was more than fans had heard directly from a BBC One Controller since Alan Yentob in the mid-1990s. Which made her mention of "all sorts of rights issues" all the more confusing.

This had never been a factor that the BBC had cited for not making the show before, even in the days when those running BBC One and the Drama department really *didn't* want to be making it. So what was the problem now?

Inevitably, there were all kinds of rumours, speculation, and outright hoaxes. The month after Heggessey's 5 Live appearance, one poster on rec.arts.drwho – identifying himself only as 'Bob' – went so far as to claim that the BBC, during the negotiations that led to the 1996 TV Movie, had somehow managed to sell Universal not just an option on *Doctor Who*, but the full rights. Forever.

"For the BBC to buy those rights back would cost millions even though the Americans have no intention of making a series. So, expect no new series," insisted 'Bob' gloomily.

This post was widely ridiculed and outright refuted by others who had contacts within the BBC. But there were also telling comments from those who felt that they wouldn't be surprised if the BBC *had* somehow managed to commit a spectacular error along these lines and accidentally sold off the family silver.

The idea that there was some issue affecting the rights, which was somehow linked to the deal with Universal to make the TV Movie in 1996, was by no means limited to anonymous online fans. Discussing the potential future of the series with *Doctor Who Magazine* in 2003, well-connected fan, actor and writer Mark Gatiss had stated that: "The accepted answer is that there are certain rights issues about what was ceded to Universal in 1996."

What is curious about such remarks is that the BBC had, in fact, already commented publicly on the rights situation following the TV Movie. In May 2000 they released a statement concerning any potential future for *Doctor Who*, which explained that:

> "Universal retained an option on making a series until the end of 1996, when the rights reverted back to the BBC. The series remains in the same position as it was in 1989 when production ceased."

This, of course, wasn't *entirely* accurate. We know from other statements released around the time that Universal had extended their option on *Doctor Who* until the end of 1997 – statements which had noted that the rights would then revert back to the BBC. Either way, it shows that at the turn of the century, the BBC – or at least their press office – believed that the rights to the programme had now definitely returned to them.

When the *Doctor Who* Appreciation Society wrote to Lorraine Heggessey early in 2003, asking her about the status of the series, the reply published in the May issue of their *Celestial Toyroom* magazine also touched on the issue of rights:

> "If there was a refreshing, affordable treatment for a new series available and we could navigate ourselves around some potentially troublesome rights issues, then I would consider reviving the series. It's only a wish, there is nothing substantial to back things up so I don't want to raise false hopes with die-hard fans! Suffice to say that *Doctor Who* has its fans among my commissioning team, most of whom spent the Seventies behind the sofa on Saturday evenings too!"

Once again there was no indication as to what these "potentially troublesome rights issues" might have been, and so the speculation and paranoia rumbled on. Even at the BBC itself there was some degree of confusion and uncertainty. Mal Young recalls what he believed to be the case at this time:

"We were told, 'Don't even go there'. I was told that there was a guy at the BBC, one of these execs who hadn't been there long, and he'd done a deal signing the rights away to *Doctor Who* to an American company. It was for a movie, and the TV rights went with the movie rights, and it meant that we couldn't touch the TV show."

The idea within the BBC that the rights to *Doctor Who* were fraught with complication was probably not helped by the Corporation finding itself in a trademark row over the original police box design used for the TARDIS. London's Metropolitan Police made a formal objection to the BBC for using the box as a trademark, in a legal argument that gained a fair amount of press coverage. In October 2002, the BBC won the case, but it can only have added to the perception that *Doctor Who*'s intellectual property was a bit of a mess.

THE LONG GAME

When producer Dan Freedman was first looking at possibly making a *Doctor Who* radio series in 1999, the BBC referred him to Universal regarding the rights to the series – despite the fact that Universal's option had by then long expired. Clayton Hickman, the editor of *Doctor Who Magazine* in the early 2000s, feels that the main problem was not that the rights situation was insoluble, but rather that, for a long time, there was nobody within the BBC with the will to properly establish the facts of the matter.

"I think there is some truth in that – the rights situation had become muddy," says Hickman. "But, the problem with it was that nobody wanted to bring back *Doctor Who* enough to just look into it properly. Nobody wanted to pay the lawyers or whatever to go through everything and find out what the situation actually was. It was easier to say it was very complicated, because they just weren't sure. I don't think anyone cared enough until there was a driving force. Until Russell came along forcing them to do this stuff, and coming in with an enthusiasm and a design for what he wanted to do with it, there wasn't enough enthusiasm within the BBC to bother sorting it out.

"It's not necessarily that something *has* been sold, it's just that they don't really *know*. There's a lot of paperwork to go through, it was all probably done by people who were there previous to them in their job position, and they were not really interested in what they were doing. So to go through it without a reason, without knowing they were going to make something – there was no incentive to look into these strange things. I think that was the truth of it. Also, it was an easy thing to say in interviews to shut people up!"

Fortunately, however, there was a small group of people within the BBC itself who had decided to get to the bottom of the issue, and being inside the Corporation they had the means to find out. They were the BBC's *Doctor Who* website team, and they had decided that, in the absence of any new film or television series, they were going to have a crack at making new *Doctor Who* themselves.

Following the success of *Death Comes to Time* in 2001 and then the series in early 2002, the website had partnered with the *Doctor Who* audio rights holders Big Finish to make *Real Time*, a Sixth Doctor adventure made available online from the summer of 2002. Then, in May and June 2003, the site had released weekly episodes of a new version of *Shada*. This had originally begun life as a fourth Doctor television story with a script by Douglas Adams, abandoned during production in 1979 due to industrial action. This new version was another collaboration with Big Finish, starring eighth Doctor Paul McGann in place of the original's Tom Baker, and was another success.

Each of these online audio dramas had included illustrations, with increasingly ambitious animation featuring more and more moving elements. This led to *Doctor Who* website producers James Goss and Martin Trickey investigating whether they might be able to get the funds to go a step further – not simply running audio dramas with accompanying artwork on the site, but making a fully animated *Doctor Who* series for the web. The idea was that this would tie in with the show's 40th anniversary in November 2003.

"*Real Time* and *Shada*, had been well-received," remembers Rob Francis, who also worked on the website. "There seemed to be very little – at least, known to us – interest in bringing *Doctor Who* back to television. James Goss and Martin Trickey always thought big, and if there were no barriers editorially, it seemed obvious that we should be as ambitious with our plans as our small online budget would allow."

"That's where I think we went to talk to the Drama guys," says Trickey. "Because by this point, we were a little bit further down the line – broadband penetration's come in, Flash is now a thing. We thought that we could potentially do a full-blown version ourselves, and we could make it in Flash. We were looking at animators, and there was Cosgrove Hall, who we all remembered from *Danger Mouse*. We thought it would be brilliant to work with them.

"Before we decided, I think – and it is *really* hazy – I think we were wondering whether or not we could make *Doctor Who*, and we decided we'd better check. So I think I wandered off and talked to some people in Drama who worked for Jane Tranter and asked if we could do a new *Doctor Who*, if anybody would mind. You do this in the BBC – you come up with ideas, and then look around and keep asking, and eventually somebody will say no. But nobody did!"

Trickey's self-confessed "hazy" recollection is backed up by a feature about the making of the serial written by Paul Cornell, the scriptwriter who was brought in to work on the project. In a piece included as an afterword to his novelisation of the serial, published by BBC Books in 2004, Cornell recalled:

> "BBC Films had been pursuing, for many years, a film deal based on the property, and that department had always previously insisted that no new Doctor be cast, thinking it would spoil any future announcement of their own new Doctor. As Martin Trickey discovered when he went to talk to them, and to people like Alan Yentob, who'd expressed an interest in *Doctor Who* in the past, every relevant department of the BBC was now happy to see a new BBC Doctor."

Trickey suspects that it was these enquiries to other parts of the BBC which alerted many to the fact that it might not be as difficult to get new *Doctor Who* off the ground as BBC Television had perhaps thought.

"I think at this point, knowing that the website wanted to make a new *Doctor Who*, that must have made people say, 'Well, I didn't think we could do it?' This is where this slight myth was discovered that the BBC were no longer able to make *Doctor Who*, which I don't think was ever the case, to be honest."

BBC Online's plans and budgets shifted and changed until, rather than being able to produce a series of twelve episodes consisting of three different serials as planned, the team were able to find the money to make a single six-episode serial. Timescales were tight, but they were also able to commission Cosgrove Hall, allowing for more sophisticated visuals than before; although, as the BBC had a public-service obligation to make its website as accessible as possible, they needed to work within the lower end of the bandwidth limitations of the period.

"Fictionlab was set up to see where we could go with Online as a legitimate broadcasting format," explains Rob Francis. "As well as providing the more traditional programme support and bonus material, we probably went off in some slightly unnecessary directions, such as trying to deliver animation to the viewer using 'web' tools such as RealPlayer and Flash, rather than using them to create video as the end product. I think our hearts were in the right place. To be fair though, bandwidth was still a big issue in the early days!"

The new project ended up being announced to the public earlier than the team behind it were expecting. Thus, on July 9 2003, the BBC *Doctor Who* website revealed that they were now making *Doctor Who* themselves – and what's more, they were doing it with a brand-new ninth Doctor, having cast Richard E. Grant in the role. The website's news page carried the statement that:

> "*Doctor Who* is back. This time he's fully animated, he's got a new body... and he's on BBCi. Richard E. Grant will play the ninth incarnation of the Time Lord. He described his interpretation as something of a 'Sherlock Holmes in Space,' and said he immensely enjoyed recording the story.
>
> "The animated adventure, featuring a star-studded cast, is scripted by Paul Cornell – regarded as one of the finest of the new breed of *Doctor Who* authors.
>
> "'I'm honoured to have the chance to set the Doctor off on another forty years of adventures,' said Paul. 'Just wait until you hear Richard! He *is* the Doctor!'"

Paul Cornell was also a regular participant on the message boards of the Outpost Gallifrey fan site, where he was quickly bombarded with questions about this new project. Cornell sought to reassure fans that just because it was animated and online, this didn't mean it wasn't the big revival they'd been waiting for:

> "This is the start of everything again, not the end. Don't be scared. The Ninth Doctor is Richard E. Grant – fully animated, not *Shada* animated... If the response is good enough, then there'll be more. (And listen: you *never know* where this could end up)."

Cornell was certainly right on that last point. *Scream of the Shalka*, as the serial came to be called, may not have led to further *Doctor Who* in a narrative sense; its 'ninth' Doctor would soon be relegated as a parallel oddity, alongside the likes of the Peter Cushing movie version. But the development of *Shalka* was an important stepping stone in *Doctor Who*'s return to television – because when the team behind the project began work, they wanted to make certain that the BBC actually *did* hold the rights to make it.

Jelena Djordjevic was the producer initially assigned to the project, having previously overseen BBC Cult's standalone online animated drama *Ghosts of Albion*. When they were embarking on what would become *Scream of the Shalka* she had gone to the relevant people in the BBC Rights Group, to establish exactly what the status of *Doctor Who* was, and whether they were free to make it. A decade later, she explained what they had told her in the documentary *Carry on Screaming*, an extra feature on the DVD release of the serial.

> "It was talked about a lot that we had a problem with the rights. And the problem with the rights were that they were hidden... And when I was told we didn't have the rights, it always came back to the Daleks. Always, always, always, people were telling us that we couldn't do it because we couldn't have the rights to the Daleks. And I said, 'We don't want to do it with the Daleks, so can we have *Doctor Who*?'"

Daniel Judd was a researcher on the BBC *Doctor Who* site at the time, who worked with Djordjevic to establish the facts of the situation. He also spoke in the *Carry on Screaming* documentary.

> "I was doing the sort of e-mail grunt work, which was e-mailing everybody to do with rights, across the BBC. That involved talking to BBC Films, who we thought maybe had an option to produce a *Doctor Who* film that we thought might have stopped anyone else working on *Doctor Who* as a project... There was one person at BBC Worldwide who gave the impression that there may not have been as big a problem as we thought. So I sort of badgered him really, so I got a definite answer... he actually said 'No, there are no real rights problems. You can sort them out, and you can do your project.'"

Interviewed for this book, Judd recalls that there was also another reason why his boss on the *Doctor Who* site, James Goss, decided to task him with looking into the rights situation.

"Every department in the BBC, if there was an external-facing e-mail address, had to answer every e-mail that came in," he explains. "So every time Lorraine Heggessey or Jane Tranter went on record saying there were rights issues, we'd suddenly get thousands of e-mails and had to answer them. The only way you'd get around that was by having a 'Frequently Asked Questions', so you could just refer them to an FAQ statement rather than having to write the same thing, or copy and paste.

"So it was really a way of just silencing that. I'd like to think James thought I was the best man for the job, but as a junior researcher he probably just thought I was the most expendable!

"I e-mailed anybody, any department, for somebody to state what the issues were, and nobody would – nobody really wanted to go on-record. But there was somebody at BBC Films at the time, and they said, 'Yes, we have got the option to do a film, but it doesn't affect any other department, it doesn't affect a TV series, it doesn't affect anything.'

THE LONG GAME

"I said, 'Do you mind being quoted on that?' So he gave a quote and James ran a news story, saying what the rights issue actually was. Basically, there wasn't really an issue – apart from the people that owned the rights to the Daleks, UNIT, the Brigadier, and things like that."

On Thursday August 21 2003, the *Doctor Who* website published a story in its news section titled "*Doctor Who* Rights". Explaining that they had put the story up because there were "all sorts of rumours flying around" about the BBC no longer owning the rights to *Doctor Who*, they related the following:

> "To put your minds at rest, we asked around the BBC Rights Group. After all, they should know. Here is their summary:
>
> - Rights to the basic property are owned by BBC and BBC Worldwide. Worldwide own the key trademarks internationally.
> - Many of the writers of the original stories retain the rights to various characters they created; e.g. Terry Nation owns the Daleks, and Victor Pemberton owns Seaweed.
> - The rights that Universal acquired to make the 1996 TV movie have reverted back to the BBC.
> - Nothing is standing in the way of the BBC making a new TV series, but, as far as we know, there is currently no movement to do so.
> - The BBC is developing a film, but it should be stressed the project is still in its very early stages.
>
> So, the BBC could commission a new *Doctor Who* series for TV if it wanted to."

The fact that this information was published in late August ended up being an interesting piece of timing. The end of that month was also when the great and the good of the British

DO I HAVE THE RIGHTS?

television industry gathered for the annual Edinburgh International Television Festival – attending seminars and screenings and launches, and generally getting together for a big industry shindig.

Unsurprisingly, Lorraine Heggessey was among those present at the 2003 Festival. While there, she gave an interview to *The Guardian* newspaper. The first half of the piece focused on BBC One's Saturday evening talent show *Fame Academy*, which had faced criticism for being too derivative of ITV's hit *Pop Idol*, against which it was now being directly scheduled.

The second half of the interview dealt with another programme which Heggessey was keen to add to the Saturday line-up:

> "Ms Heggessey also revealed that she would like to bring back *Doctor Who* to its traditional early Saturday evening slot on BBC One... However, Ms Heggessey said the complex situation surrounding the rights to the small screen character could scupper his return. 'I would like to resurrect *Doctor Who* but the rights situation is too complicated to do that at the moment. Maybe that will happen one day,' she added."

This was published on Monday August 25, just four days after the BBC website had posted its article stating quite firmly that there was no problem with the *Doctor Who* rights. As the *Guardian* piece was on the paper's website, it was easy enough for fans everywhere to read and compare the two stories, and to puzzle over this apparent contradiction.

The BBC *Doctor Who* site itself then put up a story on August 26 reporting Heggessey's comments to *The Guardian*, and reiterating their findings that the only *Doctor Who* rights which were held outside the BBC were those of individual writers in some of the monsters and characters they had created for the show; there was no issue with the format of the programme itself.

Doctor Who fans being *Doctor Who* fans, they didn't just sit and ponder this – they wrote to the BBC to point out the discrepancy.

Daniel Judd recalls how all of this led to Lorraine Heggessey's office requesting to see the research he had put together:

"When James put the initial news story up, his boss Martin Trickey – our head of department – was asked to come along to her office with James, with print-outs of all the evidence we'd found. So it was me scurrying around printing off every e-mail – I wish I had them now!"

"We came back and said yes, we have the rights to do it," says Trickey. "At which point I think they went, 'Shit! Why aren't we making *Doctor Who*, then?' I don't know what went on and what didn't, or what Lorraine Heggessey did or didn't know. But at some point – and this really is fairly foggy – I do remember having a meeting with her and Jane Tranter. I mean, James *definitely* tells me I had this meeting! I think I remember sitting over in Television Centre doing that sort of stuff."

This was how the *Doctor Who* site related what happened at the time, in a piece published in November 2003, two months after the eventual recommissioning of *Doctor Who* was announced:

> "With speculation rife within *Doctor Who* fandom (had the BBC sold the rights to the USA? Was development being blocked by a film?) BBCi Cult site researcher Daniel Judd set off to look into it. On 21 August 2003, he reported that the rights were complicated, but not really a problem.
>
> On August 26 2003 [sic] Lorraine Heggessey told the Edinburgh Television Festival: 'I would like to resurrect *Doctor Who* but the rights situation is too complicated to do that at the moment.' she said.
>
> Lorraine Heggessey runs BBC One. She's an important person. There is no reason for her to check our site on a daily basis. TV executives didn't pick up on this. But the fans did. And contacted the BBC to point out the disparity.
>
> As a result of this, Lorraine Heggessey's office approached the Cult site for details of Daniel Judd's findings regarding the rights issues. They then contacted

the various people in the Rights Group who had helped Daniel compile his report."

So, is Daniel Judd the man who saved *Doctor Who*...?

"I've never seen it like that," he insists. "I think it might have helped a little bit – helped people focus on the fact there wasn't a rights issue, or what the rights issue actually *was*. It might have just cleared the air a bit. It was a scary time, I didn't want to lose my job over it!

"People always bring it up – it's become sort of a party joke, when a friend introduces me to somebody new, that I brought back *Doctor Who*. I don't think I brought back *Doctor Who*. I think I contributed to it maybe, slightly, but I always think it would have happened anyway."

Evidence for this suggestion comes from the fact that, as we'll see in the next chapter, Russell T Davies recalls that the first approach to his agent regarding *Doctor Who* came at a launch event for BBC One's *The Canterbury Tales*. This took place in early August, some two weeks before the BBC *Doctor Who* website put Judd's findings online. So were events already in motion, even without the web team's research?

Helen O'Rahilly, who was Lorraine Heggessey's channel executive at BBC One at the time, says that things were indeed in motion – and that it was all due to a little help from a Dalek.

"There used to be a BBC Shop in Aldwych, where the BBC World Service was," she explains. "I'd pop over there to see the technological guys, for interactive TV. I was mooning about the shop one day and there was a lovely range of Daleks. I wanted this talking Dalek – I ended up buying it just for the laughs. It had about six different commands. You press the button, there were six different phrases – '*Exterminate!*' – all these different terms. It's much more sophisticated now, but it was a good voice; it was really good and quite loud!

"Anyway, I was settling into BBC One, at Television Centre on the sixth floor. I had a big double desk. As you do, you put your various bits – your awards or your whatevers – alongside your computer. I remember just putting my little Dalek on the desk. I used to get in about eight o'clock when there were very few people around. I'd get in early because I had to read all the overnight press briefings, the reviews for the shows, et cetera. Lorraine usually came in about half-eight, quarter to nine, and I wanted to be able to tell her the top three or four things she needed to concentrate on that day.

"Every time she'd come in, as she was taking her coat off, I would press the Dalek. It would come out with its '*Exterminate!*' and she'd go, 'Oh my God, that feckin' thing! Helen, you're winding me up now!' I would just continue doing it – even if I was on a phone call, I'd press the button! I'd never let up! Eventually, she got really pissed off... No, not pissed off. She just came out of her office and went, 'Right! That's it! I'm not putting up with this anymore! Go and organise a meeting. Let's find out who has the rights. We're going to do this!'

"I asked her if she was serious, and she told me she wasn't having me pressing that button anymore! It was probably in the back of her head, but I would just pull it to the forefront, you know? I basically annoyed her so much that she said it was up to me – I had to get everybody together. That was the precipice. We had to then bring Drama in – Jane was well up for it as well. She was the one obviously responsible for getting Julie and Russell. But that was the moment when the green light came on."

When I interviewed O'Rahilly, she didn't give a date for when this might have occurred. However, when writing a piece to mark *Doctor Who*'s 50th anniversary for the *Irish Times* in 2013 she was very specific that it had been in May 2003. It certainly can't have been before November 2002, as that was when she was appointed to the job working at BBC One.

Lorraine Heggessey does remember taking inspiration from O'Rahilly's desk, although in her memory it was a police box rather than a Dalek lurking there. "My channel executive Helen O'Rahilly was a bit of a *Doctor Who* fan and she had a TARDIS on her desk," says Heggessey. "One day I picked up and thought, 'We should bring back *Doctor Who*, people loved it.'"

Neither Heggessey nor Tranter recalls meeting with the web team about their research into the *Doctor Who* rights when asked about it today. However, O'Rahilly agrees that Judd's findings were very much in line with how she remembers the situation.

"That chimes with what I knew," she says. "It happens with big corporations, especially when they're disparate campuses, and it would be more likely for Drama to have more daily doings with BBC Worldwide than the channel itself – because it was up to Drama to chase rights and so forth between them. Because it was being fobbed off, it was always at the bottom of the list, and we kept being told there was something wrong with the rights.

"I don't think it was obfuscation. I genuinely think that nobody just got on the horse and rode it – until people did the work, and we were suddenly told no, there wasn't actually a problem.

"There were all sorts of rumours spreading. We thought they [the rights] were somewhere in a Hollywood vault. It just seemed to take ages – it was like walking in treacle to find out the truth. Where were they? Who had them? Really, we should have assigned our own researcher, brought somebody in for six months to find out. I remember Drama had a lot of new projects on – they were at a hundred percent capacity. Lorraine's was a very creative time at BBC One, and we were putting huge demands on Entertainment and Drama. To add on almost *the* biggest brand to it was an enormous task.

"So I think it was more that it fell between the stools, and finally it was cracked. I remember it being a hectic summer – a lot of costings had to be looked into; where were we going to shoot it? All that sort of stuff."

O'Rahilly's recollection that there was a fear of the rights to *Doctor Who* being "somewhere in a Hollywood vault" echoes the fan speculation and rumour during those years about mysterious hangovers of the TV Movie deal with Universal. Perhaps, however, the answer to that lies in simple confusion over Universal having recently been involved in discussions about *Doctor Who* again.

We know that sometime after Donna Langley's appointment as Universal's senior vice president in charge of production in June

THE LONG GAME

2001, the company was talking to BBC Worldwide about becoming involved in a *Doctor Who* feature film. Could these discussions – once again with Universal, but a different part of the organisation – have led to the rumours that the TV Movie deal from the 1990s was the source of the problem?

This perhaps becomes a more likely explanation when you consider that it was Worldwide who were in discussion with Universal, and it was Worldwide who were seemingly preventing BBC Television from embarking on any new *Doctor Who* series. It would therefore not take a great deal for the rumour mill to then decide that the issue lay on the other side of the Atlantic.

Speaking today, Jane Tranter and Lorraine Heggessey are both very clear that they never believed there was any issue with the rights to *Doctor Who* having somehow been signed away to someone outside of the BBC. They both remember that the issue was entirely to do with BBC Worldwide having primacy over the property, and being reluctant to let it go.

"The rights were looked at for absolutely ages, and there were two things, really," says Tranter. "One was what Terry Nation owned. The other was that it turned out that the rights had been assigned at some point to BBC Worldwide. I knew that there was talk of a film, and that, if I didn't go for it, the rights would potentially get snarled up. There was just an absolute nervousness within the BBC of doing *Doctor Who*. I think Worldwide knew that, and never really believed the BBC would do *Doctor Who*, and that the only way to do it then was a film.

"Timing was everything. There was a lot of talk and it was all white noise, until it just became absolutely, *glaringly* apparent to me that this is what we should do. We'd just do it and grab it; grab the nettle and just say, 'We're doing it!' and go out and do it with confidence. What was the worst thing that could happen? At that point, Lorraine was really very good and said, 'Okay, yeah, let's do it,' and it meant that we could then be very firm with Worldwide that BBC TV needed it, and away we went."

Lorraine Heggessey's memories are similar to Tranter's.

"BBC Worldwide, it transpired, owned all the rights to *Doctor*

Who. They said that we could not have it on TV because they were going to make a movie, and therefore we couldn't put it on BBC One. Which I was pretty fed up about, and ranted and raved for a bit but didn't really get anywhere.

"About a year later they still hadn't made the film, and we still hadn't found something that seemed like the right drama for Saturday early evening on BBC One. I just said, 'This is ridiculous! How can you possibly have the rights? It's a BBC One property, it should belong to the BBC. You haven't made a movie anyway. We are just going to go ahead and do it.'

"It would only happen in the BBC, wouldn't it? BBC Worldwide wouldn't let BBC TV produce it! But eventually, we just bust through that."

But what about the view from the BBC Worldwide camp? Did they really exert such a hold over *Doctor Who* in the early 2000s that it was somehow in their power to decide whether or not BBC Television could actually be allowed to make it – despite it having been a BBC Television creation in the first place? If that were true, why *were* they apparently so fixated on making a film version rather than a series?

Rupert Gavin was BBC Worldwide's Chief Executive at the time: "BBC Worldwide did not have the rights to *Doctor Who*, other than in very peripheral ways that would not have prevented a new series if one had been planned," he insists. "It was never, to my knowledge, put to Worldwide that our supposed ownership of *Doctor Who* was preventing a new series, nor was it discussed as to how Worldwide could facilitate such a new series. There just wasn't one. If there had been, we would have worked together in the normal manner to solve any issues.

"However, the rights to *Doctor Who* were not unfettered and completely open to the BBC, because of the external ownership of various characters – most notably, Terry Nation's ownership of the Daleks. This was a major obstacle at that stage, since it was thought that the Daleks were central to the TV audience's memory of *Doctor Who*."

Gavin is keen to defend BBC Worldwide's position and believes that the film proposal offered the best option to revive *Doctor Who* at that time.

"BBC Worldwide always worked closely in collaboration with BBC Production," he says. "That collaboration was always essential when it came to the funding of bigger budget ideas with global potential. BBC Films were a part of BBC Production. Worldwide agreed with BBC Films that the best opportunity to exploit *Doctor Who* was with the creation of a film. This would have global advertising that could reactivate interest in the property for TV. It would be on a budget scale that meant that the lack of Daleks was potentially not a constraint.

"In addition, we had a top mainstream movie writer in Ed Solomon, expressing great enthusiasm for the concept. Ed would open serious doors in Hollywood, and for a while, this seemed to be the most promising route. This was largely abandoned, however, when, over time, Ed failed to generate any treatments or scripts, or even a timescale for delivery. As I understood it all, it was only subsequently, that BBC Production progressed the TV-based concept from Russell T Davies."

Mike Phillips was Gavin's deputy chief executive and had been the person at BBC Worldwide most closely involved with trying to get the *Doctor Who* film off the ground. As he puts it, he had been "enthusiastic and determined" to do so. So what was his reaction when BBC Television decided that they wanted to make a series instead?

"What I remember is, at the same time I started to work on the movie, Lorraine Heggessey was saying to the Drama department that what she badly needed was what the Americans would call a 'kidult' show; an early evening show that would appeal to kids and their parents. She had seemingly had no success, or nothing that she thought would work. So of course, the inevitable thought within the BBC then always goes back to *Doctor Who*, because that was the property in that category that had always worked for them. Lorraine was prepared to wait to see if a movie deal could be done, but only for so long.

"I entirely understood her position and, at the end of the day, the needs of BBC One come first. There was no conflict in that. Obviously, I was trying to get a deal done before a new UK series was commissioned. BBC Worldwide never owned the rights to *Doctor Who*. BBC Worldwide handled the commercial exploitation, but the intellectual property rights sat with the BBC. It was a BBC-owned property. If you work in Worldwide, you know that the tail doesn't wag the dog. If it's needed for BBC One, then that takes precedence."

However, Phillips says that Worldwide still had a role to play with *Doctor Who*, providing key funding that helped to make a new series possible.

"The BBC hasn't been able to fully fund their more expensive output for a very, very long time," he explains. "That's why BBC Worldwide was constantly in the business of co-production, where that's possible, or investing upfront. So that goes across a huge swathe of the BBC's output."

One aspect of this explanation of events that doesn't quite mesh with those from the television side is the fact that Jane Tranter's recollections of Worldwide's attitude are very close to those of Heggessey's. Tranter may have been a commissioner, but she was still very much involved with the production side of things as the person in charge of BBC Drama; the department which Rupert Gavin claims would have had a better idea of the situation and the links with Worldwide. Russell T Davies also briefly talked about BBC Worldwide's investment in the initial revival of *Doctor Who* in the DVD documentary *Doctor Forever: The Unquiet Dead* in 2013, saying that the BBC's commercial arm "weren't exactly leaping up and down" about the idea.

Rupert Gavin, however, denies a lack of enthusiasm for the *Doctor Who* television revival on Worldwide's part.

"Once BBC Production were fully on board with the Russell T Davies approach, they fixed a meeting for the BBC Worldwide team to hear from Russell how the idea would work. I attended that meeting. I remember it distinctly. We were seriously impressed by the vision, the scale and the professionalism of the approach. It was a *Doctor Who* for today's audience with contemporary production standards. Although it was apparent that the shooting cost was going to be several times, in pounds-per-hour, any previous *Doctor Who* television idea, we were all immediately supportive. We embraced the idea and committed to work out a funding plan designed to make it happen, which it did."

Jane Tranter's recollection of how the matter was eventually resolved is also slightly less collaborative than Gavin's or Phillips'. Three years after the events took place, she told Gary Russell for his 2006 book *Doctor Who: The Inside Story* that she had turned to Alan Yentob to help put an end to the *Doctor Who* film project and, as Russell phrased it, "sort through the mess."

"He did, he did," Tranter tells me. "Because Alan Yentob was the sort of uber-head of BBC Films, he was the one who said this is what's going to happen, and Alan was brilliant in doing that. He just looked at it and said, 'Okay, fine, we'll shut that down.'"

After having been made Director of Television at the BBC in 1997 and then missing out on the Director-Generalship to Greg Dyke, in 2000 Yentob had been given a new role in the reshuffles conducted by Dyke during his first year in charge; these had also placed Heggessey and Tranter in their Controller jobs. Yentob was now Director of Drama, Entertainment and Children's, which meant overseeing the in-house production output in those three areas as a creative figurehead – albeit with Tranter still ultimately responsible for which drama projects were actually commissioned.

This position also gave him oversight of BBC Films, as well as a seat on the BBC's executive committee. Yentob therefore, had the necessary managerial clout within the Corporation to be able to persuade BBC Worldwide to give up their *Doctor Who* feature film ambitions for the time being and allow BBC One and the Drama department to develop a new series for the small screen.

"I don't recall much about it, but yes," says Yentob. "They hadn't managed to do anything with it. The film didn't appeal to me that much. And here were a group of people passionate about doing it, including the Controller of BBC One, and Jane, and they had writers ready to go."

So does Yentob agree that Worldwide at that time seemed to

DO I HAVE THE RIGHTS?

assume they had some degree of ownership over *Doctor Who*?

"Yes, they thought they had control. I don't know how that happened, because they were busy still trying to find an American partner. But if I'm honest, that shouldn't have happened, really. The decision should not be in the hands of the commercial division of the BBC. Eventually, that was understood. In the end, Worldwide had run out of time. We all said they'd done their bit, it hadn't worked. We needed now to take it on, and that's what happened."

Meanwhile, having actually done the work to clarify the rights situation, establishing that new *Doctor Who* could indeed be made by the BBC, the BBC Cult website team had carried on with the production of *Scream of the Shalka*. The completed six-part animated serial was due to go online from November 2003, as one of the big events to mark the programme's 40th anniversary celebrations.

A couple of months before this, BBC Information – the part of the Corporation which dealt with correspondence from viewers and listeners – prepared an 'audience answer' on the subject of the rights to *Doctor Who*, following the conflicting statements which had been made by the official website and by Lorraine Heggessey. This was a standard statement to be given to anyone who enquired about a particular subject, and the one concerning the confusion over *Doctor Who* was issued on September 9 2003.

"Please be assured there is no contradiction, but this is a very complex matter and may need some further clarification," the statement claimed, before confirming that, "Our website correctly states that the rights to the basic property are owned by the BBC, with the key international trademarks being owned by BBC Worldwide." It then explained that while BBC Drama were keen to bring *Doctor Who* back to television, BBC Films were in the early stages of developing a feature film project. This meant that:

> "Because approximately half of the funding for BBC Films derives from BBC Worldwide there are legitimate commercial reasons why it would be inappropriate to have two different *Doctor Who* projects underway at the same time. For this reason, the Controller of BBC

THE LONG GAME

> One explained that although she wants to bring the programme back as a series, there are currently rights issues which are preventing its swift return. Should BBC Films decide not to proceed with the film then other plans may well be put into motion, but it is important to clarify that no series is scheduled at the moment."

In retrospect, this last claim is a neat little technicality. While it may have been true that no new series of *Doctor Who* had yet been *scheduled*, by September 2003 there certainly *was* one already planned.

It was somewhere around this time that *Scream of the Shalka*'s author, Paul Cornell, received a telephone call from fellow writer Russell T Davies. *Shalka* was about to be overshadowed before it even debuted on the BBC website, and Davies wanted to do Cornell the courtesy of letting him know what was happening.

As Cornell explained a decade later in the *Carry on Screaming* documentary: "Russell called me and said 'I have terrible news. We're bringing back *Doctor Who*.'"

13

"RUSSELL. DOCTOR WHO. WE'RE DOING IT"

FOR THE LAST 40 OR SO YEARS of the 20th Century, Saturday night television formed one of the main battlegrounds between the BBC and their commercial rivals at ITV. Unlike many other parts of the world, Saturday had evolved into a tentpole evening for broadcasters in the UK; a night when mainstream shows could bring together large audiences and embed themselves into the collective consciousness of both the nation and its popular culture.

"If BBC One was disproportionately important to the BBC, then Saturday night was disproportionately important to BBC One," explains Lorraine Heggessey, who controlled the channel from 2000 to 2005. "The British public has certain expectations of being entertained on a Saturday night – of having programming that the family will gather around. It's still true now, even with the multiplicity of channels. Something like *Strictly* or *The X Factor* or *Britain's Got Talent* will get a massive family audience and that is still required by viewers. It's not the same in the States. It seems to be a peculiarly British phenomenon."

Alan Yentob, one of Heggessey's predecessors as Controller of BBC One, agrees.

"Saturday has become a focus for entertainment like *Strictly* and *Britain's Got Talent* and things like that. It's always been a place where you thought you could bring the family together. There's no question about how important it is."

On Saturday evenings, the focus for both the BBC and ITV would often be on entertainment shows built around spectacle and special guests, or dramas that majored on action, adventure and escapism, as opposed to the gritty realism that worked better on other nights. *Doctor Who* played its part in BBC One's Saturday line-up for most of the first two decades of the show's existence, although never really sat at the heart of primetime. It was always more of an early-evening opener, bringing the family together in the hope they would then stay with the BBC for the rest of the evening.

By the beginning of the 21st Century, though, things had begun to change. The mass Saturday night audiences were in decline – although this was also true for the mass audience for all television channels on all days of the week. While BBC One and ITV had always sat comfortably above their more specialist-interest neighbours on the analogue broadcast spectrum, BBC Two and Channel 4, the rise of multi-channel television gradually began to erode their audience shares.

Cable and especially satellite television grew massively in popularity and reach in the UK throughout the 1990s, particularly so after the introduction of digital transmission in 1998. The arrival of digital TV also brought multi-channel options to terrestrial television received through an aerial, above and beyond the traditional four or five channels. Added to this was the near-universal adoption of home video recorders and their successors; the arrival of the internet; and an increasing number of families having multiple televisions in the home, splintering the audience still further.

So the viewership was fragmented, and there was also a natural process of decay, as many of the big long-running Saturday night favourites began to show their age and were eventually judged to have had their day. As the new century dawned, it really did seem to many observers as if major Saturday night hits were a thing of the past.

There were plenty of newspaper and online articles published during these years bemoaning the death of Saturday night viewing. "Even the Independent Television Commission has recognised the problem, its last annual report pointing out the 'one-note' nature of Saturday night," wrote *The Observer* in 1999, adding:

> "'Material continues to rely on the same old faces and approaches,' the report said of ITV's Saturday evening output. This hit a chord that reverberated through the whole industry. Had there been a similar watchdog calling the BBC to account, chances are the findings would have been similar."

In 2000, the *Daily Mail* reported that:

> "Five million viewers have deserted BBC and ITV on Saturday nights because they are bored with the same old 'tired' entertainment shows... Families no longer gather round the TV set in a single unit – instead they are going to separate rooms to watch satellite channels or amuse themselves on the latest computer games."

A piece in *The Independent* in 2003 asking the question "whatever happened to Saturday night telly?" did point out that: "Of course, the question presupposes that Saturday nights used to be something to cherish. And one should be wary of such a presupposition. The TV schedules, like pretty much everything else, look a sight prettier when lit by the pink glow of nostalgia." However, it immediately went on to add:

> "But who can honestly say that an evening of Bruce Forsyth's version of *The Generation Game*, with a gaily twirling Anthea Redfern, followed by *Morecambe and Wise*, followed by the news, *Match of the Day* and *Parkinson* (with the Fred Astaires of this world as his guests, rather than the Jeremy Clarksons), is not worth a heavy, rueful sigh?"

THE LONG GAME

The BBC One Saturday night schedule was certainly in a period of transition during Lorraine Heggessey's time in charge of the channel. Their biggest Saturday evening hit of the 1990s had been the live entertainment show *Noel's House Party*, launched in 1991, which had quickly become something of a phenomenon. Its fast-paced mix of games, celebrity guests, pranks and stunts used the television medium very innovatively – all wrapped up with an air of gentle self-mockery from its host, Noel Edmonds. The show became a huge hit and, at its peak, *Noel's House Party* was watched by around fifteen million viewers.

By the end of the decade, however, there was a feeling that the programme had begun to run out of steam, with Edmonds at loggerheads with the BBC over the content of the show. BBC One controller Peter Salmon pulled the plug, and the series came to an abrupt end in early 1999.

Another of BBC One's long-running Saturday night staples had been *The Generation Game*, a game show in which teams of two, made up of different generations of the same family, competed at various tasks and activities after a demonstration by an expert – usually with anarchic and farcical results. The programme had been a big hit from 1971 until 1982, presented first by Bruce Forsyth and then Larry Grayson. It had then returned with Forsyth at the helm in 1990, although not always on Saturdays this time, before comedian Jim Davidson took over in 1995.

By the turn of the century, *The Generation Game* was another programme judged to be past its best, not helped by Davidson himself beginning to fall out of fashion with TV commissioners. Heggessey took the decision to end *The Generation Game*'s second incarnation in 2002, bringing another veteran Saturday night entertainment show to an end. BBC One did have its long-running medical drama *Casualty*, and a revolving series of different game shows built around the National Lottery draws, but not much else in terms of regular, returning hits earlier on Saturday evenings.

Heggessey's line-up also wasn't helped by the fact that for most of her time as BBC One Controller, she was without one of the programmes perhaps most associated with Saturday nights on the

"RUSSELL. DOCTOR WHO. WE'RE DOING IT"

channel – *Match of the Day*. The BBC had held the rights to show Saturday evening highlights of the day's Premier League football matches for most of the 1990s, but in 2000 – in a move perhaps predictably labelled as 'Snatch of the Day' by some of the press – ITV had outbid the BBC, and signed a three-year contract, to run from 2001 to 2004. BBC Sport were able to offer Heggessey the consolation of live football coverage, in the form of FA Cup games and England international matches. These could – especially in the case of the England games – bring enormous audiences to BBC One, but were only occasional events, rather than the regular weekly dose of *Match of the Day*.

Not, it has to be said, that ITV necessarily had an easy time of it with the Premier League highlights. Director of Programmes David Liddiment had come up with an idea to do something different with ITV's programme, called simply *The Premiership* – the name under which the Premier League was also known at the time. The BBC had always regarded the football highlights as something for the late evening, rather than primetime; Liddiment wanted to change all that, and so *The Premiership* ran at 7.00pm on ITV on Saturday evenings, right in the place where entertainment programming would usually sit.

It didn't work, and the show's ratings never took off in the early evening slot, leading to a somewhat embarrassing admission of defeat in October. Two months into ITV's contract it was announced that *The Premiership* would be moving to a more traditional late-evening slot.

It wasn't all doom and gloom, however. That same autumn, ITV launched a programme that showed that the hope of capturing both a mass audience and the public imagination on Saturday nights was perhaps not dead after all. In October 2001 they debuted the reality TV show *Pop Idol*, the successor to their star-making entertainment series *Popstars*, which had been a hit the year before.

Popstars had shown the formation of a pop group, from auditions by members of the public. *Pop Idol* followed a similar format to find a solo artist, but with a number of key differences. The show was to be presented by Ant and Dec, who would quickly become the most popular presenting duo on British television. This time, rather than it all being down to the judges, the public would get to vote. There were still judges as well, however, and among them was Simon Cowell, soon to become a hugely important figure in British entertainment, making his mark on TV for the first time.

Pop Idol was a massive success and a huge Saturday night hit for ITV. Interestingly, however, it's a show which Heggessey claims was offered to her for BBC One first.

"We had some perfectly okay game shows," she says of Saturday nights when she took over. "We had the lottery, which would normally have a game show format around it. But there was this thing of having got three game shows stacked on top of each other. They lose that shine and become a bit samey, so we needed some different kind of entertainment. ITV had *Pop Idol* – that was just going gangbusters. In fact, Simon Cowell had pitched *Pop Idol* to me and I had wanted it, but I'd lost out to ITV."

There were only two series each of *Popstars* and *Pop Idol*, before ITV partnered with Cowell in 2004 to launch a successor show, *The X Factor*. This became even more of a phenomenon, the highest-rated and perhaps most influential pop music programme on British television in the 2000s and 2010s.

So ITV had proved that, if the show was right, a big audience could still be drawn to Saturday evenings; that programmes broadcast there could still make an impact. But despite this success, there was still plenty of negativity about Saturday evening television. The BBC's own news website, for example, published an article in August 2003 reporting the results of a survey, which found that Saturdays were apparently now the least-watched night of the week on television; a huge contrast to the situation even just a few years ago.

This, then, was the arena into which Lorraine Heggessey had to pitch her new entrants in the Saturday night battle. One of her major efforts during her time at BBC One aimed squarely for the audience ITV had so successfully captured with the likes of *Pop Idol*. The BBC One equivalent, *Fame Academy*, ran for two series

"RUSSELL. DOCTOR WHO. WE'RE DOING IT"

in 2002 and 2003, to mixed success. Although there were clear attempts to add a 'BBC spin' to the format – with the contestants also being required to demonstrate skills in songwriting and playing instruments rather than simply singing – *Fame Academy* never managed to escape the accusation that it was simply too derivative of ITV's output. This put the BBC on shaky ground, as a publicly-funded broadcaster with a perceived duty to be original and distinctive. Although *Fame Academy* successfully returned for short celebrity runs in aid of Comic Relief in 2005 and 2007, the main version of the show never returned after 2003.

Much more successful was an entertainment series launched the following year, the first of Lorraine Heggessey's two great, long-lasting legacies to BBC One. On paper, *Strictly Come Dancing* didn't seem like an idea that would catch the imagination of the British public in such an enormous way, with its format of celebrities from various fields being paired with professionals in a ballroom dancing competition, with one couple voted off each week via a public vote.

The title was a combination of the dance movie *Strictly Ballroom* and the BBC's former ballroom dancing show *Come Dancing*, which had run from 1950 right through to the late 1990s. The presence of veteran presenter Bruce Forsyth evoked classic Saturday night television of the past, and the whole thing combined modern fun with charming old-school entertainment. Still going strong today, *Strictly* thrives by not taking itself too seriously, yet balances its irreverence with excellent production values and a clear sense of pride from all involved.

The whole *Strictly* format worked from the start, appealing to all ages. From a short summer run in 2004, it has gone on to become one of the major returning annual hits of BBC One's schedule.

That same summer, Channel 4 broadcast a documentary looking at the history of Saturday night television; taking in its biggest shows, its biggest failures, and the ratings wars between BBC One and ITV. Several of those taking part in the programme expressed the view that the glory days of Saturday nights were over, and there would never again be such talked-about, big-hitting programmes on that night of the week.

But the likes of *Strictly Come Dancing* and *The X Factor* would soon prove these predictions wrong, propelling Saturday nights to the top of the ratings. ITV also had another Saturday evening success with their entertainment show *Ant and Dec's Saturday Night Takeaway*, a programme that in 2005 would provide the initial opposition for the return of *Doctor Who*.

In July 2001, when she had been Controller of BBC One for less than a year, Lorraine Heggessey spoke to *The Guardian* about the future of Saturday night television. The paper reported that Heggessey's "programme-makers are developing a lot of new Saturday night shows, which she won't talk about." They also quoted her directly as she told them, "I'm looking for things which are a bit different."

In September 2002 Jana Bennett, the BBC's overall Director of Television - and Heggessey and Jane Tranter's immediate superior - spoke at a Royal Television Society dinner about the direction of BBC One's Saturday night output. As the BBC News website reported on her comments at the time:

> "The BBC has had success with *Casualty* on a Saturday night, and is now considering putting more faith in drama. Ms Bennett said: 'I want new original thinking about Saturday nights for BBC One viewers. We don't have to spend so much of Saturday nights locked up in purple and pink studios guessing the answers to the same questions. We want to throw out the conventions about Saturday nights and I will back experiments - with the schedule, with the programme mix.'"

Bennett's comments came in the same month that Heggessey had told BBC Radio 5 Live she was looking at bringing back *Doctor Who*. Indeed, later that month a gossip column in *The Observer* newspaper reported that: "One show definitely returning to TV screens is *Doctor Who*, according to microscopic-but-perfectly-formed BBC One controller Miss Lorraine Heggessey." So it seems

"RUSSELL. DOCTOR WHO. WE'RE DOING IT"

clear that a Saturday early evening drama of some sort, and quite probably *Doctor Who* itself, was definitely being considered at this point; Bennett's comments being a clear indicator of the kind of thing they were looking for.

Bennett had been made Director of Television at the BBC in February 2002, taking over from Mark Thompson who had left to run Channel 4. Jane Tranter later told *Doctor Who Magazine* in 2013 that it was after Bennett was appointed that she and Lorraine Heggessey really felt they could start to push the *Doctor Who* idea, trying to get it done while it was still "a transitional time." However, Heggessey points out that, "It wasn't that Mark or Jana tried to inhibit it. It was this thing with Worldwide. I think Jane was probably just as exasperated as I was, and we felt it was our right to be able to do it."

The momentum continued to build, and occasionally signs of it would emerge. In March 2003, Jane Tranter discussed Saturday night television for another newspaper feature – this time for *The Observer*. Asked what her perfect Saturday night BBC One line-up might consist of, Tranter told them that as part of this she would "like to do a modern version of *Doctor Who* starring someone like Judi Dench."

Lorraine Heggessey explains why she was keen to experiment by putting drama back into early Saturday evenings on BBC One, something which hadn't been attempted for some years.

"I wanted to bring light and shade into the schedule. I thought that each show would shine more by being in contrast with something completely different. If you've got an entertainment show followed by an entertainment show – whether it's two game shows, quizzes, whatever – they don't shine. Whereas if we had a very different pace and mood, with a fantastic drama that the whole family would want to watch, followed or preceded by a fantastic entertainment show that the whole family would want to watch... that would make the schedule feel much richer and would pull people in."

Mal Young enthusiastically agrees.

"I remember being in meetings with Lorraine, and we were

designing a Saturday night that would start with *Doctor Who* in its traditional slot, and I loved that," he says. "I said to Lorraine that it was a giant – it had to be on Saturday nights. That was traditionally the *Doctor Who* slot, and we could bring families back together who'd stopped watching TV as a group. It was at a time when there was a lot more time-shifting with videoing; kids had a second TV in their rooms; the family were fragmented. So we said, we could use this show to bring the family back together. They'd noticed that the family was starting to come back together on Saturday nights to watch entertainment shows like they used to."

As Mal Young remembers, the concept of putting a Drama show into what had latterly become an Entertainment slot did present its problems.

"The money was not ringfenced in Drama [as a department]. There hadn't been an early-evening drama, there was only *Casualty* on Saturday nights, so all the money was Entertainment and Entertainment hadn't come up with enough big hits. So Lorraine said, 'What if we took some of the money that was meant for Entertainment and put it into *Doctor Who*?' Because it was in the same slot, she could justify that. We said, 'Great,' and asked how much we had. I don't know exactly, but I remember it being around about £500,000 an episode.

"It wasn't enough, and we said the show was going to look pretty crap for that. At that point, I was making *Holby* for £350,000 an episode, but that was over 50 weeks a year – you could spread the cost. But your average drama costs in those days was anything between £600,000 and £800,000 per episode, and some were over a million."

The budget for *Doctor Who* would continue to be an issue and, when shooting began on the first series in the summer of 2004, full funding for the episodes had not yet been secured. As that year went on, however, Young made the decision to leave the BBC; knowing that he was going at the end of the year, he freed up money from his Drama Series budget to help make up the shortfall, and get the full series made.

"I was starting to think about what I was going do next," Young explains. "It was definitely going to be me moving to America, but no one else knew this – I kept it to myself. I was looking at it thinking, I was coming up to seven, eight years, I'd done everything I wanted to do – it might be interesting if *Doctor Who* was the last thing I did at the Beeb. I've done it, it took me a while but we got there. I could just go then.

"So I was a little more gung-ho about not worrying about the money. In the past, I'd always worried about the money, because I'm very proud to say that I take the responsibility of overspending public money quite seriously – BBC licence payers' money. It was your job to protect it.

"But I did say to them it would be fine. Thinking in the back of my mind that I wouldn't be there, so it'd be someone else's problem, but someone will find the money because they always seem to. It seems to come from somewhere, and even if the show goes into deficit to begin with, it will probably make money back as it sells around the world. But we didn't think it was going to do anything like it did. I'd love to say yes, I knew it was going to. We didn't. We were still at that stage thinking, 'I hope this works!' So we went for it and revised the budget, knowing we were going into deficit, and it did very, very well, obviously."

The question of where a new series of *Doctor Who* might sit in the schedules had been settled upon almost from the start, but as for where the show might actually be produced – that was another matter. Given Mal Young's support and enthusiasm for the revival, it might have seemed obvious for it to have been made by his Drama Series department in London, or perhaps by the drama unit in Birmingham, which had come under his aegis in early 1998. But events elsewhere in the BBC over the summer of 2003 offered up another potential home for the series, when a friend and colleague of Russell T Davies' moved to the Corporation to run an outpost of its drama empire.

In May 2003, it had been announced that Matthew Robinson was leaving his job as Head of Drama at BBC Wales. He was heading to Cambodia to oversee a project backed by the BBC World Service Trust, working with local talent to create an educational soap opera to help combat the spread of HIV in the region. The project ended up creating the successful series *Taste of Life*, and Robinson remained in Cambodia where he later formed his own production company, helping to revive the country's film industry, which had been practically wiped out under the Khmer Rouge.

Robinson's departure for this admirable endeavour meant that a successor was needed to run the Drama department at BBC Wales. On July 29 2003, the BBC Press Office announced that the job had gone to 34-year-old Julie Gardner, at the time working as a Development Producer at the ITV company LWT.

Gardner had been born and raised in South Wales, before leaving to study for a degree in English at the University of London. Returning to Wales after gaining her degree, she initially worked as a teacher before deciding that what she really wanted to do with her life was to work in the television industry.

Responding to a job advert, she managed to gain a position as a producer's secretary on the second filming block of the landmark BBC Two drama serial *Our Friends in the North*, made over a year from the end of 1994 to late 1995 and screened to huge acclaim in 1996. Generally regarded as one of the all-time great BBC dramas, it co-starred Christopher Eccleston, an actor with whom Gardner would later work more than once in a more senior capacity.

Gardner then became a script reader for BBC Drama and towards the end of the 1990s, worked in the Drama Series department under Mal Young. Here she became a script editor and worked in that capacity on a range of programmes. These included the somewhat maligned *Harbour Lights* and *Sunburn*, but also the more highly-regarded *The Mrs Bradley Mysteries*, a Sunday evening detective series set in the 1920s, starring Diana Rigg and featuring Peter Davison as Inspector Christmas.

"Julie was one of our script editors," Young recalls of Gardner's time working in Drama Series. "I was building her up to become a producer because she was great."

Gardner did indeed become a producer under Young, taking over *Sunburn* for the programme's second run in 2000, having script edited the first series. With this experience under her belt, she then left the BBC to join London Weekend Television – formerly the independent ITV franchise holder which broadcast to the capital at the weekends. LWT had been taken over by Granada Television in the mid-1990s; Gardner joined during LWT's last years as a separate entity before it was absorbed into the rest of ITV. At this point, LWT still had its own drama department, and Gardner was able to make an impact with her work there.

Her most notable project during her time there was a modern-day adaptation of Shakespeare's *Othello*, directed by the *Doctor Who* TV Movie's Geoffrey Sax. This retelling set the story in the upper ranks of London's Metropolitan Police and featured Christopher Eccleston in the Iago role – here renamed as 'Ben Jago'. *Othello* was screened on ITV in December 2001 to great acclaim, receiving a BAFTA Award nomination in the Best Single Drama category.

Othello was also nominated as Best Television Drama at *The South Bank Show* Awards, held at the Savoy Hotel in London on February 6 2002. This was to be an important event for Gardner, and for *Doctor Who*, as it was there that she met Russell T Davies for the first time.

Davies' *Bob & Rose* was also nominated in the Best Television Drama category, but both that and *Othello* lost out to *Beckett on Film*, a collaboration between Channel 4, RTE and the Irish Film Board to adapt all of Samuel Beckett's plays. Gardner explained to *Doctor Who Magazine* in 2005 that after the awards had been presented, she went over to the *Bob & Rose* table, introduced herself to Davies and told him how much she admired his work.

"We'd never met, and it was just lovely," says Gardner. "I remember an instant connection. He was very funny. I remember him saying I was so young! Which now seems laughable, but I *was* so young!"

Davies and Gardner quickly became friends, and began working together on the idea of adapting the memoirs of 18th Century Venetian adventurer Giacomo Casanova into a television drama.

"I'd had the idea to do *Casanova* when I was at London Weekend Television, working for Michelle Buck and Damien Timmer," says

Gardner. "We went to Russell, and he was very immediately very interested."

In summer 2003, with *Casanova* yet to make it into production, Gardner was approached about moving to the BBC, to take on the job of Head of Drama at BBC Wales.

"They approached me," she recalls. "At LWT, I was a producer and I was in development, sometimes in production, in the usual way. Then I was approached about the Head of Drama job by Menna Richards, who was at that time Controller of BBC Wales, and her number two, Clare Hudson.

"I remember my first thought was that they must be in trouble if they were coming to me, because I was very unqualified for the job. I'd never been an executive producer, I'd never run a department. It was a very, very different role to what I'd done."

So, were they in trouble? Menna Richards, the Controller of BBC Wales from 2000 until 2011, explains why Gardner was the one she wanted to head their Drama department in 2003.

"She was very sparky," Richards recalls. "She was full of ideas. I liked her immediately, and I thought that she had the potential to be a really great Head of Drama. It was one of those very BBC things - she and I literally met behind an aspidistra at the Langham Hotel opposite Broadcasting House, and had our first chat there. I was impressed by her and I thought she was a woman with ambition, ideas and imagination - and she delivered, in spades."

Gardner, however, wasn't initially sure whether she should take the job.

"I had this really good meeting with them - really liked them, really liked their ambition. They were very, very ambitious about drama coming out of Wales. I went to the meeting in the best possible way - not really knowing very much and not really wanting the job at that point, because I didn't know what it was. At that point BBC Wales Drama was very successful in local programming - I think they had three shows - but they weren't breaking into network [broadcast]. They'd tried in different forms - they'd tried *Drovers' Gold*, they'd tried a few. But nothing was really sticking for network, and that's what they wanted to do.

"It was the huge ambition – it was all about that. So I had a couple of meetings with Menna and Clare, and started to feel like it was possible; started to feel like I could see a path to network success. Part of that was realising they had never worked with Russell, they weren't working with Andrew Davies. There were these big characters – these big successful Welsh writers working in network, who they just weren't developing things with.

"So I did those two meetings, and then my last meeting was with Jane as Controller of Drama. That meeting was really when it completely became real, where you could see this was a significant moment, and real attention was being directed at BBC Wales Drama to break through and be on the network stage."

While Gardner's move to the BBC was ongoing in the summer of 2003, things were put in motion ahead of *Doctor Who* entering production. Jane Tranter's initial manner of informing Russell T Davies of this, however, had been somewhat oblique.

On August 6 2003 the BBC held a press launch for one of their new drama series starting that autumn, at the Baltic Bar and Restaurant on London's Blackfriars Road. *The Canterbury Tales* was a six-part anthology series, with each episode updating one of Chaucer's original 14th Century stories for a 21st Century setting. The series began on BBC One on September 11 2003, with the press launch held a month beforehand, giving plenty of time for preview features across the media.

This had no direct connection to *Doctor Who* – although Billie Piper's strong performance in the first episode may have helped her become a contender for the role of Rose Tyler. Piper was one of those present at the press launch – as was Russell T Davies' agent Bethan Evans, who happened to see Jane Tranter there.

As Davies would later tell the story, Tranter approached Evans and simply said: "Russell. *Doctor Who*. We're doing it. Tell him."

Evans rang Davies the following day, leaving an answerphone message passing on Tranter's words. But at this point, the writer was somewhat cynical about the possibility of the BBC bringing *Doctor Who* back. As he explained to *Doctor Who Magazine* in 2005:

> "[I] sort of ignored it for two days, cos I thought 'Yeah, yeah, that just means they want a potential *Doctor Who* put into development for years.' Eventually, after a week or so, I did sort of say, 'What was that about, then?' And she didn't know – all she'd had was that mention off Jane Tranter. I said something like 'Oh, tell them I'm interested and of course, I'd like to do it, but I'm busy.'"

There is one small mystery thrown up by the timing of Tranter's comments to Davies' agent, if they did indeed happen as and when Davies remembered. If Tranter did speak to Evans at the *Canterbury Tales* launch in early August as Davies recalls, why at the end of the month was Lorraine Heggessey still telling *The Guardian* at the Edinburgh Television Festival that there were rights issues preventing *Doctor Who*'s return?

Helen O'Rahilly, Heggessey's then-channel executive at BBC One, has one possible explanation – that Heggessey knew by this point the show was coming back, but wasn't yet ready to say it.

"When you work at a big channel, everything you do is scrutinised," O'Rahilly explains. "Every word out of place, anything the Controller says, anything I'd say on the phone to a journalist – *anything* could be front-page news. Without bigging myself up, it can turn into 'BBC Boss Says X.' So we had a very, very tight press operation around BBC One. Very tight. Everything was vetted, there was always a press officer there. We had strategy meetings with press and marketing and so forth. We had a very tight team. There were no leaks – everybody was very loyal to the brand and the content.

"Now, I'm not saying somebody mightn't have said something in a pub, you know? That might happen, but I certainly didn't say anything. I'm a Catholic, so it was like the Third Secret of Fatima! An on-pain-of-death type of thing.

"As you well know, fuck-ups can happen in transit – things leaking out. Edinburgh is always a huge platform for every channel controller, and the subject of *Doctor Who* would have been covered.

"RUSSELL. DOCTOR WHO. WE'RE DOING IT"

I can't remember it being covered, but I'm sure it would have been. Because we had the big news, so you would expect that would be the time to announce it, at Edinburgh.

"But I think, because other channels had their big news too, we probably thought we'd keep our powder dry. So Lorraine was probably just obfuscating, in terms of, now is not the time. It was sensible because it would have been huge anyway, but Edinburgh is a huge place. There are lots of huge announcements there, and we didn't want it to get semi-buried in anything else."

It could also simply be the case that when she spoke to *The Guardian* in Edinburgh, Heggessey wasn't yet aware of quite how far Tranter had been able to push the project along. Speaking to *Doctor Who Magazine* in 2013, however, Davies certainly suggested that Heggessey was aware of finally being able to make *Doctor Who* for some time before she made her announcement at the end of September.

"It was placed very deliberately in the *Telegraph*," Davies said, recalling Heggessey's interview. "That was planned for months."

"Months" is clearly an exaggeration – it has to be, if Davies' earlier recollection, that the press launch for *The Canterbury Tales* was when his agent was approached, is correct; it was just over seven weeks between that event and the official announcement of *Doctor Who*'s return. But it does suggest that the planning for *Doctor Who*'s comeback had already been underway for some *weeks* by the time it was officially announced.

As Julie Gardner recalls it, things seriously got underway in the first week of September. She was by now in place and working as Head of Drama at BBC Wales, and travelled to London for her first formal face-to-face meeting with Jane Tranter.

"Jane would have routine meetings with her heads of Drama," Gardner explains. "You go in and talk about all the projects in development. She very, very courteously let me go through this whole list – I can't remember what they were, but they would have been good projects – but in comparison with *Doctor Who* they would have all been small. We had an hour meeting, and maybe 30 or 40 minutes of that was me talking about these projects.

"Having done that she then said, 'I have something I need to talk to you about, which is we want to bring back *Doctor Who* as a TV series, and Russell T Davies has put his hand in the air to do this. Do you know he's been suggesting it?'"

As it turned out, this was news to Gardner.

"I didn't know that those conversations had been going on. It had never come up during our *Casanova* development – and that was the other thing that was happening. *Casanova* was stuck at ITV. We had these amazing scripts. At the time Nick Elliott, who was the decision-maker, and his second-in-command Jenny, were just really hesitant about doing a period piece about Casanova.

"I just couldn't bear it. The worst thing you can experience as a producer is to have a great piece of work that you can't get up on its feet. It's so hard to find those great pieces, and these scripts were fantastic. I can barely recognise myself in this, but when I got into my meeting with Jane to become BBC Wales Head of Drama, I said I would come, but only if they took *Casanova*.

"It's *insanity* now, to think I could march through the door and expect a project greenlit! But it was very straightforward. She read *Casanova* and she loved it, of course – the writing was always extraordinary, on the page. LWT were fantastic, in understanding. They were credited on the show, and it went to Manchester and to Nicola Shindler."

When Tranter brought up the subject of *Doctor Who*, Gardner could instantly see how it might fit into her remit at BBC Wales.

"They were thinking about *Doctor Who* and were thinking about Russell, and it would need a home, and it made sense, strategically. I was focused on network development; it made sense that this show should come out of BBC Wales and be made in Wales."

Jane Tranter explains her thinking behind wanting to place the show under Gardner's control at BBC Wales.

"I knew I had to make it in a studio somewhere," she points out. "I knew Russell was doing it. I needed more material shot outside of London. I thought it could go to Manchester; I was going to go to Manchester with it, to put it in a studio there. Then I thought, why am I doing that? A studio's a studio – why don't we just use

"RUSSELL. DOCTOR WHO. WE'RE DOING IT"

a studio in Wales? Because Russell's Welsh and why wouldn't that be a good idea? Julie Gardner had, I think, just recently been made Head of Drama for BBC Wales, and I knew that she had worked with Russell at ITV. I asked her if she wanted to do it. She said she had to have a think about it, which actually meant that she rushed off to watch lots of old *Doctor Who*. She wasn't at all sure, because she hadn't seen very much. So she watched lots and loved it, and spoke to Russell. And, of course, being Julie she became the biggest cheerleader – the most ferocious leader you could have, really."

Speaking to *Doctor Who Magazine* in 2013, Davies agreed with the early September dating of Gardner's meeting with Tranter, explaining that he could place it because when Gardner called him immediately afterwards, he was on holiday in France. There is a minor discrepancy here, however, as in that same *Doctor Who Magazine* piece Jane Tranter says that her offer to Gardner of making *Doctor Who* at BBC Wales came during a phone conversation. However, Gardner's recollection of the meeting being a face-to-face one is backed up by comments she made much nearer the time, in 2005, when she told the magazine: "That came about when I went to my first formal meeting with Jane Tranter, in the first week of September 2003."

Either way, despite his love of the show and his previous campaigns to the BBC about reviving it, Gardner remembers that there was still some doubt in Davies' mind.

"I called him immediately, and it's one of those calls that changes everything," she says. "What I remember of that call is a mix of emotions. I think there was joy, curiosity – lots of questioning. Then a moment of, 'I need to think about this, and yes, please do talk to [my agent] Bethan.'"

Davies' memory of the call is slightly different. Interviewed for a documentary in 2013, he described how Gardner initially spoke for some time about Tranter being willing for them to bring *Casanova* to the BBC, before eventually moving on to the subject of *Doctor Who*.

"We've talked about that moment subsequently," Gardner

continues. "He was always going to do it. But there's still that moment of... you want something really badly. You've said very strongly that you want to do this. It's something that has made you the writer you are today, or started that journey to becoming this great writer. The moment it's offered to you is also quite a serious moment, I think. I always felt on that call that he was going to do it, but he needed time to process it."

When Davies had told *Cult Times* magazine in 2000 that he would "rather die" than produce at the BBC, he was clearly not being serious. But it was true that, within the industry, it could be seen as a retrograde step for a writer at Davies' level to go and work on an in-house production for the BBC, as he explained to Steven Moffat when they interviewed one another for *Doctor Who Magazine* in 2020:

> "It's hard to understand from outside the industry, but for a freelancer to go from the independent sector to in-house BBC is unheard of. And let's be honest, for very successful freelancers, like you, me and Chris Chibnall... never! I've been trying to think of another show where that happens. It's just not done. It means ceding control and copyright and authorship to a higher power. It's a career in reverse. And I had massive doubts about working within the BBC, because everyone said it was full of censorship, restrictions and red tape."

So what if Davies *hadn't* wanted to work in-house at the BBC? Or if there hadn't been somewhere in-house which seemed like the right fit for making *Doctor Who*? Much of the BBC's drama output was being made by independent companies by 2003, and indeed the Corporation had indicated that this was where any future for the show would almost certainly lie when it came off the air in 1989. Could *Doctor Who* have been made by an indie on its 21st Century return?

Jane Tranter doesn't see why not – but she also doesn't think many of the independent companies around at the time would have been willing to take a risk on it.

"Yeah, for sure, but why would you?" she suggests. "Why would you do that? I mean, definitely in the right hands – an indie who really loved genre. But I think there was a feeling that it was potentially a very high-risk project. Today, there wouldn't be an indie in the world who wouldn't go, 'Fine, I'll take it!' But at the time, the indie landscape was very different. They were all doing interesting work with well-known writers and weren't going to take *that* on board. It was interesting – one for them to sit around and watch us fall flat on our faces. I think it needed to be done by a group of people who really wanted and needed it, as opposed to an indie who just didn't need it in that way."

Julie Gardner, however, doesn't believe that the Corporation would have been prepared to entrust a show of such heritage to outsiders at that time

"The BBC was never going to make it any other way than in-house," she insists. "It's too important a title for them – it's too symbolic of the BBC's history. So it was always going to have to be in-house, and Russell's love and innate understanding of the show meant he was always going to have to produce it – no question."

The time may not have been right for independently-produced *Doctor Who* at this point. But when it did eventually happen, it would end up with Tranter and Gardner running the company concerned. In September 2021 their own production company Bad Wolf were announced as the new co-producers of *Doctor Who* alongside the BBC, coming on board with an also-returning Russell T Davies.

Back in 2003, the fact that the show wasn't being made in London – and therefore had a degree of distance from the hierarchy of the BBC – was reassuring for Davies. As was the fact that Julie Gardner would be overseeing it, as he explained in *Doctor Who Magazine* 551:

"Away from London, with Julie. Perfect. I knew she

could handle the BBC side of it. And I was right – within months, she understood the arcane stuff like procurement rules and what qualifies as a substantive post. Another language! Without her, it's 50-50 whether I'd have taken the job."

"But Russell is a great producer," Gardner insists. "As much as he's a great writer, he's a great, great producer, and he really does understand the industry. I guess there was a perfect storm of considerations. Would he have done that for any other show? No. It was his profound love of *Doctor Who*, wanting to get it made, that made him work differently."

Writers, particularly of Davies' standing, have always held a lot of power in British television drama – but perhaps more so over authored one-offs and serials, rather than over the direction of a returning drama series. However, Jane Tranter explains that she had no doubt such an arrangement was the right one when it came to Davies and *Doctor Who*.

"There was never any question that Russell would be an executive producer of *Doctor Who*," she says. "'Showrunner' is a word that's bandied around; it really comes from a very significant place in American television history, and has grown into what it is today in America. But when we talk about people being showrunners in the UK, it's still not entirely the same. Not because the influence or the editorial decision-making isn't there, but in the US it's different because you've also got a lot of practical and budgetary and production responsibilities as well.

"Russell is really the only person in the UK I've ever worked with who's taken on more of a US showrunner mantle with all the responsibility. He was clearly very ably partnered by Julie Gardner in every single way, but he was responsible for everything. If there was a budget or schedule issue, he would alter a script accordingly, or he'd look at what the issue was and change the budget or schedule accordingly. He was over every piece of merchandising, every bit of everything – and why would you not? Why would you want that to be any other way? Because he just knew more than the rest of us and was better than the rest of us, so there was never an argument on that."

"It was a hybrid system," is Gardner's explanation. "We didn't have a writers' room running for weeks and weeks. We didn't have that team writing, that is very American; we didn't anoint Russell as a person who had to carry everything, in the way that American showrunners have to carry everything. We did a kind of slightly American-British hybrid, where he was – without question – the creative lead. If we want to use the word showrunner I actually would, but he always called himself 'head writer'. He was head writer and exec producer. There was not a part of *Doctor Who* that he didn't oversee."

Despite the fact that the series would be produced by BBC Wales and not by the central Drama Series department, Mal Young still ended up joining the initial team as an executive producer to help oversee the project. His recollection is that there was no argument about where the show should be produced or by whom, in spite of Drama Series' short-lived attempt to get the show off the ground with Davies five years earlier.

"We got Russell lined up," Young says. "We always promised that, if it was going to happen, it would be him. Then Jane called me and she said they really wanted to go big on this – she would put all of her support behind it, and it would become a big piece that could go across all the departments. But she was really keen that it went through Wales because, to be quite frank, there were no dramas coming out of Wales. I don't think that's a big secret – there was nothing. The spend that we were committing to Northern Ireland or Scotland wasn't matched by Wales. It was a harder task to find that. Julie was put in there to revitalise that.

"So suddenly the stars are being lined up, everyone's in the right place. I want to do it, the rights have come clean, Jane wants to do it. We all said, we're all going to need to dive in and help this, to make it happen. Because it could be a disaster – it could be our *Eldorado*! Or it could be huge. But we're going to have to get it right, because it's going to be high-profile, picked-over.

"Jane said to me, would I object if we put it through BBC

Wales? Because Julie's taking over there, it would be a great big production, and it would revitalise BBC Wales.

"I was a big fan of shooting in Birmingham or outside of London because your money could just go further. I come from the North – I get it. I said, 'That's genius, and it'll qualify for being Welsh because it's Russell!' Because it had to qualify, in those days. We had Russell, so it ticked all the boxes, everything was in. I said no, I don't have any objection to all, anything that brings it back on air, basically. So off we popped."

Julie Gardner is full of praise for Young's role in the setting-up of the series.

"Mal Young is a kind of quiet hero in the background, because he was definitely having these conversations," she says. "He was lobbying to bring back *Doctor Who*, and he was always so gracious, because I had never executive produced a show. I'd never set up a thirteen-part series. Mal had *decades* of experience in returning series. Yet the show came to Wales. Mal was an exec on the show, and was really there – quite rightly – because, could I pull it off?

"I'd started my career at the BBC, but as a script reader and script editor. I'd never worked at a senior level at the BBC, had never run a long show. I'm running a department. It's a show that has all kinds of weird kinks that need to be sorted out. So Mal was almost a safety valve. I never really felt this at the time, weirdly; I kind of knew it, but I never felt the weight of it. But he was there, I think, partly because he'd lobbied for the show; partly because he had all this experience; and, as I say, like a safety valve. He was always so gracious, because I think it would have been very difficult to get between Russell and me. Because we were already a duo by that time, and there was so much work on *Doctor Who*. My workload was absolute insanity, but Mal was so fantastic."

Gardner does, however, say that Young is mistaken in his recollection that the programme had to in some way 'qualify' as being Welsh enough to be made at BBC Wales.

"I think it was very helpful that both Russell and I were Welsh, but I don't think that was the critical thing. I think the critical thing for the nations at that time was, where is something made?

"RUSSELL. DOCTOR WHO. WE'RE DOING IT"

And how is the money controlled? Your money comes from the centre [of the BBC], but it's controlled locally."

Gardner was aware that placing *Doctor Who*'s production away from England was seen as an unusual decision at the time:

"Because England had so many shows, I think it would have been very difficult, very strange for such a big show to come out of England," she says. "The balance of commissioning would have been off. We in Wales really needed a network show. Scotland was doing fine. Northern Ireland was doing okay. Wales just didn't have anything network."

For Menna Richards, the woman in overall charge of BBC Wales, the important issue wasn't so much if or how Wales ended up being represented on-screen in the series. It was more important to ensure that bringing *Doctor Who* to Wales would provide work and opportunities for those in the industry locally.

"I remember being very firm at the time, that if it was being done in BBC Wales, we had to use as many BBC Wales and local independent skills as possible," says Richards. "I didn't go to BBC Wales in order to have stuff shipped in from London – I went in order to create a base of talent and future employment locally. It was probably quite challenging for some of my London colleagues, but it absolutely was possible to achieve it, and we did.

"One of my very clear messages to the staff was, I want us to be the best at what we do. We have a responsibility to our audiences in Wales to represent Wales as far as we can on the network, but that doesn't mean that we are exclusively about telling stories about Wales.

"There was a sense in the BBC that the nations should basically make programmes for the nations. That was never my view and actually, the two Director-Generals that I worked with, Mark Thompson and Greg Dyke, both felt very strongly that this should not be the future of the BBC. That it shouldn't be the nations just simply speaking to the nations."

Gardner agrees and suggests that *Doctor Who* helped to change the perception of BBC Wales within the rest of the BBC structure.

"I think geography makes a difference," she says. "It's hard to remember now, because BBC Wales has been so successful across all genres in network television – it's very hard to really bring to life what that time was like. When I first became Head of Drama and the network cupboard was bare, I remember very distinctly what people would pitch to me as what should be a 'Wales' drama.

"They tended to be one of two things. They would either be something warm and lovely set in Hay-on-Wye, almost the cliché, 'Oh, he's a bookseller by day and a sleuth by night, and it's feelgood and it's going to look gorgeous.' Or it was, 'They're closing the pit, and we're going to have terrible social and economic distress'. Those were the two buckets of projects that generally came through the door. I think that was the great triumph of the BBC putting *Doctor Who* into Wales with Russell – it just blew all that away immediately; because there was a show that had so much swagger and life and joy and affirmation and humanity to it. But it could also tell proper life-or-death stories; sometimes quite *moral* stories. It made BBC Wales look like you could be entertaining – you could tell almost anything.

Gardner echoes Russell T Davies' comments about having a greater sense of independence by placing the show away from the central part of the BBC in London.

"That sense of distance is helpful, and it's not like I was running a rogue operation, a black ops kind of thing! But you were able to just get on with the work. You're away from the conversation. Sometimes, in truth, I think the fact that I didn't know much about BBC management, and I was never really that interested, worked in my favour. I could just get stuff done. I think the great trick that Menna Richards and Jane Tranter played was they gave me the confidence to think I was running everything! Whereas I suspect, behind-the-scenes, there was a lot of management going on and the appropriate things getting done. But they really gave me the space to look after Russell and make him think anything was possible."

Gardner recalls there being some initial scepticism within the ranks of BBC Wales about taking on *Doctor Who*:

"What I got was some people in Wales feeling it wasn't *really* going to be a Welsh show," she says. "There was a paranoia early on that the BBC was driving shows down the M4. I would tackle that attitude head-on; I couldn't bear it – it was just such nonsense. What makes *Doctor Who* a BBC Wales show? Well, it's made in Cardiff, largely. Of course, there's always a mix of crew. But there was enormous job creation on that show, with Russell as lead writer, with me. BBC Wales were responsible for that budget, and that show, and the delivery of it. You'd never ask that question in Scotland or Northern Ireland.

"There's always a proper debate to be had about representation. I would always say, *Doctor Who*'s not able to do everything that this department needs. Of course, we are going to tell the local stories. But my argument would always be in episode three, the Victorian Charles Dickens episode, where you have Eve Myles and a cast of Welsh actors telling a story based in Cardiff, based in Wales, broadcasting to an audience of nine million. That's representation."

All of that, however, was still to come. When the deal was finally done for Russell T Davies to write new *Doctor Who* in September 2003, very little was decided at that early stage. Gardner and Davies were already pushing for a run of as many as thirteen episodes – unusually long for a non-soap BBC drama at this time, particularly for its first series. "This might be the last series of *Doctor Who* ever," was how Davies later described his thinking, wanting to cover as many different types of stories as possible.

Following the initial announcement, there was speculation about a six-episode series, and this was the number mentioned in the original *Telegraph* interview with Heggessey. The number had possibly come from her, although it wasn't presented as a direct quote. It's a number that would make sense, though, as that was a common allocation for many British drama series at the time, at least for a first run. The spy drama *Spooks*, for example, had started with six episodes in 2002, before its popularity earned it a ten-part run for its second series the following year.

Davies, however, was already thinking bigger. The initial *Doctor Who Magazine* report on the show's return mentions the possibility of an eight-or-twelve episode series – figures almost certainly given to them by Davies, given his close contact with the editorial team at the time. Julie Gardner agrees he was thinking of a higher number from very early on.

"The BBC wasn't talking about thirteen," she says. "It was Russell who went in and said, we want to do thirteen. I think there was initial talk about eight, or maybe we could be very bold and do ten. Then it was like, no – it is just such a big show, it's such a big effort to mount this, if we're going to do it, we need thirteen. I don't think he was already thinking about his arc across that thirteen at that point. It's almost like, you're going to go down fighting, you're going to crash and burn – it's either going to be a huge success or a total disaster. You just didn't know."

This was an attitude which both Jane Tranter and Mal Young enthusiastically supported:

"There's no point in doing it if you're going to do it quietly," says Tranter. "You can only do it if you do it with real conviction, and I really, really believed in it. I'm not saying I believed that it was going be the huge success that it was, but I really believed that we could make – that Russell would make – *Doctor Who* into something which would be an exceptional piece of television; that it would be there as something high-quality, should audiences want to watch it."

"I was particularly pushing for it to be thirteen forty-fives," says Young. "I was very much leaning into what it used to be like. Here's the show your dad used to watch when he was younger sitting on his sofa, and he can now sit on the sofa with you."

The 45-minute length of the episodes seems to have been locked in at this early stage, despite it being an unusual length for BBC dramas of the time. "When I walked into our first meeting, it was six episodes, 45 minutes long, early Saturday nights," Davies recalled in 2006. Mal Young explains that the nature of the Saturday evening schedules compared to weeknights allowed for this uncommon runtime for a BBC drama.

"Saturday night was more fluid," he says. "You could keep to 45 minutes, which meant it could sell to outside of the UK. Because it's hard to sell a 59-minute show – well, not anymore because of streamers, who are all running 59-minute shows now, or 65."

Davies later recalled that in their early discussions Tranter had initially thought the stories would all be two-parters, preserving the cliffhanger element which had been a constant throughout *Doctor Who*'s history – although she had been happy for him to not go with that idea. The official commission for the new series came on Wednesday September 24 2003. Things would gradually pick up pace over the coming weeks and months, as Davies put together the first outline document for the series and the first big meeting took place on December 8. Davies then began working full-time on the show in early 2004.

However, before all of that, the commission would have to be announced. The news could not be held for too long, as the more work that was done, the more people would be made aware of *Doctor Who*'s return; and, inevitably, rumours and gossip would begin to spread, as Julie Gardner explains:

"I remember sitting on a big secret and being very excited, but I don't think I ever felt we needed to sit on this longer, or that it had to be controlled. Because you just can't. You know as soon as a title's on a development list at the BBC, and you're having senior management meetings and you're talking about budgets and you're thinking about how you crew up – there is no way something is going to remain quiet."

Given the number of *Doctor Who* fans working in the industry, the news did gradually become an open secret in certain sections of fandom. However, this was not the case generally among the majority of fans – to most of whom, the eventual announcement was to come as a complete surprise.

14

MIDNIGHT

PERHAPS NO SINGLE NEWS STORY better encapsulates the frustration of the monotonous regularity with which rumours of *Doctor Who*'s return appeared in the early 2000s than one published by the show's official website in January 2001. Under the headline "Sean Bean Isn't the Doctor", BBC Online's team wearily reported:

> "Daft rumour of the month is that Sean Bean has been cast as the Doctor in a proposed film/TV series/t-shirt. See last month's equally daft 'announcement' of a whole series of Dalek films.
>
> The word from BBC Publicity is quite clear (and, it must be said, they're starting to sound bored and tired): When there is definite news of a *Doctor Who* film, TV series, or whatever, it will be announced quite clearly and firmly as soon as possible...
>
> Here on the Cult site we're just praying that something definite happens and soon. It'll put an end to these silly and, for the fans, upsetting tabloid rumours. For one thing, we are tired of wading through endless e-mails saying 'Don't you think you should announce that Sean Bean is the Doctor on your website?' We aren't because he's not. If he is, we'll tell you. Promise."

One of the reasons that rumours such as this seemed to spread so often can be explained by the yearning that so many fans felt for *Doctor Who* to return. Even after years of disappointment, many were prepared to cling to any shred of hope. Despite there being hundreds of existing episodes of *Doctor Who*, an ever-expanding library of original novels, audio productions and countless other tie-ins, there was a sense among fans that this was not enough. Over a decade after leaving regular production on television, to the devoted, *Doctor Who* remained resolutely present-tense.

Many newspapers and websites were happy to take advantage of that yearning, publishing any unfounded rumour to either fill space or attract the extra clicks from eager fans. For example, the e-mail newsletter Popbitch, as reported on by the BBC website in October 2002: "Timothy Spall is the Doctor, erm not. News that the *Auf Wiedersehen, Pet* star was about to step aboard the TARDIS spread like wildfire after it was leaked by the gossip e-mail newsletter Popbitch... We've checked with all the high-ups and they've confirmed it's bunkum."

Even the official site sounded tired of it all.

Doctor Who fans also tended to pay more-than-average attention to stories about what was going on in the media generally, and at the BBC specifically, looking for signs that often weren't there. It was just something that *Doctor Who* fans did.

As a 1999 *Doctor Who Magazine* editorial put it, "While watching a TV drama, a *Doctor Who* fan will say, 'Ooh, it's shot on film.' Real people can't do this, and don't care. *Doctor Who* fans can name the Controller of BBC One. *Doctor Who* fans know the difference between the BBC and BBC Worldwide. Real people don't."

Clayton Hickman, *Doctor Who Magazine*'s editor at the time of the show's return, explains why he thinks that so many fans took an interest in the media and television at large.

"I think part of it is because *Doctor Who* was the first franchise... God, I hate that word... where it really dug deep into the story behind the programme," he says. "*Doctor Who Weekly* was a unique thing, then it became *Doctor Who Monthly*. But even in those very early days, it was delving into the behind-the-scenes stories – who the writers were, who the directors were, who the producers were; who the guest cast were, how they were all related to each other, how they got on. Even before then, in the early Seventies you had *The Making of Doctor Who* book. That was not a normal thing. You might have got a little feature in an Annual about how your favourite TV show came to the screen – but you didn't get a whole book telling you what a production unit manager does, what a script editor does.

"We were all incredibly versed in media studies by *Doctor Who*. The production of *Doctor Who* was a fascination for us. There was such an industry around *Doctor Who*, such a level of detail and analysis – and appetite for that analysis.

"So when there wasn't a new season to speculate about – which writers are coming back, which directors are coming back, will an old enemy come back? – you've got a series with, at that point, 26 years of backstory. When you're really into fandom, it's fascinating. You want to piece everything together like a big jigsaw puzzle – you want to know *everything*!

"When *Doctor Who* was cut off, everyone just felt a bit bereft. It's like cutting off a drug supply to an addict, really. They go a bit frothing and frenzied."

This passion and interest had, of course, also led to many fans making careers for themselves in the media, which was one of the reasons why *Doctor Who* was now able to come back. As Russell T Davies put it in a piece he wrote for *Doctor Who Magazine* a few months before the new series was announced:

> "I meet more and more *Doctor Who* fans in this industry – and not just those familiar names of fandom... I've seen a drunk *Emmerdale* writer clutching his Ice Warriors box set; I've had a high-falutin' executive send me e-mails quoting Omega... Massive creativity. And I have come to tell you now: *Doctor Who* made us clever.
>
> We were brought up to fill in the gaps. We see foam and imagine the creature inside; we know that one pipe represents a vast array... We're not blind; we can still laugh at, and love, the Sellotape and plywood. All these versions play at once: we can see what is, what went

THE LONG GAME

> wrong, and what was meant to be simultaneously. And that's all TV-makers ever do – stare at plain paper and empty grids, in the hope of alchemy. No wonder the business is full of us. We've all been making TV since the age of three."

It was among those fans working within the television industry, or in other jobs connected to it or to *Doctor Who* specifically, that news of the impending return of the show began to spread as September 2003 wore on. Tom Spilsbury was Clayton Hickman's assistant editor at *Doctor Who Magazine* at the time. He recalls when they first heard the news, ahead of the official announcement on the 26th:

"Nine days earlier – it was the 17th, I think. Clayton and I and [*Doctor Who Magazine* comic strip writer] Scott Gray and Conrad Westmaas, who was my predecessor as the assistant editor – he'd left after only a few months to pursue his acting career, and had gone off to be Paul McGann's companion in the audios – the four of us, we'd had a night out together. We'd gone to see a play called *Brenda Bly: Teen Detective*, a really fun evening which we'd enjoyed a lot. At the time, Clayton and I both lived quite close together, so we were getting the same train back home from London Bridge.

"We said goodbye to the others, but Clayton got a message from Mark Gatiss. It wasn't my message so I'm paraphrasing; it said something along the lines of, '*Shalka* DVD pulled because of Russell's new series. What do you know?' I remember him mentioning the *Shalka* project being pulled; for some reason that was a little trigger that something was going on."

Clayton Hickman takes up the story.

"I came out of the theatre to find a voice-mail – I think it was a voice-mail, not a text message at that stage – from Mark Gatiss. Saying, 'I've heard rumours Russell T Davies may be doing *Doctor Who*. Find out! Find out!'

"Tom and I went to London Bridge station, waiting for the train, and I asked him if I should just phone Russell? Because I'd been friends with Russell since about 1995 or '96, and he always e-mailed the office. Every time we had a new issue we always had a big chat. So I decided to phone him!"

Spilsbury remembers then piecing together the realisation that *Doctor Who* was actually coming back from hearing Hickman's side of the ensuing conversation.

"I remember Clayton phoning Russell and hearing his side of the conversation, and it becoming obvious what it was all about. I was listening to Clayton saying things like, 'Oh so it is real then? Will the TARDIS still be a police box? What's the theme tune going to be like?' All these ridiculous questions! We were both standing up on the train – it was one of the last trains back, late at night, so it was quite full. We got off at St John's Station, which was the one midway between both of our flats. He was still on the phone as we got off the train, the conversation was still going."

All these years on, Hickman is happy to share his memories of the conversation he had with Davies that night.

"As I recall it, I dialled the number, and he went, 'Clayton Hickman, come to the front!' Which is always what he said to me, because it was something that Anthony Ainley said to me at a convention once. He was horrible to me, Anthony Ainley, for no reason, just for power; and I told this to Russell and he laughed for ten minutes. So he always answered the phone, 'Clayton Hickman, come to the front!'

"I said I'd heard on the grapevine, and he went, 'Yes?' I said that he might be bringing back *Doctor Who*? All I'd heard was this thing from Gatiss – I had no idea what was going on. He went, 'Ooo! Ooo, you're quick! Ooo, it's a relief to talk about this!' He said he was! He didn't go into much detail, he said he'd speak to me tomorrow and we'd have a proper chat. Because this was getting quite late at night.

"I remember putting the phone down. Tom was standing next to me, looking at me, and I just told him it was true! I remember us both walking away from the station and sort of skipping! Going woo-hoo-hoo!

"I got home and I phoned Gatiss and said, 'It's fucking true!' This was almost a midnight phone call. Everything else, apart from that moment, is kind of a blur. I can't remember what then happened, or when things were announced.

"I'd been friends with Russell for ages. I'd not long taken over the editorship of *Doctor Who Magazine*, and the person who was bringing *Doctor Who* back after these two strange, frightening false starts with *Shalka* and with Dan Freedman was my mate. Well, bloody hell, strike me pink!"

Many fans had become jaded about rumours of any return, due to all the exaggerations of the past. But the flip side was that this also gave them the experience to know when something felt different; when it wasn't in the same category as some wild speculation about Sean Bean or Timothy Spall being announced as the next Doctor; when it was, suddenly and wonderfully, real.

Which was how it felt to those who were around in the early hours of the morning on Friday September 26 2003.

While the news may have hit the offices of *Doctor Who Magazine* and been spreading in certain other areas of professional fandom, it doesn't appear to have leaked more widely. There were no rumours or speculation about the show's return in the usual sci-fi magazines or online. A look at the September 25 2003 archives of the rec.arts.drwho newsgroup, and the moderated version which had then recently been launched, shows that some of the active topics that day included a query about the availability of the 1993 Children in Need special *Dimensions in Time*; the distribution of BBC Books' *Doctor Who* novels in the USA; and some reactions to a post about the 1978 story *The Power of Kroll*. But no hints or rumours of any kind about a new series announcement.

Shortly after midnight, that all started to change.

The very first post in the online *Doctor Who* fan world reacting to the news appears to have been made by Steve Freestone on the rec.arts.drwho.moderated newsgroup at eighteen minutes past midnight on September 26, relaying a report he'd heard on the London radio station LBC:

> "LBC have announced breaking news of the return of *Doctor Who* in a series scripted by Russell T Davies."

By this point, newsgroups had been largely superseded as the main medium for *Doctor Who* discussion by the Outpost Gallifrey forum. Over the following two-and-a-half hours, the sole response Freestone's post attracted was a sceptical "Uh huh? Got a link?"

Over on Outpost Gallifrey, however, things became rather more active when, at 12.53am UK time that Friday morning, someone under the username 'uagibbo' posted a thread with the maniacally-excited title "NEW SERIES IS COMING!", relaying news shared in the forum's chatroom, clearly typed hastily in some excitement:

> "New series in tomorrows telegraph 26/09/03 [sic] mentioned in forum chat room today 25/09/03. Russel T davies in command. OMG!!!!"

Lee Mansfield, who was credited with breaking the story in the Outpost Gallifrey chatroom, was one of those fans who *had* heard whispers of a news story about to hit and had been looking out for it. As he explains, however, he had no idea quite what this announcement was going to be.

"I do recall the rush of elation when the news broke that night," he says. "I must have had some kind of notion that 'something' was about to break as I stayed up late, trawling the *Doctor Who* and TV forums and news sites. When I saw it pop up somewhere, I rushed into the Outpost Gallifrey chat to share the good news with fans there. Everyone was excited and deliriously happy. It is no slight exaggeration to say it is one of my happiest memories as a fan. I had only just lost my father at that time so I had been in quite a dark place; that night of the announcement was probably the first time I had felt a sense of optimism and enthusiasm for the future again."

Over the following years, *Doctor Who* fans would become used to stories about the show breaking at or just after midnight, as news services published stories they had prepared from press releases issued under embargo until a specific date. BBC Wales had in fact issued such a press release earlier that evening, strictly embargoed until one minute past midnight on September 26. *The Daily*

THE LONG GAME

Telegraph's website had clearly put the story up as soon as they were able after 12.00am, as the full text from the online version was pasted into the Outpost Gallifrey thread by a user called 'emberposse' two minutes after the first post.

The Telegraph, of course, weren't actually reacting to a press release – this was their own exclusive story. As Russell T Davies later explained to *Doctor Who Magazine*, it had been planned and arranged that Lorraine Heggessey would reveal the news in her interview with the newspaper. Its early edition would have been available, in London at least, well before midnight – and may have been where LBC picked their story up from.

On the *Telegraph*'s front page, tucked away near the bottom alongside a photograph of a rather droopy-looking Dalek, was the small headline "Guess Who's Coming Back". Promoting a full article on page three, the small piece on the cover read:

> "14 years after it last sent children scurrying behind the sofa on Saturday evening, *Doctor Who* is finally coming back to BBC One. In the most eagerly anticipated comeback in television history, channel bosses have commissioned a new series to be written by the creator of the homosexual drama *Queer As Folk*."

The full article, the one which was also reproduced on the *Telegraph*'s website, was written by their media editor Tom Leonard. Under the headline "*Doctor Who* Ready to Come Out of the TARDIS for Saturday TV Series", it read in part:

> "After aeons drifting hopelessly lost in the space/time continuum, *Doctor Who* is finally coming back to Earth. In a move that heralds the most eagerly anticipated comeback in television history, BBC One said yesterday that it is developing a new series of the sci-fi classic.
>
> The BBC hopes that *Doctor Who*... will once more become a fixture of Saturday early evening viewing.
>
> But in a development that may alarm purists, the

new series is being written by Russell T Davies, the creator of *Queer As Folk*, the controversial Channel 4 drama about gay life in Manchester... Although Davies says he wants to 'introduce the character to a modern audience', Lorraine Heggessey, the controller of BBC One, insisted yesterday that she did not expect a gay Doctor Who.

She stressed that Davies had been chosen primarily because he is an 'absolute *Doctor Who* fanatic' who had asked to write a new series...

Ms Heggessey said she had wanted to bring back the series for two years but the rights were held by BBC Worldwide... which has been trying to agree a film deal with a Hollywood studio.

'Worldwide has now agreed that, as they haven't made the film and I've been waiting for two years, it's only right that BBC One should have a crack at making a series,' she said. Davies, who also wrote the critically acclaimed ITV drama [*The*] *Second Coming*, will start writing in the New Year. The series is unlikely to be broadcast before 2005."

Even in 2003, the *Telegraph*'s mention of a "homosexual drama" and questions about "a gay Doctor Who" felt like relics from another age. The paper was certainly wrong when it claimed that Davies' involvement might "alarm purists", given that so many fans had long been aware of his love of the series and touted him as one of the likeliest candidates to helm any possible revival. Indeed, Davies' involvement instantly gave many confidence in the venture and its prospects, as fan Will Hadcroft sums up.

"It was very exciting," he remembers. "I knew that Russell T Davies was a *Doctor Who* fan, I knew he'd written *Damaged Goods*. So I knew it was somebody who understood it and who loved it."

Over on Outpost Gallifrey, those who were still awake in the UK past midnight or in other time zones were trying to take it all in. There was some understandable confusion. Was this project separate to *Scream of the Shalka*? Was it animated or live-action? Would it be six stories or a six-part serial? And, inevitably, caution from those who feared another newspaper filling their pages with baseless speculation. Forum owner Shaun Lyon quickly stepped in to offer some cautious reassurance:

> "Let me just say that I've been inundated with e-mails today about this... and that's after I got an anonymous e-mail a week ago to expect something this week. (I didn't give it much credence at the time.)
>
> This is a real article, and it's really on the *Telegraph* page, and ... let's see where this goes in the next 24 hours. But I have to say that I believe it."

These days, Lyon is happy to admit that he had been given a little advance warning of what was coming.

"I had about 48 hours' notice from friends of mine working at the BBC," he explains. "So by the time the announcement came out I had all my banners and ads ready to go. It felt like a dream, to be honest – I think in those first few days, people still didn't believe it was real. I don't think most of us really thought it was happening until we saw it."

Just before 4.00am UK time, forum member Danny Salter posted a link to a story that had just been put online on the BBC News website. Everyone could relax. *Doctor Who* definitely *was* coming back – because the BBC themselves said so.

There, on the front page of the site's entertainment section – nestled alongside such stories as "50 Cent Takes Glory at Mobos" and "Giant Queen Portrait to be Hung" – and illustrated with another slightly wrong-looking Dalek picture – was the headline "*Doctor Who* Returns to TV", and the teaser: "A new series of cult science fiction drama *Doctor Who* is to be made, 14 years after it was axed."

The story itself was based around the BBC Wales press release, which had been put out under embargo the previous evening by their Head of Press and Publicity, David Cartwright. A second,

MIDNIGHT

more general, press release – including the quotes from Russell T Davies and Mal Young which had been in the BBC Wales release, but not those from Julie Gardner – was issued by the main BBC Press Office later in the day on September 26. This one was interesting, however, for specifically stating that "all rights issues regarding *Doctor Who* have been resolved."

Over on Outpost Gallifrey, as morning broke in the UK and the bedlam continued, Shaun Lyon revealed to those posting on his forum that he'd now had his own private confirmation of the news from an unimpeachable source.

> "I just wanted to add this: Earlier tonight, after I heard, I sent off a congratulatory e-mail to Russell Davies, whom I haven't talked to in quite a while, and just got a nice note back from him. 'All true' as he says... and I can tell he's quite excited about it.
>
> *Doctor Who*'s coming back, yes, that's good news. But... in such good hands as Russell Davies, and under the eyes of a controller of BBC One that actually likes our show (Lorraine Heggessey... our hero!) What an unbelievable bit of great news we have today.
>
> It's a great time to be a *Doctor Who* fan."

The official BBC *Doctor Who* website also joined in the fun and games, finally able to relay the news fans had craved for so long, rather than having to wearily dismiss another wild rumour. They perhaps summed-up the feelings of fans all over the world best, with a little animated message cycling a few short sentences on their front page. It read:

> "*Doctor Who* is coming back. Saturdays, BBC One, 2005. It's by Russell T Davies. Yes, it is real, no you're not dreaming. Now sit down, have another biscuit, it's a special day."

The news was now everywhere – being discussed on radio

programmes, on breakfast television, and of course online. And not just in the UK, either; the Outpost Gallifrey news page collated dozens of online news stories about the announcement from across the world.

Even the *Doctor Who Magazine* team found themselves making the news. Having heard about the impending new series earlier in the month, they had completed their latest issue and sent it off to print – only to have to hurriedly stop the presses that Friday to reflect the official announcement. Then assistant editor Tom Spilsbury, recalls the excitement.

"If you look at the dates, we knew that this was happening, and we already must have been fairly close to finishing that issue at the time of that train journey and the phone call hearing all about it. The issue wasn't finished, but because it wasn't an official announcement at that point there was no question about including any of that in the magazine.

"Anyway, we did finish the issue. Then pretty much the day after we'd sent it to the printers, we saw the official announcements on September 26. They hadn't printed it at that stage, so it was possible to make some changes. We didn't change the cover picture, but we did add a little flash in a circle. Clayton also made some changes to his editorial on whatever page that was, and of course the little bit in Gallifrey Guardian – that all swapped around slightly. It probably affected about three or four different pages – the rest of the magazine was able to stay exactly as it was."

Such was the interest in the return of *Doctor Who* that the BBC's regional *South East Today* television news programme sent a reporter to film a piece with the magazine's team that afternoon.

"*South East Today* was always quite keen to talk to us because we were local – they basically had their office down the bottom of the hill opposite the Tunbridge Wells train station," recalls Spilsbury. "So they asked if they could come and interview us and get our reaction and so on. We said yes, but could they leave it until the afternoon? Because that morning we were really busy, trying to redo all the pages that we then had to get done very quickly!

"After we'd sorted all the stop-press stuff for the printers, they came in the afternoon and basically asked if we could re-create what we did that morning. So Clayton and I sort of pretended to be sitting around a monitor – not really how it worked at all, but the way something might look on TV is never really how things actually happen. We acted out how we might have reacted for the purposes of the cameras! They got a few quotes from Clayton, it was quite funny. I think it must have gone out on the local news that evening – that clip probably does still exist somewhere."

For the fans, it was a day of tremendous excitement. But how did it feel for those at the centre of it all, for whom the hard work was only just beginning?

"Oh, it was completely daunting!" is Julie Gardner's verdict. "I had the good fortune to not really know what I was getting into, because I wasn't steeped in that world. I had a vague inkling of how important and confusing and difficult it was going to be, but I didn't really know. I remember the excitement – but also the terror – of when the show was announced as coming back. The press just went completely nuts! It was absolutely everywhere!

"I think the most instructive moment was when a tabloid ran a story about who should be cast as the Doctor, and Paul Daniels was a suggestion! I remember looking at that being very confused. I mean, I loved Paul Daniels – I love a good magician. But I remember Russell and I discussing it; there was a moment of thinking that this was what the show had become, to the press and the outside world. They thought it was like entertainment – they didn't think it was drama. That was one of the things that would really, *really* need to be addressed."

For the woman who'd made the announcement, the reaction that the news had received prompted a mixture of emotions.

"I was really pleased, but I was also very nervous. Because of its heritage, there was a huge burden of expectation. In one way, it felt like an obvious thing to do. In another, it felt extremely risky.

"You know it has a big fan base, a very strong core of die-hard fans who are completely hooked on the show and know everything about it. So you don't want to let them down – it's got to deliver for them. Then there are the ones who aren't dyed-in-the-wool fans –

the families who remember it; the adults who remember it as part of their childhood; grandparents who remember sitting down with the family watching it. Cosy memories of a day when there were only two channels and that was one of the big shows that you watched. It was a big part of growing up for a lot of people – it ran for a long, long time, it was a mainstay of the BBC One schedule for a long time.

"So the excitement made me nervous, because it's very exposed putting anything on BBC One. Putting anything on Saturday night is even more exposed, and bringing back a much-loved, iconic show is another risk."

Jane Tranter says she was a little taken aback by the amount of attention the newly-announced project received.

"That was a surprising thing, really, about *Doctor Who* – from then onwards, the amount of scrutiny that we had. Who was going to be the Doctor? Were we going to bring the Daleks back? Were the BBC going to decommission it before I'd even got to make it?"

The latter point could, in fact, have happened if history had gone slightly differently. When Greg Dyke had to leave the BBC in January 2004, he was succeeded later that year by Mark Thompson – a former Director of Television at the corporation, who returned after having spent two years as the chief executive of Channel 4. When Thompson took over as Director-General, he actually asked Tranter if the *Doctor Who* project could be stopped.

"He asked if it was possible to stop it," Tranter recalls. "I told him, 'No, no, no! We are way too far gone!'"

Tranter felt that the reason for Thompson asking her to bring the project to a halt was came from elsewhere within the BBC. At the same time as Dyke had left as Director-General, the BBC's Chairman Gavyn Davies had also resigned because of the same controversy. The Chairman is a non-executive role with no official involvement in programming matters, but Tranter claims that Thompson's desire to stop *Doctor Who* came from the fact that the vacant Chairmanship had been filled by someone with a known antipathy towards the programme – Michael Grade.

But, as Heggessey puts it, "Well, it was too late by then!"

The reason it was too late was the fact that Heggessey herself had announced the news so firmly and so publicly. It would have been difficult, and embarrassing, for the BBC to backtrack on the commission, even if they had wanted to. This was something of which Russell T Davies was well aware, as he later explained to *Doctor Who Magazine* in 2013:

> "Once it was announced in the press by the Controller of BBC One there was no turning back. That interview was huge, the moment that cemented the entire future of *Doctor Who*, although there were still a lot of battles to be won."

But won they were. The decision had been taken, and the process – at long last, after all of those years of rumours and disappointments – had finally, genuinely begun. A process which would lead to *Doctor Who* returning to BBC One on Saturday March 26 2005, exactly eighteen months after the official announcement of its recommissioning.

What a return it was, too – *Doctor Who* was not only brought back, but it was brought back as an *enormous* success; one that was to usher in an extraordinary new period of popularity for the programme, internationally as well as in the United Kingdom, with its future on television secured for many more years to come.

That, of course, is another story, but one which – oddly, as this book is prepared for print – has come full circle. Almost exactly eighteen years on from the announcement of *Doctor Who*'s return, and once again on a final Friday in September, it was revealed that Russell T Davies will take control of a new version of the show – as with the previous announcement, due on screen the year after next, which will be 2023 this time around. As before, he will be working alongside Julie Gardner and Jane Tranter.

Fittingly perhaps for a time travel show, it seems that the events of *Doctor Who*'s past as told here now look set to have an enormous impact on its future, too.

BBC POSITIONS

A SUMMARY OF WHO HELD SOME OF THE KEY POSITIONS in the BBC relevant to this book during the time period covered. Most of these roles, of course, had long histories and other occupants both before and after these points, but a few - the BBC Broadcast and BBC Production chief executive posts, the Director of Programmes/Production role at BBC Production and Alan Yentob's Director of Drama, Entertainment and Children's position - only existed for the durations given below.

CONTROLLER OF BBC ONE
1993-1996: Alan Yentob
1996-1997: Michael Jackson
1997-2000: Peter Salmon
2000-2005: Lorraine Heggessey

DIRECTOR OF TELEVISION
1996-1997: Michael Jackson
1997-2000: Alan Yentob
2000-2002: Mark Thompson
2002-2006: Jana Bennett

CHIEF EXECUTIVE, BBC BROADCAST
1996-1999: Will Wyatt

CHIEF EXECUTIVE, BBC PRODUCTION
1996-1998: Ron Neil
1998-2000: Matthew Bannister

DIRECTOR OF PROGRAMMES (1996–1997, 1999–2000)
DIRECTOR OF PRODUCTION, BBC PRODUCTION (1997–1999)
1996–1997: Alan Yentob
1997–1999: Jana Bennett
1999–2000: Lorraine Heggessey

DIRECTOR-GENERAL OF THE BBC
1993–2000: John Birt
2000–2004: Greg Dyke

DIRECTOR OF DRAMA, ENTERTAINMENT AND CHILDREN'S
2000–2006: Alan Yentob

CONTROLLER OF DRAMA PRODUCTION (1997–00)
CONTROLLER OF DRAMA COMMISSIONING (2000–06)
1997–1999: Colin Adams
1999–2000: Susan Spindler
2000–2006: Jane Tranter

HEAD OF DRAMA SERIES (1996–2000)
CONTROLLER OF CONTINUING DRAMA SERIES (2000–2004)
1996–1997: Jo Wright
1997–2004: Mal Young

HEAD OF DRAMA, BBC WALES
1995–1997: Karl Francis
1997–2000: Pedr James
2000–2003: Matthew Robinson
2003–2009: Julie Gardner

TIMELINE

1996

DECEMBER

Universal Television's rights option on *Doctor Who* is originally due to expire at the end of this month. However, they are able to negotiate a one-year extension on the option with BBC Worldwide. This gives them until the end of 1997 to attempt to find another broadcast partner for the series in the United States.

1997

JULY

Jane Tranter re-joins the BBC from commercial television, to work as an executive producer on single drama projects for BBC One.

SEPTEMBER 2

Peter Salmon is named as the new Controller of BBC One.

OCTOBER

Mal Young is announced as the new Head of Drama Series at BBC Television.

OCTOBER 14

The *Daily Record* newspaper in Scotland reports that the US Sci-Fi Channel is to enter a co-production deal with the BBC for a new series of 30-minute episodes of *Doctor Who*. This turns out to be a groundless rumour, presumably originating from BBC Scotland and the Sci-Fi Channel collaborating on the science fiction serial *Invasion: Earth*, in production at the time and eventually shown in May and June 1998.

THE LONG GAME

DECEMBER 31
With no new broadcast partner having been found, Universal's option on *Doctor Who* following the TV Movie expires, and all rights now revert to the BBC.

1998

MAY 18
At the Cannes Film Festival, the BBC's Head of Film and Single Drama David Thompson comments that a *Doctor Who* feature film is in the early stages of development; remarks widely picked up and reported by the media. *Doctor Who Magazine* subsequently reports that the BBC have been in discussions with Miramax and a company called HAL Films about such a venture.

"MAY OR JUNE"
Patrick Spence, then the Head of Development in the BBC's Drama Series department, recalls that it is around this time when he first comes into contact with Russell T Davies. At the instigation of Davies' friend Tony Wood, a producer in the department, Spence speaks to Davies on the phone about the possibility of rewriting the scripts for the troubled drama series *Harbour Lights*. Davies, however, has no interest in *Harbour Lights*, and says that he would rather be involved with reviving *Doctor Who* – an idea about which Spence is immediately enthusiastic.

Spence recalls this being eight-to-twelve weeks before *Harbour Lights* went into production, which according to a report at the time in *The Sun* newspaper was in August that year.

SOMETIME BETWEEN EARLY SEPTEMBER 1998 AND THE END OF JANUARY 1999
Russell T Davies has his first in-person meeting at the BBC about the possibility of reviving *Doctor Who*, with Patrick Spence.

"Some provisional ideas were discussed," Davies later tells *Doctor Who Magazine*, but during the meeting he expresses concern that the rights to the series may be tied-up, either with Universal or with BBC Films' efforts to make a movie version of the show. The meeting ends after approximately 20 minutes when Davies' friend Tony Wood, who has resigned from the BBC that day, arrives and takes Davies off to a bar.

Wood was still at the BBC in early September 1998 – when the drama series *Sunburn*, which he oversaw, was announced – but had departed by the beginning of February 1999, when it was reported he was setting up an independent production company with support from Channel 4. The day of his resignation, and Davies' face-to-face meeting with Spence, must therefore have occurred within that period. The official partwork *Doctor Who: The Complete History* from 2016 dates the meeting as taking place in December 1998.

Both Spence's head of department Mal Young and BBC One controller Peter Salmon are enthusiastic about the idea of a *Doctor Who* series. However, Spence subsequently discovers that BBC Films are indeed developing a project, and that any TV version will have to wait to see what happens with the film.

1999

"EARLY"

According to *Doctor Who: The Complete History*, Peter Salmon makes further direct contact with Russell T Davies about the *Doctor Who* idea.

FEBRUARY 23

Russell T Davies' drama series *Queer as Folk* begins transmission on Channel 4, with Davies as both writer and – for the first time on a drama he's written – co-producer.

MAY

The film director Paul WS Anderson tells *Total Film* magazine that his next project is likely to be a *Doctor Who* movie.

THE LONG GAME

JUNE

Doctor Who Magazine 279 is published, with the main feature *We're Gonna Be Bigger Than Star Wars!* This takes several fans now working in the TV industry – Russell T Davies, Steven Moffat, Mark Gatiss, Paul Cornell, Gareth Roberts and Lance Parkin – and asks them about how *Doctor Who* could be revived for modern television. "God help anyone in charge of bringing it back," says Davies at the article's conclusion. "What a responsibility!"

AUGUST 29

Mike Phillips of BBC Worldwide tells the *Independent on Sunday* newspaper that they have "made a deal" with Anderson and his producing partner Jeremy Bolt, and are attempting to interest American partners in a potential *Doctor Who* film.

SEPTEMBER

Doctor Who Magazine 283 is published, and in a news article reveals that BBC Films' proposed venture with Paul WS Anderson and Jeremy Bolt has "temporarily sidelined a mooted new television series of *Doctor Who*, which BBC One Controller Peter Salmon had approached Russell T Davies to write... These plans, which were at a very early stage indeed, were put on hold several months ago when it was realised that rights issued precluded their continuation until it is known whether the movie is a 'go' project or not."

NOVEMBER

On November 4, the website of *SFX* magazine reveals that the involvement of Anderson and Bolt in the film project has come to an end.

Doctor Who Magazine 285 claims in a *Gallifrey Guardian* article that the Russell T Davies series had the proposed title *Doctor Who 2000*. Four years later, Davies tells the magazine: "It was certainly never called *Doctor Who 2000* – that title only sprang into existence when the papers somehow got wind of this meeting."

Jane Tranter is promoted to Head of Drama Serials at the BBC.

TIMELINE

2000

JANUARY 28

Greg Dyke officially takes over from John Birt as the new Director-General of the BBC.

MAY 18

Variety publishes an article claiming that the BBC Films are now in discussions with the Mutual Film Company, producers of *Saving Private Ryan*, about a potential *Doctor Who* feature film.

MAY 23

Issue 57 of *Cult Times* contains a small update from Russell T Davies about his discussion with the BBC about a new television version of *Doctor Who*. "I get an e-mail from them every six months saying, 'We haven't forgotten you,' so it might happen," he tells the magazine. But he also adds that he would only write for any such series and not be involved in producing it: "I wouldn't produce it. I would never produce for the BBC, I would rather die."

JUNE 8

Russell T Davies dismisses reports that he is to write the screenplay for a *Doctor Who* film to be directed by *Highlander* director Russell Mulcahy, telling *SFX* magazine: "Russell Mulcahy is actually directing the first three hours of the *Queer as Folk* American remake. So that's how the two Russells have come to be linked!"

JUNE 29

Doctor Who Magazine 293 is published, containing the results of a readers' poll concerning the show's future. One question asks who the readers would like to see producing a new TV series of *Doctor Who* – the joint winners, each with sixteen percent of the vote, are Russell T Davies and Verity Lambert. "Several, in fact, suggested that Lambert and Davies should work on a new series together," the magazine reveals.

THE LONG GAME

SEPTEMBER 13

Lorraine Heggessey is announced as the new Controller of BBC One, replacing Peter Salmon. She will take up the job from November 1.

OCTOBER 12

Jane Tranter is announced as the BBC's new Controller of Drama Commissioning, ultimately responsible for all of the BBC's television drama output.

At the same time, Mal Young's role in the BBC Drama department is upgraded from Head of Drama Series to Controller of Continuing Drama Series.

NOVEMBER 30

Gay.com UK publishes an interview with Russell T Davies, where Davies says of *Doctor Who*: "That was Peter Salmon wanting that, bless him, and now he's no longer Controller of BBC One I expect that's dead. I haven't heard anything for about six months. Apparently, there's a film deal still ticking away, which would stop any television versions, so I think it just had the support of Peter Salmon and I don't know who to talk to now. Lorraine Heggessey, I don't know at all, wouldn't know her to look at her, so I think that's dead."

2001

"AROUND 2000 OR 2001"

Davies has another meeting about *Doctor Who*, with drama department executive Pippa Harris. He uses the recent *Walking With Dinosaurs* to suggest what can now be done with CGI on a television budget, and also suggests an episode involving a version of the *Weakest Link* game show. "I'd just been to New York for the launch of *Queer as Folk* USA. Anne Robinson was plastered all over the city for the American version of the *Weakest Link*," he later tells *Doctor Who Magazine*; The US version of *Queer as Folk* was launched in December 2000. Davies later says of the meeting, "I suspect

TIMELINE

they weren't that interested and used *Doctor Who* as a pretext to talk to me about other projects, but I had plenty of work from ITV and Channel 4. For me, it was *Doctor Who* or nothing."

Given that at the time of his Gay.com interview in November 2000 he thought the project was dead, and that the American *Queer as Folk* debuted in December that year, this meeting was almost certainly in 2001.

JULY 2

The Guardian publishes a feature about the future of Saturday night television, with Lorraine Heggessey among those interviewed. "Heggessey says her programme makers are developing a lot of new Saturday night shows, which she won't talk about... 'I'm looking for things which are a bit different,' she says."

JULY 12

The first episode of the *Doctor Who* audio drama *Death Comes to Time* – originally a rejected radio pilot for BBC Radio 4 – is released on the BBC *Doctor Who* website. It is produced by Dan Freedman.

AUGUST 30

The BBC announces that a full serial of *Death Comes to Time* is to be produced, taking on and concluding the story begun in the pilot episode. It will be made available on the *Doctor Who* website in early 2002.

MID-OCTOBER

The BBC holds a press launch event for new drama *Linda Green* at The Lowry in Manchester. *Linda Green* is produced by Nicola Shindler's Red Production Company for BBC One, with one episode written by Russell T Davies. It is at this event that Shindler introduces Davies to Jane Tranter for the first time, and they briefly discuss the idea of reviving *Doctor Who*. Despite Davies' earlier BBC *Doctor Who* meetings, Tranter later claims that had it not been for this encounter, she would not necessarily have realised that Davies wanted to write *Doctor Who*. "It was literally that *Linda Green* press launch in the Lowry hotel that forged the entire creation of *Doctor Who*," Davies later states.

Before Tranter can make any headway with Davies on *Doctor Who* she leaves the BBC for a period of maternity leave, giving birth to twins in December.

DECEMBER

Doctor Who Magazine 312 is published in which – in an article about the possible future of the show – writer Jonathan Blum claims that there are "four proposals for a new series of *Doctor Who*... currently doing the rounds at the BBC." Only one of these is specifically identified – that of Dan Freedman, producer of the *Death Comes to Time* webcast drama.

"BACK WHEN *DEATH COMES TO TIME* WAS AROUND"
– Mark Gatiss, Doctor Who Magazine *335*

Feeling "a little concerned about the content" of Freedman's plans for the series, Mark Gatiss draws up his own proposal for reviving *Doctor Who*, in collaboration with fellow writer Gareth Roberts and *Doctor Who Magazine* editor Clayton Hickman. Gatiss submits this pitch to Jon Plowman, the Controller of Comedy Entertainment at BBC Television, who passes it on to Jane Tranter. "All the right noises were made," Gatiss later claims, "but it is incredibly hard to get a straight answer."

2002

"EARLY"

Russell T Davies meets with Laura Mackie, the Head of Drama Serials in the BBC drama department. "[She] said 'I love *Bob & Rose*, and I'd like to work with you.' I said 'Well, I'd only like to do *Doctor Who*.'"

Around this time, the BBC are keen for Davies to write "a science fiction version of *A Tale of Two Cities*" in collaboration with the novelist China Miéville.

Davies later says there was then another *Doctor Who* meeting where "I went in again and had a meeting and talked about how I'd do it." In the interview where he discusses this, he again mentions his *Walking with Dinosaurs* and *Weakest Link* ideas.

Davies either pitched these notions twice or has, in the years since, confused the details of his meetings with Mackie and his earlier meeting with Pippa Harris.

"I was very excited, but they said, 'We've got to inquire about the rights,' and still nothing happened."

FEBRUARY 5

Jana Bennett is named as the new overall Director of Television at the BBC. She succeeds Mark Thompson, who has departed to become Chief Executive of Channel 4.

FEBRUARY 14

The *Death Comes to Time* webcast series begins on the BBC *Doctor Who* website. Producer Dan Freedman tells *Doctor Who Magazine* about his plans for a television revival of the show: "We have cast [the Doctor] – theoretically – but I can't say who... It's not that the BBC aren't willing, it's that the BBC doesn't exist. The BBC is full of departments, and the people that make programmes are completely separate to the people that make money... For the first time now there is a coherent plan in motion for bringing *Doctor Who* back." Nev Fountain tells the magazine that Freedman has asked him to script edit the series, should it happen.

SOMETIME BETWEEN MAY 2002 AND FEBRUARY 2003

Writer Matthew Graham, later co-creator of *Life on Mars* and *Ashes to Ashes* and writer of three episodes of the modern *Doctor Who* "batted a few ideas around" for a revival of the series. "I think I would have kept the sense of invention that Russell did, but probably made it a bit more Gothic. And darker," he later recalls.

In *Doctor Who Magazine* 370, published in May 2006, Graham confirms that it was John Yorke with whom he discussed *Doctor Who*. Yorke was promoted to Head of Drama Series under

THE LONG GAME

Mal Young in May 2002, and left the BBC to move to Channel 4 around February 2003. Therefore, Graham's discussion with him was almost certainly sometime during this period.

MAY 17
Death Comes to Time producer Dan Freedman states in a post on the official BBC's *Doctor Who* website's message board that he is no longer interested in trying to make a TV revival of the series. "The TV thing is really over now, for me... I've kind of decided to drop out, given the strength of feeling amongst the majority of fans, and leave it to [Mark] Gatiss, Big Finish and co. I'm sure someone will do it eventually, so don't give up hope!" he writes. "But don't overestimate my importance here, I'm just not going to do any more *Doctor Who*, that doesn't mean other people can't, and they might have more success. It's not as if it was on TV and I pulled out. It still wasn't on and it still isn't, so nothing drastic has happened. I'm happy to be able to do other programmes so I'm going to concentrate on that."

MAY 24
The BBC *Doctor Who* website relates a *Financial Times* report of BBC Films having invested "a six-figure sum" to develop a *Doctor Who* film with the Mutual Film Company. However, a BBC Films spokesman tells the website that although the film is indeed an ongoing project for them, "these things take years to develop."

SEPTEMBER 17
Appearing on Simon Mayo's show on BBC Radio 5 Live, Lorraine Heggessey discusses *Doctor Who*: "I think we should be looking at how we could reinvent it... I have been actively talking to some people about reinventing and writing some new *Doctor Who*s. At this moment it's in incredibly early stages, and there are all sorts of rights issues that have to be overcome, but there is hope, all you people out there."

TIMELINE

SEPTEMBER 29
The Observer's "Pendennis" column reports: "One show definitely returning to TV screens is *Doctor Who*, according to microscopic-but-perfectly-formed BBC One controller Miss Lorraine Heggessey."

2003

FEBRUARY 9 AND 10
Russell T Davies' two-part drama *The Second Coming*, starring Christopher Eccleston, is broadcast on ITV.

MARCH 16
In a feature for *The Observer* newspaper about Saturday night TV, Jane Tranter says that she would "like to do a modern version of *Doctor Who* starring someone like Judi Dench."

MAY
BBC One channel executive Helen O'Rahilly recalls in a 2013 piece for *The Irish Times* that this was when Lorraine Heggessey asked her to look into the *Doctor Who* rights situation, so that work could start on a new series.

JULY 9
The BBC *Doctor Who* website announces the production of their forthcoming fully-animated webcast drama *Scream of the Shalka*, starring Richard E. Grant as an apparently official new ninth Doctor.

JULY 29
Julie Gardner is announced as the new Head of Drama for BBC Wales, leaving her role as a Development Producer at LWT to join the Corporation; she succeeds former *Doctor Who* director Matthew Robinson in the role.

AUGUST 6
At a press launch for the BBC's series of modern-day adaptations

of Chaucer's *The Canterbury Tales* at Baltic in London, Jane Tranter tells Russell T Davies' agent Bethan Evans: "Russell. *Doctor Who*. We're doing it. Tell him." Evans leaves Davies an answerphone message passing on this news, but he "sort of ignored it for two days, cos I thought 'Yeah, yeah, that just means they want a potential *Doctor Who* put into development for years... Eventually, after a week or so, I did sort of say, 'What was that about, then?' And she didn't know – all she'd had was that mention off Jane Tranter. I said something like 'Oh, tell them I'm interested and of course, I'd like to do it, but I'm busy.'"

AUGUST 21

The BBC *Doctor Who* website publishes a news article clarifying the current rights status of *Doctor Who*. Having made enquiries with the BBC Rights Group, the article concludes that the BBC "could commission a new *Doctor Who* series for TV if it wanted to." The article claims that the research was conducted because, "There are all sorts of rumours flying around – many of them suggesting that the BBC no longer owns the rights to make the series."

AUGUST 25

The Guardian's media website interviews Lorraine Heggessey at the Edinburgh International Television Festival, where she claims that: "I would like to resurrect *Doctor Who* but the rights situation is too complicated to do that at the moment. Maybe that will happen one day."

AUGUST 26

The BBC *Doctor Who* website reports on Heggessey's *Guardian* interview of the previous day, reiterating that: "We recently looked into the rights concerning *Doctor Who* and discovered that there is nothing to prevent the show's return."

Following this, some fans contact the BBC to point out the disparity between Heggessey's comments and the BBC *Doctor Who* website's statement that the series rights are not in dispute. BBC website producer Martin Trickey is summoned to a meeting where he takes a copy of the research conducted by the site's researcher Daniel Judd, to demonstrate that the rights are fully available.

THE FIRST WEEK OF SEPTEMBER

Jane Tranter formally offers Julie Gardner the opportunity to produce *Doctor Who* at BBC Wales, working with Russell T Davies. Immediately after speaking to Tranter, Gardner calls Davies, who is on holiday in France, to tell him that the BBC are serious about wanting to bring *Doctor Who* back, and want them to make it together at BBC Wales. After considering the idea, he accepts.

"EARLY SEPTEMBER"

Davies, Gardner and Tranter meet together for the first time to discuss their plans for the series.

SEPTEMBER 9

BBC Information issues an 'audience answer' about *Doctor Who*, stating that: "Should BBC Films decide not to proceed with the film then other plans may well be put into motion, but it is important to clarify that no series is scheduled at the moment."

SEPTEMBER 24

According to *Doctor Who: The Complete History*, this is the date on which Lorraine Heggessey officially commissions a new series of the programme.

SEPTEMBER 26

In an interview with *The Daily Telegraph*, Lorraine Heggessey announces that a new series of *Doctor Who* is to be made, written and produced by Russell T Davies.

Heggessey tells the *Telegraph* that "Worldwide has now agreed that, as they haven't made the film and I've been waiting for two years, it's only right that BBC One should have a crack at making a series."

SOURCES

AUTHOR'S INTERVIEWS AND CORRESPONDENCE

Joe Ahearne, Colin Brake, Steve Cole, Nev Fountain, Rob Francis, David Fury, Julie Gardner, Rupert Gavin, Gary Gillatt, Matthew Graham, Will Hadcroft, Lorraine Heggessey, Clayton Hickman, Michael Jackson, Daniel Judd, Shaun Lyon, Lee Mansfield, Andrew Marshall, Saul Nassé, Helen O'Rahilly, Mike Phillips, Damian Rafferty, Menna Richards, Mark Rogers, Andrew Mark Sewell, Patrick Spence, Tom Spilsbury, Shannon Patrick Sullivan, David Thompson, Jane Tranter, Martin Trickey, Jo Wright, Alan Yentob, Mal Young

CHAPTER 1

Broadcast, November 4 1988 – "BBC Television's Drama Group is Being Restructured" Page 2

The Times, August 2 1989 – "Drama at the BBC" Andrew Lycett, page 30

The Independent, November 6 1991 – "Long Queue For Short Shrift at BBC For Independent Radio Producers" Kent Barker, page 15

Screen Finance, May 5 1993 – "BBC Theatrical Slate to Remain Small Says Shivas" Page 5

Broadcast, July 23 1993 – "Wearing Takes Centre Stage – BBC Drama" Page 3

Broadcast, April 29 1994 – "Indies are Victors in BBC Regional Cash Injection" Steve Busfield, page 5

Broadcast, July 29 1994 – "Denton Stands By Cap on Indie Drama Quota" Richard Life, page 2

THE LONG GAME

Broadcast, May 10 1996 – "Caleb Takes Up Top Drama Post" Matt Baker, page 2

Associated Press, May 15 1996 – "List of Week's TV Ratings"

Associated Press, May 21 1996 – "List of Week's TV Ratings"

The Times, June 12 1996 – "Why is Birt Killing Off a Top Team?" Alexandra Frean, page 23

The Independent, June 15 1996 – "Michael Jackson is the BBC's New Director of Television" Matthew Horsman, page 2

Broadcast, June 21 1996 – "BBC Chiefs Aim for Simplicity" Jason Deans, page 1

Broadcast, June 21 1996 – "Broadcast Ratings" William Phillips, page 25

Doctor Who Magazine Issue 241, July 31 1996 – "Which Way Now?" Page 4

Broadcast, October 4 1996 – "Martin Takes Top TV Sports Position at BBC Broadcast" Jason Deans, page 6

Broadcast, January 10 1997 – "Wall to Wall Stake up for Sale as BBC Grasps Root" Jason Deans, page 3

Doctor Who Magazine Issue 248, February 12 1997 – "Universal Extends Option on New *Doctor Who*" Page 4

The Guardian, February 18 1997 – "False Steps" Maggie Brown, page 25

The Guardian, May 5 1997 – "Small Step For Manna" John Dugdale, page 20

Broadcast, June 6 1997 – "Drama Decision 'Soon'" Page 1

Broadcast, June 13 1997 – "BBC Saga Ends With Adams" Jason Deans, page 1

Broadcast, July 11 1997 – "Return to the BBC on the Cards if Elliott Misses Out on ITV Post" Page 1

Broadcast, August 29 1997 – "BBC May Line Up New Drama Tsar" Jason Deans, page 5

Broadcast, October 10 1997 – "Elliott Turns Down BBC Drama Part" Matt Baker, page 1

Broadcast, June 2 2000 – "Ross Replaces C4 Drama Chief Neal" Colin Robertson, page 1

SOURCES

The Guardian, October 16 2000, *Media Guardian* supplement – "Dramatis Personae" Maggie Brown, page 5

Doctor Who Magazine Special Edition: The Complete Eighth Doctor, September 3 2003 – "DWM Archive: *Doctor Who – The Movie*" Andrew Pixley, page 67

rec.arts.drwho, July 23 1996 – "For Who, the Bell Tolls" Elizabeth Danna

rec.arts.drwho, July 27 1996 – "Dreamwatch says 2 more films". Simon Jerram

rec.arts.drwho, August 2 1996 – "New BBC series rumor" Greg Motte

rec.arts.drwho, April 8 1997 – "Letter From the BBC, No Big News". Lance Hall

Variety.com, June 12 1997 – "BBC Drama Post to Adams" Adam Dawtrey

rec.arts.drwho, July 20 1997 – "Beeb.com announcement" Corey Klemow

The Fun Factory: A Life in the BBC, Will Wyatt. Aurum Press Ltd, 2003, pages 169 and 236

Uncertain Vision: Birt, Dyke and the Reinvention of the BBC, Georgina Born. Secker & Warburg, 2004, pages 175, 321-323

A Critical Survey of BBC Films: 1988-2013, Anne Woods. University of Portsmouth, 2015, pages 73-75

CHAPTER 2

Broadcast, March 3 1989 – "BBC Appointments" Page 34

The Times, August 2 1989 – "Drama at the BBC" Andrew Lycett, page 30

Media Week, December 8 1989 – "BBC Television Features Appointment" Page 44

Broadcast, January 25 1991 – "Channel 4 to Revamp *Brookside* in Bid to Secure Larger Audience" Page 22

Marketing, January 16 1992 – "Marketing Moves – Carlton Announces Five New Appointments" Page 35

Evening Standard, March 10 1993 – "Salmon Opts for C4" Page 33

The Guardian, July 26 1993 – "Group Captain's Dramatic Flare" James Saynor, page 14

Broadcast, October 1 1993 – "Carlton Completes Its Restructuring" Andy Fry, page 3

Evening Standard, June 30 1994 – "BBC Bid to Win Back Drama Chief Who Quit" Tim Cooper, page 6

Broadcast, July 1 1994 – "Popularity Stakes – BBC Loses Ratings Battle" Mike Jones, page 18

The Guardian, July 13 1994 – "New Drama Gets Dressed For Action" Andrew Culf, page 10

The Guardian, April 26 1995 – "BBC Loses Man With Golden Touch" Andrew Culf, page 2

The Independent, August 8 1995 – "Dramatic Choice". Page 16

The Guardian, August 28 1995, *G2* supplement – "A V-Sign to the M People" John Dugdale, page 14

Financial Times, January 4 1996 – "Prebble in Granada Satellite Slot" Raymond Snoddy, page 4

The Guardian, June 18 1996 – "BBC Drama Chief Demoted Over Loan" Andrew Culf, page 8

Broadcast, June 21 1996 – "Parr Exits as Drama Unfolds" Claire Atkinson, page 3

Broadcast, October 4 1996 – "Brookie's Young in Pearson Role" Sarah Littlejohn, page 1

The Times, November 13 1996 – "Passion and Channel 5" Maggie Brown, page 23

Broadcast, December 20 1996 – "BBC Drama Chief Quits to Take Film Role" Christine Smith, page 3

Broadcast, April 11 1997 – "Singular Thompson Wins BBC Job" Jason Deans, page 1

The Guardian, May 3 1997 – "BBC Bereft as Channel 4 Picks Grade's Successor" Andrew Culf, page 4

Broadcast, May 23 1997 – "The Wright Stuff?" Jason Deans, page 27

SOURCES

The Hollywood Reporter, August 21 1997 – "BBC Duo Go Away for Weekend" Monika Maurer, page 5

The Guardian, September 3 1997 – "BBC1 'People's Channel'" Clare Longrigg, page 10

The Guardian, September 8 1997, Media Guardian supplement – "Big Fish Makes a Fine Catch" Maggie Brown, page 10

Broadcast, October 31 1997 – "BBC Poaches Young to Fill TV Drama Role" Christine Smith, page 5

The Guardian, September 17 1999 – "Soaps Are Now 'Soul of the Nation'" Janine Gibson and Julia Hartley-Brewer, page 3

Broadcast, November 19 1999 – "Leading Lady" Tim Dams, page 13

The Guardian, September 4 2000, *Media Guardian* supplement – "One Hell of a Drama" Matt Wells and Maggie Brown, pages 2-3

The Guardian, October 16 2000, *Media Guardian* supplement – "If I Say it Will Happen, it Will Happen" Maggie Brown, pages 4-5

The Guardian, September 29 2004 – "News Roundup – Media: Young to Leave BBC for 19 TV" Sam Jones, page 10

Nothing at the End of the Lane issue 3, January 2012 – "Illuminating *The Dark Dimension*" Richard Bignell, page 109

Doctor Who Magazine Issue 463, September 2013 – "The Way Back – Part One: Bring Me to Life" Cavan Scott, page 23

British Film Institute website – "Jane Tranter"

Debretts.co.uk, October 19 2004 – "Debrett's People of Today – Young, Mal"

TheGuardian.com, June 15 2007 – "Farewell, Nick Elliott" Maggie Brown

TheGuardian.com, October 1 2008 – "How I Would Run BBC Drama" Nick Elliott

GamesRadar.co.uk, December 7 2009 – "Russell T Davies and the Line That Must Never Be Uttered" Nick Setchfield

bbc.co.uk, March 13 2013 – "Could *Eldorado* Make a Comeback?" Justin Parkinson bbc.co.uk, July 20 2015 – "Peter Salmon to be New Director of BBC Studios"

NPR.org, 31 October 2019 – "*His Dark Materials* Producer Jane Tranter Stays True to the Story" Audie Cornish

Royal Television Society, January 2020 – "Soap Opera Showrunner Mal Young Gives a Masterclass in Drama Production" Roz Laws

TheGuardian.com, November 10 2020 – "Super Producer Jane Tranter: 'Women are Finally Getting the Chance in TV'" Sarah Hughes

Doctor Who: The Inside Story, Gary Russell. BBC Books, 2006, pages 18-19

Gallifrey Stands, episode 60, June 10 2015 – "Mal Young: From *Brookside* to Gallifrey"

Endgame. Extra feature on *Doctor Who - Survival* DVD, BBC Worldwide, 2007. Written and produced by Richard Molesworth

Doctor Forever: The Unquiet Dead. Extra feature on *Doctor Who - The Green Death: Special Edition* DVD, Pup Ltd for BBC Worldwide, 2013. Edited and produced by James Goss

CHAPTER 3

The Times, February 15 1997 – "*Dr Who* Lands in the Middle of a £22 Million Lawsuit" Joanna Bale, page 9

Doctor Who Magazine Issue 263, April 8 1998 – "Philip Segal Moves Toward Securing *Who* Movie Rights" Page 4

The Guardian, May 19 1998 – "BBC Banks on Warrior Queen in Costliest Film" Dan Glaister, page 7

The Sun, May 19 1998 – "Bizarre: Victoria Reports From the Cannes Film Festival" Victoria Newton, page 14

Daily Mail, May 26 1998 – "She's Won a BAFTA But Can Daniela Take on the TARDIS Time Travel and Daleks?" Paul Ruddell, page 31

SOURCES

Doctor Who Magazine Issue 266, July 1 1998 – "Stop Press" Page 4

Doctor Who Magazine Issue 267, July 29 1998 – "Gallifrey Guardian" Page 4

Doctor Who Magazine Issue 268, August 26 1998 – "'We Are Examining Film Possibilities' – BBC" Page 5

The Evening Standard, February 10 1999 – "Many Happy Returns for the European Dream Team" Sue Summers, page 27

The Independent on Sunday, August 29 1999 – "TARDIS Ready for Take-Off Again" Matthew Sweet, page 4

The Sunday Times, September 19 1999 – "*Dr Who* Conquers Time to Land on Planet Hollywood" Nicholas Hellen, page 11

Doctor Who Magazine Issue 282, September 22 1999 – "Denzel Washington to Play Big Screen Doctor?" Page 4

The Sunday Times, October 17 1999 – "BBC Ploughs £40m into Movies" Nicholas Hellen, page 2

Radio Times, November 13-19 1999 – "What's the Future for the Doctor?" Page 32

Doctor Who Magazine Issue 284, November 17 1999 – "Scary Movie?" Page 4; "Hollywood Babble-On" – Neville Watkins, page 6.

Doctor Who Magazine Issue 285, December 15 1999 – "Is the *Who* Movie Dead?" Page 4

The Sunday Times, November 26 2000 – "Dyke Calls Up Daleks to Take on Hollywood" Nicholas Hellen, page 7

The Hollywood Reporter, June 15 2001 – "Langley Named Sr. VP Prod'n at Universal Pictures" Zorianna Kit, page 4

Financial Times, May 14 2002 – "Auntie Goes to Hollywood With Three Entries at Cannes" Boyd Farrow, page 6

bbc.co.uk, November 24 1998 – "*Dr Who* Back on the BBC"
rec.arts.drwho, May 4 1999 – "The New Movie?" Dan Garrett
Ain't It Cool News, November 5 1999 – "Is Paul Anderson's *Dr Who* Movie Dead?"
Variety.com, February 1 2000 – "HAL, Miramax Confirm Split" Adam Dawtrey

Variety.com, May 18 2000 – "*Who* Materializing for BBC Films" Adam Dawtrey and Dana Harris

Archive.org – capture of "*Who* Film Taking Time" on bbc.co.uk. Page dated May 24 2002. Capture dated June 1 2002

TheAge.com.au, November 11 2004 – "Digging for Plot" Brian Courtis

bbc.co.uk, November 14 2011 – "*Doctor Who* 'To be Made into Hollywood Feature Film'"

Doctor Who: The Sixties David J. Howe, Mark Stammers and Stephen James Walker. Doctor Who Books, 1992, pages 127-132

Doctor Who: The Seventies David J. Howe, Mark Stammers and Stephen James Walker. Doctor Who Books, 1994, page 73

Doctor Who: The Eighties David J. Howe, Mark Stammers and Stephen James Walker. Doctor Who Books, 1996, page 173

Doctor Who: Regeneration, Philip Segal with Gary Russell. HarperCollins Entertainment, 2000, page 157

Now on the Big Screen: The Unofficial and Unauthorised Guide to Doctor Who at the Cinema, by Charles Norton. Telos Publishing, 2013, Kindle Edition. Chapter Ten: 'Back Home'. Section: 'Chaos Theory'

CHAPTER 4

Broadcast, May 15 1998 – "Beeb Unveils Berry's Role" Jason Deans, page 2

The Sun, July 6 1998 – "New BBC Jobley For Tina Hobley" Sarah Crosbie, page 15

Broadcast, September 4 1998 – "Collins Cast in BBC Holiday Rep Drama" Jason Deans, page 2

Broadcast, September 18 1998 – "Profile: TV Soap's Mr Fix-It" John Dugdale, page 20

Broadcast, February 5 1999 – "C4 Finances Indies in Drama Initiative" Tim Dams, page 5

SOURCES

The Independent on Sunday, August 29 1999 – "TARDIS Ready for Take-Off Again" Matthew Sweet, page 4

Doctor Who Magazine issue 283, cover dated October 20 1999 – "Movie Production Steps Up a Gear". Page 5

Cult Times issue 57, June 2000 – "Isn't it Time for Some New Who?" David Richardson, page 5

Doctor Who Magazine Issue 317, May 29 2002 – "Tales From the Fiction Factory: Chapter Five – From Cradle to Grave" David J. Howe, pages 12-13

The Guardian, September 15 2003. G2 supplement – "Transmission Was Madness. Honestly" Russell T Davies, pages 16-17

Doctor Who Magazine Issue 338, January 7 2004 – "Lucky Thirteen?" Page 4

Doctor Who Magazine Issue 359, August 17 2005 – "A Long Game" Benjamin Cook, page 34

Doctor Who: The Complete History Volume 48, February 10 2016 – "*Rose*: Pre-Production", page 22

rec.arts.drwho, August 29 1999 – "Independent on Sunday Article" Stephen Graves

Archive.org – capture of "*Queer as Folk*: Exclusive Interview With Russell T Davies" on bbc.co.uk. Capture dated October 23 1999

Ain't It Cool News, June 6 2000 – "Another *Dr Who* Update From IronEagle

rec.arts.drwho, June 6 2000 – "Russell T Davis [sic] Scotches Who Flick Talk" 'Hazzer'

rec.arts.drwho, August 31 2000 – "Peter Salmon Loses BBC1 Controller Position!" Gareth Parker

Gay.com UK, November 30 2000 – "*Folk* Off to America" Scott Matthewman

TheGuardian.com, July 24 2016 – "*Happy Valley* Producer: 'Gritty North? I Get Very Cross About That Phrase'" Frances Parraudin

THE LONG GAME

T is for Television: The Small Screen Adventures of Russell T Davies Mark Aldridge and Andy Murray. Reynolds & Hearn Ltd, 2008, pages 9, 23, 32-37, 43-45, 60, 69, 74-75, 86-87, 106

On Show: Russell T Davies. BBC Wales for BBC 2W. March 17 2005, Produced by Steve Freer, directed by Gwyndaf Roberts
Russell T Davies: Unscripted. BBC Bristol for BBC Four. April 11 2005. Produced and directed by Merryn Threadgould
Mark Lawson Talks to Russell T Davies. BBC Television for BBC Four. January 16 2008. Produced and directed by Helen Partridge
Doctor Forever: The Unquiet Dead. Extra feature on *Doctor Who - The Green Death: Special Edition DVD*, Pup Ltd for BBC Worldwide, 2013. Edited and produced by James Goss

CHAPTER 5

Doctor Who Magazine Issue 241, July 31 1996 – "BBC Books to Take Over from Virgin" Page 5
Electronics Times, September 28 1998 – "Vision On" Miller Freeman, page 3
Evening Standard, October 2 1998 – "The Idiot's Guide to a Digital Revolution" Nicole Swengley, page 25
The Times, November 13 1998 – "A Party? When We Hit 1m" Raymond Snoddy, page 40
The Times, November 16 1998 – "First Digital TV Service Walks On Air" Raymond Snoddy, page 4
Radio Times, March 6-12 1999 – "Everybody's Talking About... Doctor Who" Page 15
Doctor Who Magazine Issue 278, June 2 1999 – "Can You Still Love Me in My New Body?" Alan Barnes, page 8
Radio Times, November 13-19 1999 – "From the Editor" Sue Robinson, page 4
Doctor Who Magazine Issue 305, May 29 2001 – "Tales From the Fiction Factory: Chapter One – Dancing in the Dark" David J. Howe, page 6

SOURCES

Doctor Who Magazine Issue 313, February 6 2002 - "Tales From the Fiction Factory: Chapter Four - The Gap Band" David J. Howe, page 14

Doctor Who Magazine Issue 328, April 2 2003 - "DWM Archive Extra: *The Curse of Fatal Death*" Andrew Pixley, pages 23-25

Doctor Who Magazine Special Edition: The Complete Eighth Doctor, September 3 2003 - "DWM Archive: *Doctor Who - The Movie*" Andrew Pixley, page 68; "Further Adventures: Comics" Stuart Duncan, page 81

Doctor Who Magazine Issue 335, October 15 2003 - "Gentleman's Excuse Me". Anthony K McCail, page 27

Doctor Who Magazine issue 353, March 2 2005 - "Further Adventures: To the Slaughter" David Darlington, page 21

rec.arts.drwho, June 4 1996 - "Movie Novel is US & Oz" Gary Russell

bbc.co.uk, September 23 1998 - "A New Channel is Born"

bbc.co.uk, November 20 1998 - "Children's Classics Go Back to the Future"

rec.arts.drwho, February 22 1999 - "Re: Rowan Atkinson in New Who Episode!!!!!" Corey Klemow

bbc.co.uk, May 24 1999 - "Mercury and Moore Head Millennium Stamps"

bbc.co.uk, September 5 2000 - "*Fawlty Towers* Tops TV Hits"

Archive.org - capture of "We Want *Who*" on bbc.co.uk. Page dated September 22 2003. Capture dated October 3 2003

Doctor Who: The Handbook - The First Doctor, The William Hartnell Years: 1963-1966 David J. Howe, Mark Stammers and Stephen James Walker. Doctor Who Books, 1994, page 189

Auntie's TV Favourites: Drama. BBC North for BBC One. October 11 1996. Produced by Richard Fell, directed by John Rooney

Auntie's All-Time Greats. BBC Television for BBC One. November 3 1996. Directed by Stuart McDonald

THE LONG GAME

Right to Reply. Channel 4 Television for Channel 4, November 7 1998. Edited by Jerry Foulkes

CHAPTER 6

The Guardian, September 26 1996, Online supplement – "Beeb Casts its Net" Andrew Culf, page 6

The Guardian, November 17 1997, *Media Guardian* supplement – "News Box of Tricks". Simon Waldman, page 13

Doctor Who Magazine issue 258, cover dated November 19 1997 – "More News in Brief..." Page 5

New Media Age, 7 May 1998 – "BBC Hitting Massive Traffic" Page 1

Beeb.com press release, November 20 1998 – "What Was it Like Looking Down the Barrel of a Dalek Gun?" Matthew Turmaine

The Guardian, October 16 2000, *Media Guardian* supplement – "Shopping With Auntie" Meg Carter, pages 58-59

New Media Age, June 27 2002 – "Comparison Sites Make New Moves to Beat the Downturn" Page 16

SFX Issue 128, March 2005 – "Regeneration Failure" Nick Setchfield, page 49

bbc.co.uk – "Dreams, Data and Downloads"

rec.arts.tv.uk, November 3 1994 – "Tomorrow's World on BBC's WWW?" Rob May

rec.arts.drwho, May 30 1996 – "Doctor Who News Home Page" Shannon Patrick Sullivan

The Independent, June 3 1997, online version – "Auntie Goes For Gold" Sophia Chauchard-Stuart

rec.arts.drwho, July 20 1997 – "Beeb.com Announcement" Peter Anghelides

rec.arts.drwho, July 27 1997 – "BBC Radio Times Doctor Who Vote!!" Jennifer Guest Billingsley

rec.arts.drwho, November 14 1997 – "Destiny of the Doctors" 'Ian'

rec.arts.drwho, December 4 1997 – "Dr Who on Beeb" 'M.E. Levy2'

SOURCES

alt.tv.space-a-n-b, February 23 1998 – "BBC Cult TV" Matt McCarthy

Archive.org – capture of Cult homepage on bbc.co.uk. Capture dated May 20 1998

rec.arts.drwho, May 24 1998 – "Movie News and Other Questions" Corey Klemow

rec.arts.drwho, September 14 1998 – "Send a FREE Doctor Who Postcard!" 'Sebastian'

uk.media.tv.sf.drwho, November 19 1998 – "BBC Doctor Who Web-site Advert" 'Paul'

rec.arts.drwho, November 19 1998 – "My GOD a DW Ad!!!!" 'Tlotoxl'

rec.arts.drwho, November 20 1998 – "Official BBC Home of Doctor Who is Now Live" Damian Rafferty

Archive.org – capture of "Doctor Who: Destiny of the Doctors" on beeb.com. Capture dated January 17 1999

rec.arts.drwho, March 11 1999 – "Watch the Doctor Who Comic Relief Special *Live* Online" Andrew Wong

rec.arts.drwho, March 15 1999 – "All Parts of Comic Relief Doctor Who Sketch Now Online!" Andrew Wong

alt.fan.philippa.forrester, October 23 1999 – "Revealed" 'Mark_H'

Archive.org – capture of "Sean Bean Isn't the Doctor" on bbc.co.uk. Page dated January 2001. Capture dated January 23 2001

Archive.org – capture of "*Who* Messageboards End" on bbc.co.uk. Page dated April 20 2004. Capture dated April 23 2004

bbc.co.uk, December 4 2007 – "Revolution Not Evolution". Alan Connor

bbc.co.uk, December 18 2007 – "Brandon's History of Online BBC" Brandon Butterworth

The Register, November 28 2012 – "The Inside Story of the News Website that Saved the BBC" Andrew Orlowski

Twitter.com, @gossjam, May 23 2020 – 10.55am; 10.59am; 11.20am

CHAPTER 7

The Guardian, May 15 1989 – "Dramatic Decline at the BBC" Bob Woffinden, page 21

Broadcast, October 28 1994 – "Heggessey Becomes QED Editor" Louise Bateman, page 2

The Guardian, December 23 1996, G2 supplement – "Who's Lost the Plot?" Richard Brooks, page 9

Broadcast, May 23 1997 – "MBC Lifts Heggessey from BBC1 Hospital" Jason Deans and Christine Smith, page 5

Broadcast, June 27 1997 – "BBC Kids' Job Tempts Heggessey from MBC" Christine Smith, page 1

The Times, November 7 1997 – "Chains of Command" Sue Summers, page 41

Broadcast, November 28 1997 – "BBC Awards Drama Execs More Power" Jason Deans, page 6

The Times, January 13 1999 – "BBC1's Ratings Fall Below 30% For First Time" Carol Midgley, page 6

The Times, January 14 1999 – "BBC Seeks New Birt" Raymond Snoddy, page 6

The Independent, March 9 1999 – "The Reviled Revolutionary" Ian Hargreaves, page 12

Broadcast, March 12 1999 – "Off the Record: End Credits" Trevor Goodchild, page 32

The Independent, May 29 1999 – "Profile: Alan Yentob – The Insider's Extrovert" David Lister, page 5

The Times, August 30 1999 – "BBC1 in Dramatic Plea For £100m" Carol Midgley, page 7

The Guardian, September 10 1999 – "ITV Game Show Pushes BBC1 to All-Time Low" Janine Gibson, page 6

Broadcast, October 22 1999 – "Spindler Replaces Adams at BBC Drama" Tim Dams, page 3

Televisual, November 1 1999 – "Interview: Creative Director" Keely Winstone, page 18

Broadcast, November 12 1999 – "Tranter to Take on BBC Drama Role" Tim Dams, page 3

SOURCES

The Observer, November 14 1999, Screen supplement – "Hidden Casualties". Josephine Monroe, pages 2-3

The Independent, March 17 2000 – "Hundreds of BBC Jobs May Go in Dyke Shake-Up" Jane Robins, page 9

The Guardian, June 22 2000 – "BBC1 Controller Under Fire After Governors Damn Channel's Output" Matt Wells, page 2

The Times, September 1 2000, *Times 2* supplement – "Fresh Air for Flagging Flagship" Michael Leapman, page 20

The Guardian, September 4 2000, *Media Guardian* supplement – "One Hell of a Drama" Matt Wells and Maggie Brown, pages 2-3

Broadcast, September 15 2000 – "Thompson Announces Retirement" Tara Conlan, page 1

The Times, October 6 2000, *Times 2* supplement – "The BBC's Loveable Hatchet Man" Steve Clarke, page 14

The Guardian, October 16 2000, *Media Guardian* supplement – "If I Say It Will Happen, It Will Happen" Maggie Brown, pages 4-5

Broadcast, November 24 2000 – "*Waking the Dead* to Become a Series" Page 10

The Guardian, February 12 2001, *Media Guardian* supplement – "Bubbling Over" Maggie Brown, page 4

The Guardian, November 19 2001, *Media Guardian* supplement – "Getting One Over" Maggie Brown, pages 2-3

The Times, January 4 2002 – "Why ITV Has Lost Its Edge" Steve Clarke, pages 18-19

Doctor Who Magazine Issue 312, January 9 2002 – "50 Essential Questions: TV" Jonathan Blum, page 7

Doctor Who Magazine Issue 337, December 10 2003 – "Gallifrey Guardian Extra!" Clayton Hickman, page 7

Broadcast, May 1 2009 – "The Broadcast Interview: Lorraine Heggessey" Steve Clarke, page 30

Doctor Who Magazine Issue 463, September 2013 – "The Way Back – Part One: Bring Me to Life" Cavan Scott, page 23

The Sunday Telegraph, June 21 2020 – "'I Was Invited to Elton John's Party. I Had to Borrow a Tiara'" John Wright, page 12

bbc.co.uk – "History of the BBC: John Birt, Director-General 1992-2000"
Variety.com, February 8 1998 – "Patience Wearing Thin at BBC" Adam Dawtrey
bbc.co.uk, October 19 1998 – "CBBC Chief Comes Clean Over *Blue Peter* Sacking"
bbc.co.uk, June 25 1999 – "Greg Dyke is New BBC Boss"
bbc.co.uk, January 31 2000 – "Dyke Pledges BBC Spending Boost"
TheGuardian.com, April 3 2000 – "The BBC Memo in Full"
TheGuardian.com, June 21 2000 – "Shake-Up Time for Auntie" Matt Wells
bbc.co.uk, August 25 2000 – "BBC Shifts *Nine O'Clock News*"
TheGuardian.com, August 31 2000 – "BBC Timeline: Dyke's First Year" Jason Deans
TheGuardian.com, August 31 2000 – "Heggessey Heads Contenders for BBC1 Role" Jason Deans
bbc.co.uk, September 13 2000 – "Salmon Leaps into BBC Sport"
bbc.co.uk, September 14 2000 – "First Woman to Run BBC One"
TheGuardian.com, September 15 2000 – "Two Halves of a Zodiac Coin at the BBC" Maggie Hyde
bbc.co.uk, October 3 2000 – "BBC News Move 'Senseless'"
TheGuardian.com, October 12 2000 – "Tranter Takes BBC TV Drama Role" Jason Deans
Archive.org – capture of "BBC News Release: Lorraine Heggessey to be Controller of BBC One" on bbc.co.uk. Capture dated October 23 2000
bbc.co.uk, October 4 2001 – "This Week's TV: *Holby City* Back Forever" William Gallagher
bbc.co.uk, February 7 2002 – "One BBC: Making it Happen" Greg Dyke
TheGuardan.com, April 11 2002 – "Thompson Steps Up War of Words With Dyke" Jason Deans
bbc.co.uk, February 14 2005 – "How Heggessey Rose Through BBC Ranks"
WhatNoise.co.uk, February 7 2007 – "Script Doctors: Chris Chibnall 2007" David Darlington

SOURCES

Archive.org – capture of "Getting to Work in TV... Lorraine Heggessey" on BroadcastFreelancer.com. Capture dated October 9 2007

BridportNews.co.uk, September 7 2019 – "Looking Back to *Harbour Lights* in West Bay"

bbc.co.uk, June 2 2021 – "*Holby City*: BBC Medical Drama to End in 2022"

A Shrinking Iceberg Travelling South – Changing Trends in British Television: A Case Study of Drama and Current Affairs, Steven Barnett and Emily Seymour. University of Westminster/Campaign for Quality Television, 1999, page 52

The World of Jonathan Creek, Steve Clark. BBC Books, 1999, page 10

The Harder Path: The Autobiography, John Birt. Time Warner Books, 2002, page 363

The Fun Factory: A Life in the BBC, Will Wyatt. Aurum Press Ltd, 2003, pages 217-219, 276-277

Uncertain Vision: Birt, Dyke and the Reinvention of the BBC, Georgina Born. Secker & Warburg, 2004, pages 358, 363

Inside Story, Greg Dyke. Harper Perennial, 2004, Kindle edition. Chapter Eight: 'The BBC Years (1)'

Nicky Campbell (Brian Alexander sitting-in), BBC Radio 5 Live, September 14 2000, 9am-12 midday

Points of View. BBC Television for BBC One. September 21 1994. Produced by Bernard Newnham.

Points of View. BBC Television for BBC One. October 19 1994. Produced by Bernard Newnham

CHAPTER 8

Radio Times, April 1-7 1995 – "*Avengers* for the 90s" Richard Johnson, page 22

TV Zone Issue 79, June 1996 – "Colin Brake: All Under Control" David Bailey, page 14

The Sunday Times, September 29 1996, *ST* supplement – "The X Factory" Steve Clarke, page 20

Televisual, January 2 1997 – "Morrissey Vanishes for ITV" Page 7

The Guardian, March 29 1997, *The Guide* supplement – "Preview: The Vanishing Man" AB, page 94

Doctor Who Magazine Issue 254, July 30 1997 – "The Life and Times of Jackie Jenkins" Page 42

Doctor Who Magazine Issue 256, September 24 1997 – "Timelines" Compiled by Alan Barnes, page 23

Doctor Who Magazine, Issue 259, December 17 1997 – "Newspaper Fuels *Who* Rumours Frenzy" Page 4

Radio Times, May 2-8 1998 – "Alien Alert" Nick Griffiths, pages 20-23; "Editor's Letter" Sue Robinson, page 126

Doctor Who Magazine issue 279, cover dated June 30 1999 – "We're Gonna Be Bigger Than *Star Wars!*" Gary Gillatt, page 12

Broadcast, December 17 2004 – "Sci-Fi on Spending Spree" Susan Thompson, page 11

The Independent, May 9 1998, online version – "Out of This World" James Rampton

rec.arts.drwho, May 20 1998 – "Invasion Earth" Donald Campbell

bbc.co.uk, June 17 2003 – "*Sea of Souls*: Thrilling New Drama from BBC Scotland"

Doctor Who: From A to Z, Gary Gillatt. BBC Books, 1998, page 167

A Shrinking Iceberg Travelling South – Changing Trends in British Television: A Case Study of Drama and Current Affairs, Steven Barnett and Emily Seymour. University of Westminster/Campaign for Quality Television, 1999, page 48

Endgame. Extra feature on *Doctor Who – Survival* DVD, BBC Worldwide, 2007. Written and produced by Richard Molesworth

SOURCES

CHAPTER 9

Newsday, December 3 2000 – "Controversy? That's Not All, 'Folk'" Marvin Kitman, page 35

Broadcast, April 27 2001 – "More *Linda Green* Episodes Ordered By BBC1" Page 9

The Guardian, October 15 2001, *Media Guardian* supplement – "Media Monkey's Diary" Page 7

The Guardian, December 16 2002, *Media Guardian* supplement – "Drama Queen" Maggie Brown, page 9

The Daily Telegraph, September 26 2003 – "*Doctor Who* Ready to Come Out of the Tardis for Saturday TV Series" Tom Leonard, page 3

Doctor Who Magazine Issue 359, August 17 2005 – "A Long Game" Benjamin Cook, pages 34-35

Doctor Who Magazine Issue 463, September 2013 – "The Way Back – Part One: Bring Me to Life" Cavan Scott, page 17

T is for Television: The Small Screen Adventures of Russell T Davies, Mark Aldridge and Andy Murray. Reynolds & Hearn Ltd, 2008, pages 129-130, 143

Doctor Forever: The Unquiet Dead. Extra feature on *Doctor Who – The Green Death: Special Edition DVD*, Pup Ltd for BBC Worldwide, 2013. Edited and produced by James Goss

CHAPTER 10

Doctor Who Magazine Issue 279, June 30 1999. "We're Gonna Be Bigger Than *Star Wars!*" Gary Gillatt, pages 8-12

Broadcast, January 14 2000 – "Robinson to Head Drama at Wales" Tim Dams, page 6

Doctor Who Magazine Issue 287, February 9 2000 – "The 1999 DWM Awards" Page 37

Doctor Who Magazine Issue 293, July 26 2000 – "Hollywood... Or Bust!" Page 9; "Coming Soon to a Cinema Near You..." Pages 10-11; "Starring... Hugh Grant" Steven Moffat, page 11;

THE LONG GAME

"New Producers of TV *Doctor Who*" Page 12; "And Now, on BBC1..." Pages 12-13; "Starring... Ian Richardson" Paul Cornell, page 13

Doctor Who Magazine Issue 312, January 9 2002 – "50 Essential Questions: TV" Jonathan Blum, pages 4-7

rec.arts.drwho, May 31 2000 – "Official! Paul McGann Audio" Martin Wicks

Archive.org – capture of "Release Schedule" on bbc.co.uk. Capture dated January 25 2001

CHAPTER 11

Doctor Who Magazine Issue 288, March 8 2000 – "New *Who* Radio Series Commissioned" Page 4

Doctor Who Magazine Issue 292, June 28 2000 – "Radio Serial Static" Page 4

Broadcast, October 13 2000 – "Tranter Takes Key Role at BBC Drama" Tara Conlan, page 1

Doctor Who Magazine Issue 298, December 13 2000 – "Pilot Ready for Take-Off!" Nev Fountain, page 5

Doctor Who Magazine Issue 312, January 9 2002 – "50 Essential Questions: TV" Jonathan Blum, pages 5-6

Doctor Who Magazine Issue 314, March 6 2002 – "Life After Death?" Benjamin Cook, pages 26-30

Daily Express, July 2 2002 – "Return of *Dr Who*" Mark Jagasia, page 15

Doctor Who Magazine Issue 335, October 15 2003 – "Gentleman's Excuse Me" Anthony K McCail, pages 30-31

Doctor Who Magazine Issue 351, January 5 2005 – "DWM Archive Extra: *Death Comes to Time*" Andrew Pixley, pages 24-25

Doctor Who Magazine Issue 370, June 21 2006 – "Script Doctors: Matthew Graham" David Darlington, pages 45-46

Doctor Who Magazine Issue 377, January 3 2007 – "Script Doctors: Gareth Roberts" Rex Duis, page 17

Doctor Who Magazine Issue 500, July 2016 – "*Doctor Who*: 2001" Graham Kibble-White, page 70

SOURCES

Archive.org – capture of "Pilot Canned by Radio 4" on bbc.co.uk, by Julian Knott. Page dated January 25 2001. Capture dated April 5 2001.

Archive.org – capture of "*Death Comes to Time*: The Radio Pilot" on bbc.co.uk. Capture dated April 5 2001

Archive.org – capture of "Giles Spin-Off Latest" on bbc.co.uk, by Rob Francis. Page dated May 14 2001. Capture dated August 16 2001

Archive.org – capture of "*Doctor Who* Returns to BBC Online" on bbc.co.uk. Paged dated June 10 2001. Capture dated August 6 2001

Archive.org – capture of "BBC Says Thanks for Webcast Success" on bbc.co.uk. Page dated July 23 2001. Capture dated August 1 2001

Archive.org – capture of "Extra 'Time' for Online *Doctor Who*" on bbc.co.uk. Page dated August 30 2001. Capture dated September 13 2001

Archive.org – capture of "New Series Rumor Goes Further" on the Doctor Who News Page at Outpost Gallifrey. Page dated October 5 2001. Capture dated October 25 2001

Archive.org – capture of "*Death Comes to Time* Recorded" on bbc.co.uk. Page dated December 20 2001. Capture dated March 28 2002

Archive.org – capture of "He's Back: New Episode Now Online" on bbc.co.uk. Paged dated February 14 2002. Capture dated February 24 2002

Archive.org – capture of "Online Who From Big Finish" on bbc.co.uk. Page dated February 16 2002. Capture dated February 23 2002

Archive.org – capture of "*Dr Who* News" on TomAndNev.co.uk. Page dated March 27 2002. Capture dated April 5 2002

Archive.org – capture of "*Death*: The Final Teaser" on bbc.co.uk. Page dated April 30 2002. Capture dated May 23 2002

bbc.co.uk, May 16 2002 – "John Yorke Takes Up New Role"

Archive.org – capture of "Dan Says Telly Bye-Bye?" on bbc.co.uk. Page dated May 17 2002. Capture dated June 1 2002

THE LONG GAME

alt.babylon5.uk, July 5 2002 – "New Who?" John Mosby

rec.arts.drwho, August 2 2002 – "TWIDW Update: Real Time Trailers on the BBC" Benjamin F. Elliott

Archive.org – capture of "More From the Minister?" on bbc.co.uk. Page dated October 24 2002. Capture dated November 4 2002

bbc.co.uk, February 12 2003 – "BBC Head Moves to Channel 4"

Archive.org – capture of "Interview: Russell T Davies" on bbc.co.uk. Capture dated December 25 2003

Outpost Gallifrey forum, April 30 2005. Rob Shearman.

Doctor Who: Regeneration, Philip Segal with Gary Russell. HarperCollins Entertainment, 2000, page 12

Doctor Who: The Inside Story, by Gary Russell. BBC Books, 2006, page 14

T is for Television: The Small Screen Adventures of Russell T Davies, Mark Aldridge and Andy Murray. Reynolds & Hearn Ltd, 2008, page 185

Drama and Delight: The Life of Verity Lambert, Richard Marson. Miwk Publishing, 2015, pages 272-273

Red, White and Who: The Story of Doctor Who in America, by Steven Warren Hill and Jennifer Adams Kelly, Nicholas Seidler and Robert Warnock, with Janine Fennick and John Lavalie. ATB Publishing, 2017, pages 417-426

CHAPTER 12

Broadcast, November 22 2002 – "Heggessey Boosts Team" Page 5

Doctor Who Magazine Issue 335, October 15 2003 – "Gentleman's Excuse Me" Anthony K McCail, page 31

Doctor Who Magazine Issue 351, January 5 2005 – "DWM Archive Extra: *Death Comes to Time*" Andrew Pixley, page 24

The Irish Times, November 23 2013 – "From Glasnevin to Gallifrey: An Irish *Doctor Who* Adventure". Helen O'Rahilly, page 9

rec.arts.drwho, October 2 2002 – "No New Series – Ever!" 'Bob'

bbc.co.uk, October 23 2002 – "BBC Wins Police Tardis Case"

SOURCES

Outpost Gallifrey, May 3 2003 – "Heggessey on the Record" Shaun Lyon

Outpost Gallifrey, July 9 2003 – "BBCi: Richard E. Grant is the Ninth Doctor" Shaun Lyon

Archive.org – capture of "BBCi's Ninth Doctor" on bbc.co.uk. Page dated July 11 2003 (sic). Capture dated July 14 2003

Archive.org – capture of "*Doctor Who* Rights" on bbc.co.uk. Page dated August 21 2003. Capture dated September 18 2003

TheGuardian.com, August 25 2003 – "Heggessey: Jury's Out on *Fame Academy*" John Plunkett

Archive.org – capture of "*Who* May Come Back" on bbc.co.uk. Page dated August 26 2003. Capture dated August 29 2003

Archive.org – capture of "Why Now?" on bbc.co.uk. Page dated November 11 2003. Capture dated December 2 2003

Doctor Who: Regeneration, Philip Segal with Gary Russell. HarperCollins Entertainment, 2000, page 157

Doctor Who: Scream of the Shalka, Paul Cornell. BBC Books, 2004, page 196

Doctor Who: The Inside Story, Gary Russell. BBC Books, 2006, page 19

Nicky Campbell, BBC Radio 5 Live, October 18 2000

Simon Mayo, BBC Radio 5 Live, September 17 2002

Carry on Screaming. Extra feature on *Doctor Who – Scream of the Shalka* DVD, Pup Ltd for BBC Worldwide, 2013. Edited and directed by James Brailsford

Doctor Forever: The Unquiet Dead. Extra feature on *Doctor Who – The Green Death: Special Edition* DVD, Pup Ltd for BBC Worldwide, 2013. Edited and produced by James Goss

CHAPTER 13

The Observer, February 21 1999, *Screen* supplement – "Keep it in the Family" Michael Collins, pages 6-7

THE LONG GAME

Birmingham Post, April 12 1999 – "BBC Bosses Still Grinding 'Em Down at Pebble Mill" Page 15

Daily Mail, September 30 2000 – "The Great Saturday Night Switch-Off" Lisa O'Carroll, page 23

The Guardian, July 2 2001, *Media Guardian* supplement – "Saturday Night is Not All Right" Maggie Brown, page 9

The Observer, September 29 2002 – "IDS: Kiss Me Kate?" 'Pendennis', page 31

The Observer, March 16 2003, *Review* supplement – "The Weekend Stops Here" Liz Hoggard, page 8

Broadcast, May 30 2003 – "UK TV Execs to Produce Soap in Cambodia" Page 1

The Independent, July 25 2003 – "Give Us Back Our Saturday Night Telly" Brian Viner, page 4

The Daily Telegraph, September 26 2003 – "*Doctor Who* Ready to Come Out of the Tardis for Saturday TV Series" Tom Leonard, page 3

Doctor Who Magazine Issue 336, November 12 2003 – "He's Back!" Page 5

Doctor Who Magazine issue 338, January 7 2004 – "Lucky Thirteen?" Page 4

Doctor Who Magazine Issue 354, March 30 2005 – "Gardner's World" Clayton Hickman, Benjamin Cook, pages 14-15

Doctor Who Magazine Issue 359, August 17 2005 – "A Long Game" Benjamin Cook, page 35

Doctor Who Magazine Issue 463, September 2013 – "The Way Back – Part One: Bring Me to Life" Cavan Scott, pages 18 and 20-21

Doctor Who: The Complete History Volume 48, February 10 2016 – "*Rose*: Pre-Production", page 27

Doctor Who Magazine, Issue 551, June 2020 – "Russell T Davies and Steven Moffat" Russell T Davies, Steven Moffat, page 19

bbc.co.uk, February 25 1999 – "The Party's Over For Edmonds' Show"

bbc.co.uk, June 15 2000 – "BBC 'Sour' Over Football Deal"
bbc.co.uk, June 15 2000 – "BBC Nets Equaliser"

SOURCES

TheGuardian.com, October 22 2001 – "ITV Scraps 7pm Premiership" Jason Deans
bbc.co.uk, September 20 2002 – "BBC Plans New Saturday Night"
bbc.co.uk, July 29 2003 – "Othello Award-Winner Returns Home to BBC Wales Post"
bbc.co.uk, August 29 2003 – "Saturday Night TV Least Popular"
Outpost Gallifrey, November 5 2003 – "SFX Interview" Shaun Lyon
Independent.co.uk, November 16 2003 – "*Doctor Who*: The Tenth Coming" Matthew Sweet
Outpost Gallifrey, December 23 2003 – "Davies in Welsh" Shaun Lyon

Doctor Who: The Inside Story, Gary Russell. BBC Books, 2006, page 20

Who Killed Saturday Night TV? At It Productions for Channel 4. July 10 2004. Produced and directed by Christopher Bruce
Doctor Forever: The Unquiet Dead. Extra feature on *Doctor Who – The Green Death: Special Edition* DVD, Pup Ltd for BBC Worldwide, 2013. Edited and produced by James Goss

CHAPTER 14

Doctor Who Magazine, Issue 285, December 15 1999 – editorial. Gary Gillatt, Alan Barnes, page 6
Doctor Who Magazine Special Edition: The Complete Second Doctor, June 4 2003 – "Classical Gas" Russell T Davies, page 48
BBC Press & Publicity, September 25 2003 – "*Dr Who*: Strict Embargo" David Cartwright
The Daily Telegraph, September 26 2003 – "Guess Who's Coming Back" Page 1
The Daily Telegraph, September 26 2003 – "*Doctor Who Ready* to Come Out of the Tardis for Saturday TV Series" Tom Leonard, page 3
Doctor Who Magazine Issue 463, September 2013 – "The Way Back – Part One: Bring Me to Life". Cavan Scott, pages 20-21

Archive.org – capture of "Sean Bean Isn't the Doctor" on
bbc.co.uk. Page dated January 2001. Capture dated January
23 2001
Archive.org – capture of "Auf Wiedersehen, Doctor" on bbc.co.uk.
Page dated October 18 2002. Capture dated November 1 2002
rec.arts.drwho, September 25 2003 – "Dimensions in Time"
Lee Hubbard
rec.arts.drwho.moderated, September 25 2003 – "Books in USA –
Any Sign?" Nicholas Fitzpatrick
rec.arts.drwho.moderated, September 25 2003 – "The Power of
Kroll – Part 1" 'J2rider'
rec.arts.drwho.moderated, September 26 2003 – "LBC Report"
Steve Freestone, 'Macfadyan'
Outpost Gallifrey forum, September 26 2003, – "NEW SERIES
IS COMING!" 'uagibbo', 'Cessair of Diplos', 'Shaft of
Gigsville', Craven Moorehead, Danny Salter, Shaun Lyon
bbc.co.uk, September 26 2003 – BBC News, entertainment
homepage.
bbc.co.uk, September 26 2003 – "*Doctor Who* Returns to BBC One"
bbc.co.uk, September 26 2003 – *Doctor Who* homepage

Doctor Forever: The Unquiet Dead. Extra feature on *Doctor Who –
The Green Death: Special Edition* DVD, Pup Ltd for BBC
Worldwide, 2013. Edited and produced by James Goss

INDEX

2point4 Children: 173
3rd Rock From the Sun: 115
30 Years in the TARDIS: 12
1990 Broadcasting Act: 20, 42
Aardman Animations: 42
Aaronovitch: Ben, 155
Abbott, Paul: 72, 180, 183
ABTV: 165
Academy Awards: 52, 54, 59, 62
Adams, Colin: 23-4, 27, 29, 147-8
Adams, Douglas: 235
Ahearne, Joe: 167-70, 173-4
Ainley, Anthony: 287
Airport: 144
Aldred, Sophie: 202, 204
Aldridge, Mark: 183
Alex Rider: 158
Alexander, Brian: 150
All Creatures Great and Small: 40, 91
AltaVista: 125
Amblin Entertainment: 14
Ambrosia Books: 108
And the Beat Goes On: 32
Anderson, Gerry: 41
Anderson, Paul: 57-8, 61-2, 66, 83
Angel: 122, 208
Animal Hospital: 145
Annett, Chloë: 158
Ansorge, Peter: 136

Ant and Dec: 258
Ant and Dec's Saturday Night Takeaway: 260
AOL: 125-6
Arc of Infinity: 193, 218
Artisan Entertainment: 59-60, 62
Astaire, Fred: 255
Atkinson, Rowan: 98-100, 192
Attack of the Cybermen: 193
Auf Wiedersehen, Pet: 284
Aukin, David: 54
Auntie's All-Time Greats: 91
Avengers, The: 156
Bad Wolf (production company): 273
Badger: 135
Back to the Future: 63-4
Bacon, Richard: 146
BAFTA: 52, 139, 214, 265
Baker, Colin: 102, 115, 213
Baker, Tom: 49, 93, 101, 172, 174, 179, 235
Balhetchet, Sophie: 168
Ballykissangel: 91, 136
Barnett, Steven: 164
Batman: 41
Battlestar Galactica: 164
Baxendale, Helen: 53
BBC
  – attitude to 1996 *Doctor Who* TV Movie: 12-13

- attitude to science fiction and fantasy programmes: 157, 167, 169-73, 175
- audience share: 140, 154
- Broadcast/Production split: 22-3, 142
- change of Director-Generalship at in 2000: 142-3, 146-7; change of Director-Generalship at in 2004: 296
- change of schedule on BBC One in 2000: 151-2
- commercial arm helping to fund output of: 249
- *Doctor Who* fans' attitudes to executives of: 31-2, 44
- drama output in the late 1990s: 129-39
- Duty Log: 116
- expansion into feature film production: 50-1
- facilities of being hired out to other companies: 165
- Granada Television, making programmes for: 43
- Greg Dyke's influence on: 33, 150
- hiring of Julie Gardner: 266-7
- hiring of Mal Young: 33
- impact of 1990 Broadcasting Act on: 20
- Independent Commissioning Group: 21, 148
- involvement with *Lost in the Dark Dimension*: 12-13
- involvement with proposed *Buffy the Vampire Slayer* spin-off: 209-10
- launch of digital television services: 94
- launch of online services: 110-13
- legal action against by *Doctor Who* film rights holders: 49
- legal argument concerning police box trademark: 233
- licence fee: 130
- online broadcasting: 205-07, 213, 235-7
- perceived financial status of in early 2000s: 150, 207
- Producer Choice system: 141
- production methods for drama programmes: 132-4
- receiving proposals for revival of *Doctor Who*: 201
- regional production quotas: 20
- rejection of Russell T Davies' *The Second Coming* scripts: 187
- Saturday evening television schedules: 253-62
- statements from regarding *Doctor Who* rights: 232, 251-2
- use of *Doctor Who* in promotional trailers: 93
- Viewer and Listener Correspondence unit: 28, 113

BBC Audio: 103
BBC Birmingham: 34-5
BBC Books: 88-9, 93, 95, 109, 115, 236, 288

INDEX

BBC Bristol: 42
BBC Broadcast: 22-3, 25, 142, 145
BBC Children's Books: 87, 91
BBC Choice: 93-4, 101, 140
BBC Cult website: 115-17, 121-23, 205-07, 238, 242, 251, 283
BBC Drama: 16-17, 19-27, 34-41, 46-8, 50, 75, 77, 80, 84-5, 97, 121, 130, 136, 138, 148, 154-5, 169, 181, 186, 222, 235-6, 244-5, 248-9, 251, 262, 264
BBC Enterprises: 12-13, 87
BBC Entertainment: 121
BBC Factual Books: 91
BBC Films: 20-1, 48, 50-4, 56, 58-60, 64-5, 79-80, 236, 239, 248, 250-2
BBC Information: 251
BBC Manchester: 70
BBC Natural History Unit: 42
BBC News 24/News Channel: 140
BBC News Online: 113, 260, 292
BBC North: 23
BBC North Acton Rehearsal Rooms: 44-5, 69
BBC Northern Ireland: 136, 275, 277, 279
BBC One: 11-13, 17, 19, 22-3, 34, 37-8, 41-3, 45-7, 67, 72-3, 75, 81-5, 91, 97, 100, 114, 128, 130-1, 134, 136, 138-40, 143-7, 149-51, 154-5, 157-8, 160-1, 163-4, 172-83, 192, 195, 210, 214, 217, 223, 225, 229-31, 233, 241-5, 247, 249-50, 253-4, 256-61, 267-8, 284, 290-1, 293, 296-7
BBC Online: 113-121, 207, 213, 236-7, 242, 283
BBC Press Office: 232, 264, 293
BBC Production: 22-3, 25, 36, 142-3, 145-6, 248-9
BBC Publicity: 283
BBC Radio 4: 202-05, 207
BBC Radio 5 Live: 150, 229, 232, 260
BBC Rights Group: 238, 240, 243
BBC Scotland: 136, 161, 175, 275, 277, 279
BBC Shop: 112-13, 243
BBC Sport: 257
BBC Studios: 23
BBC Television Centre: 34, 43, 46, 72, 87, 121, 136, 155, 221, 242-3
BBC Two: 18-19, 46, 52, 60, 94, 101-02, 110, 115, 138-9, 157, 164, 168, 172, 192, 196, 210, 216, 254, 264
BBC Video: 95
BBC Visual Effects: 165
BBC Wales: 23, 69-70, 193, 263-4, 266-7, 269-71, 275-9, 289, 292-3
BBC World Service: 117, 243

BBC World Service Trust: 263
BBC Worldwide: 12-14, 16, 23, 27, 57-66, 80, 87-91, 95-6, 103, 111, 112-14, 118-19, 128, 181, 190, 207, 239-40, 245-51, 261, 284, 291
BBC Worldwide Americas: 124
BBC Written Archives Centre: 123
BBCi – *see 'BBC Online'*
Bean, Sean: 283, 288
Beckett on Film: 265
Beckett, Samuel: 265
beeb.com: 28, 111-15, 118-19, 128, 162
Bennett, Jana: 260-1
Bergerac: 41, 91, 189
Berry, Nick: 75-7
Big Finish Productions: 102-04, 109, 190-2, 202, 204, 213, 235
Bill, The: 33, 131
Billy Elliot: 50
Birmingham: 20, 34-5, 179, 263, 276
Birt, John: 22, 24, 111-13, 131, 137, 140-3, 145-7, 150
Black and White Minstrel Show, The: 230-1
Blackadder: 98
Blair Witch Project, The: 59
Blake's 7: 162, 167, 189, 204, 223
Bland, Christopher: 24, 144
Bland, Robin – *see 'Dicks, Terrance'*
Blue Peter: 146
Blum, Jonathan: 153, 199, 218, 221, 224-5
Boaden, Helen: 205
Boak, Keith: 137
Bob & Rose: 186, 265
Bodies: 163
Bolt, Jeremy: 57-62, 66, 83
Bonanza: 177
Born and Bred: 160, 225-6
Born, Georgina: 21, 138
Bowker, Peter: 165
Boyle, James: 202, 204
Boys from the Blackstuff: 137
Brake, Colin: 155-9, 169
Bramwell: 11, 45
Breakfast Serials: 70
Brenda Bly: Teen Detective: 286
Brickner, George: 108
Britain's Got Talent: 253
British Academy of Film and Television Arts – *see 'BAFTA'*
British Film Institute: 92
Broadbent, Jim: 98
Broadcast magazine: 20, 24, 46, 78, 81, 182, 193
Broadcasting House: 203-04, 266
Broke, Richard: 19
Brookside: 32, 39, 196
Brown, Maggie: 24
Buck, Michelle: 265
Buffini: Nuala: 87, 89
Buffy the Vampire Slayer: 120-22, 208-11
Bugs: 155-9, 169, 172
Bullmore, Amelia: 168
Byker Grove: 193

INDEX

Byron: 154
Bush House: 117
Butterworth, Brandon: 110
Cahill, Martin: 56
Caleb, Ruth: 23
Campbell, Nicky: 231
Cannes Film Festival: 48, 51-5, 57
Canterbury Tales, The: 243, 267-9
Capaldi, Peter: 192
Cardiac Arrest: 161
Cardiff: 279
Carlton Television: 42, 45, 139, 161
Carnival Films: 156, 158
Carry on Screaming: 238-9, 252
Cartmel, Andrew: 45, 155-6
Cartwright, David: 292
Casanova: 265-66, 270-1
Casanova, Giacomo: 265
Cason, Jamie: 122
Casualty: 27, 31, 36, 45, 91, 131-3, 152, 156, 222, 256, 260, 262
Cathy Come Home: 47, 92
Celestial Toyroom: 233
Centre House: 34, 121
Century Falls: 71, 182
Chalk: 196
Changing Rooms: 144
Channel 4: 21, 32, 42-3, 50, 54, 73, 77-8, 82, 94, 122, 136, 145, 150, 167-8, 170, 180, 182, 187, 196, 222, 254, 259, 261, 265, 291, 296
Channel 5: 33
Chaos Films: 55-6

Chaucer, Geoffrey: 267
Chibnall, Chris: 135, 160, 193, 226, 272
Children of the Stones: 167
Children's Ward: 71, 76
Churchill's People: 129
Cinema Verity: 38, 201
Clark Productions: 145
Clarke, Steve: 161, 176
Clarkson, Jeremy: 255
Clemens, Brian: 156-8
Clocking Off: 180-1
Clough, Chris: 226
Coast-to-Coast: 49
Colditz: 91
Cole, Steve: 87, 89-91, 95-7, 103-05
Collins, Tim: 54-5
Collinson, Phil: 160, 175, 225
Come Dancing: 259
Comic Relief: 97-100, 115, 128, 191, 259
CompuServe: 108, 125
Condon, Paul: 124
Cook, Ben: 215
Cornell, Paul: 166, 192, 195-8, 206, 226, 236-8, 252
Coronation Street: 42, 57, 71, 196
Cosgrove Hall Films: 235-6
Coupling: 172, 196
Cowell, Simon: 258
Coyle, Richard: 172
Cracker: 46, 51, 135
Cracking Crime Day: 229
Craig, Daniel: 138
Creature, The: 50

Cregeen, Peter: 34, 38, 169
Crime Traveller: 158-60, 165, 176, 197
Crimewatch: 42
Crusade, The: 97
Cult Times: 73, 78, 83-4, 272
Cura, John: 123
Curse of Fatal Death, The: 98-9, 128, 191-2
Curse of Fenric, The: 18
Curtis, Richard: 99-100
Cushing, Peter: 49, 225, 238
Cutting It: 154
Cybermen: 193, 211, 213, 224
Daily Express: 209
Daily Mail: 52, 74, 109, 255
Daily Mirror: 109
Daily Record: 163
Daily Telegraph: 185, 269, 279, 289-92
Daldry, Stephen: 51
Dalek: 225
Daleks: 47, 52, 55, 74, 93, 95, 98, 101, 104, 121, 141, 156, 193, 197-8, 211, 216, 218, 224, 230, 238, 240, 243-4, 247-8, 283, 290, 292, 296
Daleks' Invasion Earth 2150 AD: 49
Daltenreys: 49
Damaged Goods: 71, 74, 291
Danger Mouse: 235
Daniels, Paul: 295
Dark Season: 71
Darlington, David: 135
Davenport, Jack: 167
Davidson, Jim: 256

Davies, Alan: 160, 186, 192
Davies, Andrew: 267
Davies, Russell (broadcaster): 69
Davies, Russell T
- approach from the BBC to write *Doctor Who* in 2003, 243-4, 248, 267-72
- as an example of a *Doctor Who* fan in the TV industry, 123
- BBC Worldwide's early contact with regarding revival: 249-50
- career in children's television: 69-71
- closure of BBC *Doctor Who* message boards: 126-7
- comments made on day of *Doctor Who* revival announcement: 293
- communication with fan websites: 110
- compared to writers of 1990s science fiction series: 159
- consulted by *Doctor Who Magazine* in 1999 on how the show might be revived: 194-7
- convenience of being Welsh for working with BBC Wales: 276
- dealing with continuity in *Doctor Who* revival: 198
- decision over whether to work for the BBC on *Doctor Who*: 272-4, 278
- discussing media perception of *Doctor Who* with Julie

INDEX

Gardner: 295
- dismissing idea of people 'bidding' to make *Doctor Who*: 201
- early life: 69
- fan reaction to his being in charge of *Doctor Who*: 289, 291
- friendship with Julie Gardner: 263, 265
- Gary Gillatt on: 193
- invitation to write for *Harbour Lights*: 76-7, 135
- involvement with *Casanova* project: 266
- Jane Tranter's enthusiasm for him to write *Doctor Who*: 177
- Julie Gardner's realisation BBC Wales were not working with: 267
- making *Queer as Folk*: 73-5
- meeting Jane Tranter at *Linda Green* launch: 183-85
- meeting with Laura Mackie regarding *Doctor Who*: 186
- meeting with Pippa Harris regarding *Doctor Who*: 181-2, 186
- on breadth of BBC drama in early 2000s: 154
- on BBC's inability to reverse revival announcement: 297
- on fan interest in production of *Doctor Who*: 285-6
- on Jane Tranter's attitude to *Doctor Who*: 47
- on Mal Young's attitude to *Doctor Who*: 31
- phone call with Clayton Hickman confirming *Doctor Who*'s return: 286-8
- phoning Paul Cornell to inform him of *Doctor Who* revival: 252
- position as 'showrunner' of *Doctor Who*: 274-5
- position in fan poll for who should run *Doctor Who*: 194
- possibility of writing *Doctor Who* in 1999, 43, 67, 73, 76-84, 172, 191, 195
- possibly prompting the BBC into investigating *Doctor Who* rights: 234
- reason for wanting as long a series of *Doctor Who* as possible: 279
- return to *Doctor Who* from 2023: 273, 297
- rumour linking to *Doctor Who* film: 84
- suggestion of Michael French as *Doctor Who* lead: 160
- thoughts on series and episode lengths of new *Doctor Who*: 279-81
- use of Nicola Shindler as messenger to the BBC regarding *Doctor Who*: 180-81
- view on prospects of *Doctor Who*'s return in 2000: 83-5

- work on *Doctor Who* compared with other revival proposals for the show: 217-20, 223-5
- work with Granada Television: 71-3
- writing *Damaged Goods* novel: 71-2
- writing for *Linda Green*: 182-83
- writing *The Second Coming*, 187

Davies, Gavyn: 296
Davis, Gerry: 201
Davison, Peter: 92, 101-02, 218, 264
Death Comes to Time: 204-13, 234
Decalog: 98
Dench, Judi: 261
Denton, Charles: 20-3
Destiny of the Daleks: 156
Destiny of the Doctors: 113
Dickens, Charles: 279
Dicks, Terrance: 90, 115, 192
Dimensions in Time: 288
Discovery Channel: 174
Disney: 54
Dispatches: 145
Dixon of Dock Green: 47, 170
Djordjevic, Jelena: 238-9
Doctor Forever: The Unquiet Dead: 79, 183, 185-6, 249
Doctor, The: 28, 48, 52, 55, 57, 60, 77, 82, 88, 98-9, 101-03, 159-60, 191-2, 198-9, 202, 204, 209-13, 216, 224, 235-8, 283-4, 288, 291, 295-6
Doctor Who (1996) – *see* 'TV Movie'
Doctor Who (character) – *see* 'Doctor, The'
Doctor Who
- 35th anniversary of: 93-4, 101, 115
- 40th anniversary of: 208, 235, 251
- 50th anniversary of: 244
- 1990s BBC One controllers' attitudes towards: 42
- announcement of revival in *The Daily Telegraph*, 185, 269, 289-91
- argument used by some fans for BBC revival of: 130
- BBC approaches Russell T Davies to write in 2003: 243-4, 248, 267-72
- BBC Films' interest in: 52, 236, 239, 251-2
- BBC Worldwide's reasons for interest in film of: 58, 66
- BBC Worldwide's film proposals preventing new television version of: 181, 246-51, 261, 291
- book ranges: 88-91, 95-7
- budget for revived version of: 262-3
- cancellation of in 1989: 34, 161, 177-8, 272
- Colin Brake as potential script editor of: 155-6
- Comic Relief parody version of: 97-100, 128
- comparisons to and with

INDEX

- other programmes: 156-7, 159-60, 162, 167, 172, 175-6
- conditions at the BBC in the early 2000s to allow for return of: 150
- 'crown jewel' of BBC Drama: 41
- revival attempt in 1999, 43, 77-83
- decision on where new version would be produced: 263, 270-1, 275-6
- decisions over length and episode running time of new series: 279-81
- departments made by during original run: 17, 41, 186
- differing fan views on format for any revival of: 189
- discussion of possible revival of in BBC One meetings: 179-80
- *Doctor Who 2000* rumoured title: 82-3
- *Doctor Who* Books imprint: 88
- early 1990s revival proposals for: 201
- fan embarrassment about: 217
- fan reaction to revival announcement: 288-9, 291-2
- fans' attitudes to potential film version of: 66-7
- fans' interest in production of: 284-86
- fans' desire for return of: 230, 284
- fans' possible preference for Director-General role: 142-3
- fans' views on who should create and star in any new version of: 191-94
- film proposal with HAL Films and Miramax: 54-6
- film proposal with Impact Films: 57-61
- film proposal with Mutual Film Company: 62-5
- film version announced at 1998 Cannes Festival: 48, 51-3
- film versions attempted during the series' run: 49-50
- future prospects after 1996 TV Movie: 11-16, 22-3, 27-8
- Helen O'Rahilly's enthusiasm for: 179
- importance of to BBC Wales: 276-9
- Jane Tranter asks Julie Gardner to make at BBC Wales: 269-71
- Jane Tranter's views of: 44
- Joe Ahearne's work on as director on: 167, 174
- Julie Gardner on Mal Young's importance to: 276
- launch of Big Finish audio dramas: 102-04
- launch and rise of official BBC websites for: 113-123
- legacy rights from 1960s films: 55-6

- longest-lasting BBC science fiction shows during absence of: 156
- Lorraine Heggessey and Jane Tranter begin to consider reviving: 177-78, 185
- Mal Young's views of: 31, 41
- Mark Thompson's request to stop the new series of: 154, 296-7
- media reaction to revival announcement: 290-5
- online message boards about: 124-7
- online streaming of television versions of: 128
- online versions of on BBC website: 205-07, 213, 235-8
- people employed full-time to work on: 87
- personnel involved with future production of working on *Harbour Lights*: 137
- possibility of being made as an independent production: 272-3
- possibility of reviving with someone other than Russell T Davies: 226-7
- proposal for animated series of: 201-02
- public perception of: 91-3
- radio versions of: 202-05, 234
- regularity of revival proposals being submitted to the BBC: 224
- relationship between fan and official websites: 124
- return of Russell T Davies, Julie Gardner and Jane Tranter to from 2023: 273, 297
- repeats of on BBC Two: 101-02, 157, 164
- rights issues regarding: 187, 227, 230-34, 236, 238-47, 251-2
- rise of fan-run news websites about: 107-10
- rumours of return ahead of official announcement: 281
- Russell T Davies and Jane Tranter discussing at *Linda Green* launch: 183-85, 221
- Russell T Davies' fandom of: 69-70, 74-5
- Russell T Davies telling the BBC it was the only thing he wanted to write for them: 182, 186
- Saturday evening scheduling of, 155, 230-31, 254, 260-2, 280
- shooting format of 1989 series: 18
- shooting format of 21st Century series: 134
- 'showrunner' role on: 274-5
- success of magazine about: 189-90
- success of revival of: 297
- suggestion that Granada

Television should produce: 71
theme night on BBC Two in
1999: 62, 100-01, 192
- television revival proposal by
Dan Freedman, 207-13: 221
- television revival proposal
by Gatiss, Hickman and
Roberts: 214-21
- television revival proposal by
Matthew Graham: 221-4
- unfounded rumours of
revivals of: 163-4, 210, 283-4,
288
- views of BBC executives on
response to announcement of
revival of: 295-6
- views of fans working in TV
industry on how could be
revived: 194-9
Dr. Who and the Daleks: 49
Doctor Who Appreciation
Society: 233
Doctor Who: From A to Z: 176
Doctor Who Magazine: 15-16, 27,
31, 54-5, 57, 60, 67, 71, 77-9,
82-3, 87, 89, 92-3, 95, 97-101,
104, 107, 109, 124, 135, 153-4,
160, 163, 181-2, 186-7, 189-92,
194-6, 198, 202-03, 208,
210-11, 213-15, 218-22, 224,
232, 234, 261, 265, 267, 269,
271-3, 279, 284-6, 288, 290,
294, 297
Doctor Who Meets Scratchman: 49
Doctor Who News Page, The:
107-10

Doctor Who Online: 126
Doctor Who Restoration Team:
126
Doctor Who: The Complete History:
79
Doctor Who: The Inside Story: 47,
250
Doughty, Stuart: 158
Dreamwatch: 209
Drovers' Gold: 266
Dundas, James: 123
Dunn, Ben: 115
Durham University: 145
Dyke, Greg: 32-3, 62, 85, 131,
134, 143-51, 154, 250, 277,
296
EastEnders: 27, 31, 36, 38, 91,
116, 121-22, 130-1, 155,
158-9, 165, 193, 222-4
Eastman, Brian: 156-7, 159
Eccleston, Christopher: 138,
187, 264-5
Edge of Darkness: 137
Edinburgh Festival: 202
Edinburgh International
Television Festival: 134, 140,
144, 241-2, 268-9
Edmonds, Noel: 91, 256
Edwards, Julie: 45
Elba, Idris: 167
Eldorado: 38-9, 130, 275
Elliott, Benjamin: 125
Elliott, Nick: 25, 34-5, 37, 136,
148, 166, 270
Emmerdale: 196, 214, 285
English Patient, The: 54

Evans, Bethan: 267-8, 271
Event Horizon: 57, 60
FA Cup: 231
Faber, George: 19, 48
Fame Academy: 241, 258-9
Family Affairs: 33
Farscape: 210
Fawlty Towers: 92
Fell, Richard: 121
Fictionlab: 121, 237
Financial Times, The: 64
Fishburne, Laurence: 59
Five Faces of Doctor Who, The: 94
Flannery, Peter: 138
Flash (animation technique): 215, 235, 237
Forbidden Planet: 117, 120
Forsyth, Bruce: 255-6, 259
Fountain, Nev: 203-08, 210-12, 225-6
Four Weddings and a Funeral: 191
Fox Network: 11-12, 15, 27-8
Foyle's War: 158
Francis, Rob: 122-4, 127, 235, 237
Freedman, Dan: 202-04, 206-13, 215-16, 221, 223-4, 234, 288
Freestone, Steve: 288-9
French, Michael: 152, 158-60
Friends: 53
Fry, Stephen: 204, 211-13
Fujitsu: 111
Fury, David: 208-09, 211-13
Gaiman, Neil: 164
Gallagher, Stephen: 156, 158
Gallifrey Base forum: 126-7

Gallifrey One convention: 28, 108
Gardner, Julie: 137, 244, 264-7, 269-81, 293, 295, 297
Gatiss, Mark: 101, 123, 172, 192, 195-7, 214-16, 218-21, 223-4, 232, 286-7
Gavin, Rupert: 58, 63, 66, 112, 247-50
Gay.com: 85, 180
Generation Game, The: 230-1, 255-6
Genesis of the Daleks: 74, 101-02
Gentleman Thief: 152-3, 159, 223
Ghost Light: 155
Ghost Squad: 223
Ghosts of Albion: 238
Gillatt, Gary: 15, 95, 97, 104, 176, 189, 193-5
Gold, Murray: 172
Goodchild, Peter: 19
Gordon, Mark: 62
Goss, James: 122, 124, 126-7, 206, 235, 239-40, 242
Grade, Michael: 42, 296
Graham, Matthew: 153, 166-8, 171, 221-4
Granada Television: 42-3, 54, 71-3, 76, 129, 143, 180, 265
Grand, The: 72-3, 77
Grange Hill: 56
Grant, Brian: 156
Grant, Hugh: 98, 191
Grant, Richard E., 98-9, 192, 237-8
Grantham, Leslie: 165

Gray, Scott: 286
Grayson, Larry: 256
Green Light: 49
Greengrass, Paul: 51
Grieve, Ken: 156
Gruffudd, Ioan: 139
Guardian, The: 24-5, 35, 43, 73-4, 132, 134, 136, 139, 144, 148, 165, 241, 260, 268-9
Gunpowder, Treason & Plot: 51
Hadcroft, Will: 94, 291
Haigh-Ellery, Jason: 102
HAL Films: 54-6, 61
Hamish Macbeth: 136
Hammer Film Productions: 50, 168
Handerson, Mitchell: 56
Harbour Lights: 75-8, 134-5, 137, 144, 264
Hard News: 145
Hare, David: 132
Harker, Susannah: 167
Harris, Pippa: 181, 186-7
Harry Potter: 49
Hartnell, William: 62, 216
Havers, Nigel: 152, 159
Head, Anthony: 209-10
Heartbeat: 75-6
Heggessey, Lorraine: 85, 145-7, 149-52, 154, 175-82, 185, 220, 226, 229-33, 239, 241-51, 253, 256-62, 268-9, 279, 290-1, 293, 295-7
Hetty Wainthropp Investigates: 43
Hickman, Clayton: 189-90, 214-21, 223, 234, 284-7, 294-5

Highlander: 84
Higson, Charlie: 172
Hill, James: 49
Hill, Steve: 126-7
Hillsborough: 51
Hinchcliffe, Philip: 192
Hogg, Susan: 226
Holby City: 131-4, 153-4, 159, 222, 262
Holding On: 138
Holland, Tony: 38
Hollingworth, Corinne: 133
Hollywood: 52, 59, 62, 67, 162, 245, 248, 291
Holmes, Sherlock: 237
Home, Anna: 70, 145
Hooper, Tom: 51
Hopkins, Anthony: 59, 64
Horning, EW: 152
Horowitz, Anthony: 158, 165
Hour of the Pig, The: 55
House of Cards, 138: 192
House of Eliott, The: 18
Hoving, Petrea: 54
Hudson, Clare: 266
Hustle: 152
Hutton Report: 154
I Love the 70s: 122
I Love the 80s: 122
Iannucci, Armando: 51
Ice Warriors: 285
ICL: 111-12
Impact Films: 57, 60
Impossible Pictures: 174
Independence Day: 162
Independent, The: 143, 162, 255

Independent on Sunday: 57, 59, 82-3
Independent Television Commission: 255
Indiana Jones: 56
Inspector Morse: 22, 167, 170
International Computers Limited – *see 'ICL'*
Invasion: Earth: 114, 161-3, 176
Invisible Man, The: 164
Irish Film Board: 265
Irish Times, The: 244
ITC Entertainment: 172
ITV: 11, 22, 25-6, 33-5, 37, 42-3, 45-7, 51, 71-2, 75-6, 129, 132, 134-5, 139-40, 143, 145-8, 150-2, 154, 156-8, 164-7, 172, 182, 186-7, 196, 214, 222-3, 231, 241, 253-5, 257-60, 264-5, 270-1, 291
Ivory, William: 139
Jackanory: 206
Jackson, Michael: 22-3, 37, 41-2, 138
Jane Eyre: 21
Janus, Samantha: 172
Joking Apart: 196
Jonathan Creek: 136, 160, 173, 194, 197
Jones, Matt: 199
Jordan, Tony: 165
Judd, Daniel: 122, 239-43, 245
Judge John Deed: 152-3
Juliet Bravo: 75
K9: 74, 137
Kane, David: 175

Kelly, Anne: 122
Kelly, Craig: 74
Kelley, Jennifer Adams: 126
Kibble-White, Graham: 219-20
Kneale, Nigel: 50
Kosminsky, Peter: 139
Kudos (production company): 152
Laing, Moray: 124
Lambert, Verity: 38, 87, 194, 196, 201
Langham Hotel: 266
Langley, Donna: 63-5, 245
Lanning, Steve: 75
Last Train, The: 166, 168, 222
LBC: 288, 290
League of Gentlemen, The: 101, 196, 214
Leonard, Tom: 290
Levene, Lesley: 96
Levine, Ian: 126
Leventhal, Colin: 54
Levinsohn, Gary: 62
Lewis, Damian: 139
Liddiment, David: 257
Life on Mars: 165, 221
Linda Green: 176, 180-1, 183-5, 221
Line of Duty: 163
Lion, The: 97
Liverpool: 32
Lofficier, Jean-Marc: 125
Lofficier, Randy: 125
Logopolis.com: 110
London: 19-20, 26, 32, 34, 39, 42, 45, 54, 61, 70, 84, 87,

117, 136, 145, 164, 185, 190, 203, 223, 233, 263, 264-5, 267, 269, 270, 273, 276-8, 286, 288, 290
London Weekend Television – see 'LWT'
London's Burning: 34
Long Game, The: 156
Los Angeles: 28, 108
Lost in the Dark Dimension: 12
Lumley, Joanna: 98
LWT: 34, 37, 54, 129, 143, 264-6, 270
Lyon, Shaun: 108-10, 123-7, 292-3
Macfadyen, Matthew: 139
Machin, Barbara: 152
Mackenzie, Catriona: 73
Mackie, Laura: 186-7
Mackinnon, Douglas: 72
Magician's House, The: 192
Maid Marian and Her Merry Men: 70
Making of Doctor Who, The: 285
Manchester: 70-3, 84, 180, 183, 187, 270, 291
Mansfield, Lee: 289
Mansfield Park: 21
Marchant, Tony: 138
Marshall, Andrew: 172-3
Marter, Ian: 49
Martin, Dave: 137
Marvel: 168, 189
Mary, Queen of Scots: 51, 53
Master, The: 60, 98, 192
Match of the Day: 230-1, 255, 257

Matthewman, Scott: 85
Mayo, Simon: 229-31
MBC: 146
McCoy, Karen: 201-02
McCoy, Sylvester: 92, 102, 155-6, 202, 223
McGann, Paul: 13, 28, 63, 67, 89-90, 103, 177-8, 191, 216, 235, 286
McGovern, Jimmy: 51
Me, You and Doctor Who: 57
Meek, Colin – see 'Freedman, Dan'
Men Behaving Badly: 165
Men in Black: 62
Mercurio, Jed: 161-3, 171
Mersey Television: 32, 38
Metropolitan Police: 233, 265
Middlemarch: 138
Miéville, China: 186
Mill, The: 99, 165
Minghella, Anthony: 54
Minister of Chance (character), 212-13; (proposed television series): 221
Ministry of Time, The: 220
Miramax: 54-6, 59, 61
Missing Adventures, The: 88
Moffat, Steven: 98-100, 123, 172, 191-3, 195-6, 198, 223, 272
Morbius: 90
Morecambe and Wise: 255
Morgan, Siobahn: 125
Morrissey, Neil: 165
Mortal Kombat: 57
Mortimer, Bob: 172
Move Over Darling: 142

Mr Bean: 98
Mrs Bradley Mysteries, The: 264
Mrs Brown: 50
Mulcahy, Russell: 84
Murray, Andy: 183
Mutual Film Company: 62, 64, 66
My Left Foot: 54
Myles, Eve: 279
Naked Eye Productions: 114
Nardini, Daniela: 52
Nassé, Saul: 114-15, 119
Nathan-Turner, John: 44
Nation, Terry: 166, 201, 240, 246-7
National Lottery: 197, 256, 258
Neal, Gub: 73
Neel, Janet: 138
Net, The: 110
Netflix: 174
Never Say Never Again: 56
Neverwhere: 164
New Adventures, The: 71, 88, 102, 166, 194, 199
New Line Cinema: 63
New Tricks: 152
New York: 61, 182
Newman, GF: 152
Newman, Sydney: 17, 20
News at Ten: 151
Newsround: 189
Nine O'Clock News: 72, 144, 151
Nitro Nine website: 125
Noddy: 87
Noel's House Party: 256
Nostromo: 27, 135

Notting Hill: 191
O'Rahilly, Helen: 178-80, 243-5, 268-9
Observer, The: 139, 255, 260-1
Olympic Games: 32
Omega: 285
Onedin Line, The: 91
Oscars – *see 'Academy Awards'*
Othello: 265
Outpost Gallifrey: 108, 110, 123-4, 126-7, 208, 225, 237, 289-91, 293-4
Our Friends in the North: 46, 129, 138, 264
P.O.W.: 223
Palmer, Laura: 124
Panini (publishing company): 189-90
Panorama: 145
Paradise Towers: 69
Parker, Gareth: 85
Parkin, Lance: 189, 195-7
Parkinson: 230-1, 255
Parks, Karen: 124
Parr, Chris: 35
Pearce, Jacqueline: 204
Pearson Television: 33, 39-40
Pebble Mill Studios: 20, 179
Pemberton, Victor: 240
Performance: 18
Pertwee, Jon: 101, 179, 202, 210
Phantom Menace, The: 194
Pharoah, Ashley: 171
Phillips, Mike: 57-8, 62-6, 248-50
Phippen, Mark: 110

Pidgeon, John: 203
Pingu: 87
Piper, Billie: 267
Pixley, Andrew: 199
Platt, Marc: 155
Play for Today: 19, 32, 41
Play on One, The: 17
Play School: 69-70
Playdays: 87
Plowman, Jon: 220
Poirot: 34, 158
Pop Idol: 241, 257-8
Popbitch: 284
Popstars: 257-8
Potter, Dennis: 141
Powell, Jonathan: 34, 38, 42, 161
Power of Kroll, The: 288
Power of the Daleks, The: 93
Premier League: 231, 257
Premiership, The: 257
Press Gang: 196
Pride and Prejudice: 129, 138
Prime Suspect: 46, 135
Professionals, The: 170
Pryce, Jonathan: 98
Pugh, Ed: 70
Pyramids of Mars: 74
Quatermass: 165, 167, 223
Quatermass Experiment, The: 50
QED: 145
Queer as Folk: 73-4, 76-8, 80-2, 84-5, 180, 182, 187, 194, 199, 290-1
Queer as Fuck – see 'Queer as Folk'
Quirke, Pauline: 93

Radio Times: 41, 61, 88, 93, 100-01, 112-13, 156-7, 162
Rafferty, Damian: 116-120
Raffles (character): 152, 159
Randall & Hopkirk (Deceased): 172, 214
Rayner, Jac: 96, 124
RealPlayer: 206, 237
Real Time: 213, 235
rec.arts.drwho: 12, 92, 98, 107-08, 125, 232, 288
rec.arts.drwho.moderated: 288
Red Dwarf: 90-1, 156-8
Red Production Company: 73, 180-1, 183, 187
Redfern, Anthea: 255
Redgrave, Jemma: 45
Reeks, Jenny: 166, 270
Reeves, Vic: 172
Register, The: 111-12
Renwick, David: 136
Resurrection of the Daleks: 193
Revelations: 71, 76
Rhodes: 27, 129, 135
Richards, Justin: 96
Richards, Menna: 266, 277-8
Richardson, Ian: 191-2
Rickman, Alan: 98
Rigg, Diana: 264
Right to Reply: 94-5, 104
Ripper: 210
Roache, Linus: 57
Roberts, Gareth: 172, 195-7, 214-16, 218-21, 223
Robin of Sherwood: 158
Robinson, Anne: 182

Robinson, Matthew: 193, 222, 263-4
Robinson, Sue: 162
Robinson, Tony: 70
Rock and Roll Years, The: 122
Rogers, Mark: 116-18, 120
Roobarb's forum: 126
Root, Antony: 72
Rose: 127
Rosenberg, Max J.: 49
Ross, Tessa: 21, 148
Royal Opera House: 143
Royal Television Society: 31, 260
RTÉ: 178, 265
Russell, Gary: 89, 102, 250
S4C: 167
Salmon, Peter: 42-4, 47, 72, 75-6, 79-81, 83-5, 138-40, 144-7, 150-2, 172-3, 182, 195, 256
Salter, Danny: 292
Sangster, Jim: 124
Sapphire & Steel: 167
Saving Private Ryan: 62
Sawalha, Julia: 98
Sax, Geoffrey: 265
Schulman, Barry: 163
Sci-Fi Channel, The: 161-2, 166
Scream of the Shalka: 238, 251-2, 286, 288, 292
Screen One: 19, 25, 45
Screen Two: 19, 25, 45
Screenplay: 18
Sea of Souls: 175
Second Coming, The: 187, 291

Segal, Philip: 14-15, 28, 55, 125, 192, 201
Selby, Rona: 90
Sessions, John: 204
Sewell, Andrew Mark: 114-15, 119
Seymour, Emily: 164
SFX magazine: 60, 84, 124, 206, 208
Shada: 235, 238
Sharp, Lesley: 186
Sheard, Michael: 56
Shearman, Robert: 225
Shindler, Nicola: 73, 180-1, 183-5, 187, 270
Shivas, Mark: 21, 34, 48, 50
Silent Witness: 35, 39-40, 135-6, 167
Simm, John: 192
Simpsons, The: 115, 117, 121
Sins, The: 139
Sky One: 210
Sky Television: 94
Sliders: 15
Smith, Julia: 38
Smith, Zadie: 21
Snaith, Stuart: 104
Snowdon, Lord: 101
Solomon, Ed: 62-4, 66, 248
Soundhouse Studios: 204
South Bank Show Awards, The: 265
South East Today: 294
Space: Above and Beyond: 115
Space Odyssey: Voyage to the Planets: 174

Spall, Timothy: 284, 288
Spearhead from Space: 101
Spence, Patrick: 39-40, 46-7, 75-82, 135-7, 152-3, 187
Spielberg, Steven: 14
Spilsbury, Tom: 286-7, 294-5
Spindler, Susan: 148
Spooks: 152, 223, 279
Springhill: 71
Star Trek: 115, 122, 157, 162
Star Trek: Deep Space Nine: 115, 117
Star Trek: The Next Generation: 164
Star Wars: 56, 194-5, 224
State of Play: 154
Strange: 154, 172-5
Street-Porter, Janet: 142
Strictly Ballroom: 259
Strictly Come Dancing: 177, 253, 259-60
Subotsky, Milton: 49, 55-6
Sullivan, Lee: 206
Sullivan, Shannon Patrick: 15, 28, 107-10, 124-5
Summerfield, Bernice: 102
Sun, The: 52, 78, 109
Sunburn: 78, 134-5, 144, 264-5
Sunday Times, The: 59-60, 62, 161, 164, 166, 176
Survival: 18
Survivors: 166
Swansea: 69
Sweeney, The: 170
Sweet, Matthew: 57, 59, 82
Talalay, Rachel: 172
Tale of Two Cities, A: 186

Talkback Thames (production company): 154
Tall Guy, The: 54
Tarbuck, Liza: 180
TARDIS: 12, 45, 53, 192, 216, 218-19, 224-5, 233, 244, 284, 287, 290
TARDISCam: 123
Target Books: 88
Taste of Life: 264
Terminus: 156
Thames Television: 33, 40, 57, 145
This Life: 46, 52, 129, 168
This Week: 145
This Week in Doctor Who: 125
Thompson, David: 25, 48, 50-5, 57-61, 63, 65, 79-80
Thompson, Mark: 144, 148, 150, 154, 261, 277, 296
Thompson, Roy: 145
Time Lords: 50, 82, 162, 193, 197-8, 212, 218, 237
Time Meddlers of Los Angeles: 108
Times, The: 109, 140, 142, 145, 147
Timmer, Damien: 265-6
Tomorrow People, The: 167
Tomorrow's World: 114, 120
Tomorrow's World Plus: 114, 119, 128
Top Gear: 89, 112, 119
Top of the Pops: 112, 121
Toronto International Film Festival: 60
Total Film: 57

Touch of Frost, A: 167
Touching Evil: 72
Tranter, Jane: 44-8, 133, 139, 148-52, 154, 170-1, 173, 176-8, 181, 183-6, 220-22, 226, 236, 239, 242, 244-6, 249-50, 260-1, 267-75, 278, 280-81, 296-7
Traylen, Steve: 108
Trickey, Martin: 121-2, 206-07, 235-6, 242
Truly, Madly, Deeply: 19-20
Tucker, Mike: 123
TV 60: 91, 93
TV Movie: 11-16, 19, 22, 27-8, 32, 36, 41, 45, 48-9, 55, 63, 67, 79-80, 88-91, 101, 107-09, 125, 155, 159, 177-8, 191, 201-02, 217-18, 220, 232, 240, 245-6, 265
TV Zone: 155-6
Twitter: 126
Tyler, Rose: 267
Tyne Tees Television: 129
UKTV Horizons: 114
Ultraviolet: 167-8, 170, 174
Uncertain Vision: Birt, Dyke and the Reinvention of the BBC: 21
Uninvited, The: 165-6
UNIT: 240
Universal Pictures: 63-6, 245-6
Universal Television: 12, 27-8, 63, 79, 220, 232, 234, 240, 245
University of London: 264
University of Westminster: 129, 164

Untouchables, The: 223
Usenet: 107, 125-6
Valentine Productions: 75
Vancouver: 15
Vanishing Man, The: 164-5, 176
Variety: 24, 54, 61-2, 137-8
Vertue, Sue: 98
Vincent and the Doctor: 99
Virgin Publishing: 71, 88-9, 98, 102, 109, 123, 157
Viva Las Vegas!: 71
Waking the Dead: 152-3
Walking With Dinosaurs: 182, 186-7
Wall to Wall (production company): 152
Wallace & Gromit: 42
Walpole, Sophie: 121
Warriors: 139
Warriors' Gate: 156
Washington, Denzel: 57, 59
Watchdog: 116
Wavelength: 196
Weakest Link: 182, 186-7
Wearing, Michael: 34, 36, 137-9
Westmaas, Conrad: 286
Wheldon, Huw: 31
When the Boat Comes In: 91
White, Carol: 47
White Teeth: 21
Why Don't You?: 69-70
Winslet, Kate: 71, 98
Woffinden, Bob: 132
Wonfor, Andrea: 37
Wood, Tony: 76-8
Worcester College, Oxford: 69

INDEX

Working Title Television: 172
World Productions: 167-8
Wright, Jo: 13-14, 23, 26, 35-7, 39, 141-2, 159
Wrong Trousers, The: 143
X Factor, The: 253, 258, 260
X-Files, The: 114, 122, 161-2, 164, 175, 210
Yates, David: 49
Yentob, Alan: 12-14, 22-4, 26, 31, 36, 38, 42, 55, 80, 143, 231, 236, 250-1, 253
Yorke, John: 222-4
Yorkshire Television: 37, 129
Young, Mal: 31-4, 37-41, 43-4, 47, 75-7, 80-1, 130-4, 136-7, 152-3, 159, 171-2, 222-3, 226-7, 233, 261-4, 275-6, 280-1, 293
Z Cars: 91, 170
Zajdlic, Richard: 168
Zenith Productions: 22

ACKNOWLEDGEMENTS

THIS BOOK WOULD NOT HAVE BEEN POSSIBLE without the help, co-operation, advice or assistance of the following people – either for speaking to me themselves, helping to arrange interviews, aiding with assorted queries, reading through draft versions, or providing facts and useful information. I am extremely grateful to them all.

Joe Ahearne, Flynn Aislin, Alan Barnes, Steve Barnett, Jonathan Blum, Colin Brake, Steve Cole, Serena Cullen, Theresa Cutts, Kate Emmerson, Nev Fountain, Rob Francis, David Fury, Julie Gardner, Rupert Gavin, Gary Gillatt, Matthew Graham, Will Hadcroft, Unity Haggard, Elin Hampton, Clayton Hickman, Lorraine Heggessey, John Hoare, Susan Hogg, Tanya Hudson, Laura Hutchinson, Michael Jackson, Daniel Judd, Shaun Lyon, Laura Mackie, Lee Mansfield, Andrew Marshall, Saul Nassé, Helen O'Rahilly, Andrea Ortiz, Mike Phillips, Damian Rafferty, Bill Rawcliffe, Menna Richards, Mark Rogers, Andrew Mark Sewell, Tom Spilsbury, Shannon Patrick Sullivan, Cat Taylor, David Thompson, Talia Tobias, Jane Tranter, Martin Trickey, Tom Webb, Steve Williams, Jo Wright, Alan Yentob, Mal Young.

Special thanks are due, of course, to Stuart Manning at Ten Acre for being so kind about and keen on the idea, and for turning this into a real, actual book. Stuart is the one responsible for getting this out into the world to be read, for which I will always be incredibly grateful.

I also wish to give particular thanks to Graham Kibble-White, who, without knowing me at all, was extremely generous in opening the doors to interviews which otherwise would not have happened. He also helped to make this publication possible by introducing me to Stuart, and was generally a great encouragement.

Thank you also to all of those on the Gallifrey Base forum who were so enthusiastic about the timeline I put together for fun, which was how this idea all started. Their positive reactions first made me wonder if there might be a book in it!

My sincere apologies and heartfelt thanks to anybody else who assisted with the book if you were inadvertently missed from the above list.

ABOUT THE AUTHOR

PAUL HAYES was born and raised in West Sussex and now lives in Norwich. A writer and broadcaster, he has contributed feature articles to the likes of *Doctor Who Magazine*, BBC Online, *The Stage* and the *Eastern Daily Press*. For the BBC he has produced and presented a variety of radio documentaries, on subjects including The Beatles, motor racing, broadcasting history, politics, film, football and, of course, *Doctor Who*, a programme which he has loved for as long as he can remember.